MANAG
ORGANI

Contemporary sport could not function without the involvement of voluntary organisations, from local grass-roots clubs to international agencies such as the International Olympic Committee. Management of this sector continues to undergo profound change, largely in response to the challenges of professionalisation and increasing expectations in terms of transparency, accountability and ethical behaviour. This book fills a significant gap in the literature on sport management by setting out the principles and practices necessary for effective management of voluntary sport organisations around the world.

In addition to applying and adapting established management strategies and techniques to voluntary sport organisations, this book is the first to fully relate mainstream organisational theory to this important sector of sport management. With contributions from an international team of researchers and management practitioners, the book explores key functional areas such as:

- governance;
- strategy and planning;
- human resources;
- finance;
- managing change;
- marketing;
- event management;
- risk management.

Each chapter discusses best practice and some also include case study material, self-test questions and guides to further reading. As the only book to outline a professional, theoretically informed and practically focused curriculum for voluntary sport management, this book is essential reading for all students of sport management and all managers working in or alongside the voluntary sector.

Leigh Robinson is a Professor of Sport Management in the Department of Sport Studies, University of Stirling. She has carried out research with a wide range of organisations in the voluntary, commercial and public sectors, including Olympic Solidarity, British Olympic Association, Sport England, British Judo and the Amateur Swimming Association. She works extensively with the International Olympic Committee funded MEMOS network.

Dick Palmer is an independent sports consultant, based in the UK. He was Technical Director of the London 2012 Olympic Bid and an adviser to the Commonwealth Games Federation serving on their Coordination Commission for the Games of Kuala Lumpur, Manchester and Melbourne. He was also International Consultant to the successful Glasgow Bid for the 2014 Commonwealth Games. He remains an Executive Vice President of the British Olympic Association and a Board Director of the British Olympic Foundation and Sports Coach UK.

MANAGING VOLUNTARY SPORT ORGANISATIONS

**EDITED BY LEIGH ROBINSON
AND DICK PALMER**

 Routledge
Taylor & Francis Group

LONDON AND NEW YORK

First published 2011 by Routledge

2 Park Square, Milton Park, Abingdon, Oxon, OX14 4RN

Simultaneously published in the USA and Canada by Routledge 270 Madison Avenue, New York, NY 10016

Routledge is an imprint of the Taylor & Francis Group, an informa business

The right of Leigh Robinson and Dick Palmer to be identified as the authors of the editorial material and the authors for their individual chapters has been asserted by them in accordance with sections 77 and 78 of the Copyright, Designs and Patents Act 1988.

Typeset in Zapf Humanist and Eras by
HWA Text and Data Management, London

Printed and bound in Great Britain by
CPI Antony Rowe, Chippenham, Wiltshire

British Library Cataloguing in Publication Data
A catalogue record for this book is available from the British Library

Library of Congress Cataloging-in-Publication Data
Managing voluntary sport organisations / edited by Leigh Robinson and Richard Palmer.
      p. cm.
   1. Sports administration—United States. 2. Sports—United States—Management. I. Robinson, Leigh, 1965– II. Palmer, Richard.
   GV713.M364 2010
   796.06′9—dc22   2010008668

ISBN: 978-0-415-48944-7 (hbk)
ISBN: 978-0-415-48945-4 (pbk)
ISBN: 978-0-203-88135-4 (ebk)

CONTENTS

v
contents

ILLUSTRATIONS

FIGURES

TABLES

CONTRIBUTORS

Leigh Robinson PhD (editor) is Professor of Sport Management at the University of Stirling, Scotland. A graduate in physical education from the University of Otago, New Zealand, she obtained her PhD from Loughborough University in the area of quality management and local authority leisure facilities. Her principal research interest is in the management and measurement of performance, governance and quality in voluntary sport organisations. She works with voluntary organisations in order to improve performance and organisational change and is a member of England's Amateur Swimming Association's Board. She works extensively with the Olympic Solidarity funded MEMOS network and is a member of the Steering Committee for their advanced sport management courses. Leigh is author of *Managing Public Sport and Leisure Services* and co-editor of *Managing Olympic Sport Organisations*.

Dick Palmer CBE, M.ed, FRSA (editor) began his career as a physical education teacher. He moved into sports management, becoming Secretary General of British Universities Sports Federation. In 1975 he was appointed Deputy Secretary General of the British Olympic Association and in 1977 Secretary General, a post he held for 20 years until his retirement in 1997. During that time he was Deputy Chef de Mission of the British teams at ten Summer and Winter Olympic Games. For many years Dick has been advisor to the International Olympic Committee and Olympic Solidarity. He has been Vice President of the European Olympic Committees, and was a member of the Association of National Olympic Committees Board for many years. He was Technical Director of the London 2012 Olympic Bid and an adviser to the Commonwealth Games Federation serving on their Co-ordination Commission for the Games of Kuala Lumpur, Manchester and Melbourne. He was also International Consultant to the successful Glasgow Bid for the 2014 Commonwealth Games and Rio for the 2016 Olympic Games. He remains an Executive Vice President of the British Olympic Association and a Board Director of the British Olympic Foundation and Sports Coach UK. He is also a member of the Sports Council for Wales and Chair of their Performance & Excellence Committee. He is co-author of the first *IOC Olympic Village Guide* and the *Sports Administration Manual* and made a number of contributions to the book *Managing Olympic Sports Organisations*.

Guillaume Bodet PhD is a Lecturer in sport policy and management at Loughborough University. A graduate of the Sport Sciences Faculty of the University of Burgundy, France, he obtained his PhD from the Burgundy Centre for Marketing Research (CERMAB) at the University of Burgundy. His research primarily deals with sport marketing and particularly with consumer behaviour regarding sport organisations, sporting events and sport brands. He has published several papers in peer-reviewed journals such as *European Sport Management Quarterly, Journal of Retailing and Consumer Services, International Journal of Sport Management and Marketing, International Journal of Sport Marketing and Sponsorship*, and *Qualitative Market Research*. He has volunteered in sport organisations, both in France and in the United Kingdom, since his early twenties, and is still an active participant and coach in his current handball club.

Jean-Loup Chappelet PhD is a Professor of public management and Director of the Swiss Graduate School of Public Administration associated with the University of Lausanne. He has been IDHEAP Dean since 2003. Professor Chappelet specialises in sport management and sport policy with a particular emphasis on the organisations of Olympic Games and other sport events. He has written several books on sport organisations and is on the editorial boards of two sport management journals and a member of the board of the Lausanne-based International Academy of Sport Sciences and Technology (AISTS). For more than ten years he was the Director of the MEMOS programme, an executive masters in sport organisation management supported by Olympic Solidarity.

Andy Gray LLB is a solicitor and has been the in-house Head of Legal Affairs to British Swimming since 1996. He advises on a broad range of commercial, disciplinary and regulatory issues with both a national and international dimension, with a particular interest in doping control and child protection. He was appointed in 2006 as Sports Regulatory Consultant to Brabners Chaffe Street solicitors whose clients include world and national sports bodies and Manchester United Football Club. Andy is a member of the Panel of Arbitrators of the Sports Dispute Resolution Panel. He is a member of the British Association for Sport and the Law, and on the editorial board of World Sports Law Report.

Sarah James LLB is an in-house legal adviser to the Amateur Swimming Association and British Swimming, principally in the area of governance and regulation. Previously she worked at De Montfort University in the law faculty, and has contributed widely to the study materials of the university's successful sports law and practice LLM. She retains links to the university as an associate member of its Sports Law Unit.

Peter McGraw MA is Director of the Labour-Management Studies Foundation and a faculty member in the Department of Business at Macquarie University. He is the author of many academic papers on a broad range of human resource issues and a well known consultant and executive educator. Peter is a recipient of a Macquarie University Outstanding Teacher Award.

Brian Minikin MSc is the Regional Sport Development Manager for the Oceania National Olympic Committees. He is responsible for supporting the development and professionalisation of the Oceania Island Nations Olympic Committees. He oversees the Oceania Sport Education Programme and is a regular presenter at National Olympic Committee conferences. His particular interests are in strategic preparation and planning and performance evaluation.

Simon Shibli CIMA is currently employed at Sheffield Hallam University as a Director of the Sport Industry Research Centre (SIRC). He is a graduate in Physical Education, Sport Science and Recreation Management from Loughborough University and is also a qualified management accountant with the Chartered Institute of Management Accountants (CIMA). In 2007 Simon was awarded the title of Professor in Sport Management at Sheffield Hallam University and is also a visiting Professor at Waseda University in Tokyo, Japan. He has been involved in research and consultancy relating to the economics and finance of the sport industry since the start of his academic career in 1992. As a one-time club rugby player he has always had an interest in the management of voluntary sector sports clubs, notably anything concerned with finance.

Tracy Taylor PhD is currently the Deputy Dean in the Faculty of Business at the University of Technology, Sydney. Tracy has a significant research profile in the area of sport management and is on the editorial board of several international sport management journals including the position of Associate Editor of *Sport Management Review*. Her most recent book is *Managing People in Sport Organizations: A Strategic Human Resource Management Perspective* (2008). Her teaching areas are leadership and teamwork, human resource management in sport and sport management. Tracy also conducts corporate executive leadership training programmes.

Eleni Theodoraki PhD is Director of the Edinburgh Institute for Festival and Event Management where she oversees a range of research and continuing professional development programmes and is a Reader in Festival and Event Management at Edinburgh Napier University's Business School. She is a Member of the Vancouver 2010 Olympic Games Impacts Expert Resource Group and has worked for the London 2012 Olympic Games Bid Committee and Athens 2004 Olympic Games Organising Committee on Olympic education, and strategic planning and development issues, respectively. In 2001 she received the International Year of Volunteers IOC Diploma for her contribution to the development of sport and Olympism. She is author of *Olympic Event Organisation*.

PREFACE

The voluntary sport sector underpins sport internationally and is responsible for the delivery of sport opportunities from grass-roots mass participation to elite performance across the globe. The organisations within this sector are extremely diverse, including local clubs and their leagues, national governing bodies of sport and international agencies, such as the International Olympic Committee.

The management of this sector has undergone, and is still undergoing, fundamental change. Members are becoming increasingly demanding of the services they require in exchange for their membership, professionalisation has led to the presence of paid human resources in many voluntary organisations previously run entirely by volunteers, and the delivery of sport has been challenged in terms of transparency, accountability and ethical behaviour. A key response to these changes has been the increasing adoption of management approaches and techniques, such as marketing, sponsorship and performance management, which have been traditionally associated with other sectors.

The adaptations made, and lessons learned, by those working and researching in the voluntary sector have been communicated in a piecemeal and haphazard fashion and information on possible management strategies is often a mixture of rhetoric and/or prescriptive information. There has been little attempt to systematically consider the application of techniques that are traditionally associated with the commercial sector to the voluntary sector.

This book aims to fill this gap and attempts to consider and analyse the issues facing the management of contemporary voluntary sport organisations. The book will also discuss and adapt traditionally commercial management strategies and techniques in order to present best practice in the management of voluntary sport services.

The book will be arranged in three parts containing 14 chapters. Part 1 will be an introductory section consisting of three chapters. Chapter 1 establishes what is meant by voluntary sport organisations and their management. It sets out the nature of the voluntary sport sector, the role of the main organisations that make up the sector and the characteristics common to all voluntary sport organisations.

It then provides a discussion of the context impacting on the management of voluntary sport organisations and the personal skills required for managers to be effective.

To understand how voluntary sport organisations can be managed effectively requires an understanding of their internal and external operating environment. This is the purpose of Chapter 2, which will firstly discuss the nature of organisations and then present and discuss factors in the operating environments that need to be taken into account when managing a voluntary sport organisation. It will go on to present structures for managers to use to analyse their operating contexts.

Chapter 3 will introduce the concept of governance that has emerged as being of importance to the voluntary sport sector. It will set out the development of the concept and will deal, in detail, with the role of boards in governance. Finally, it considers the aspects of organisations that might impact on governance activities.

Part 2 will contain seven chapters that consider key management dimensions, presenting perceived best practice and then applying and adapting this to the voluntary sport context. Chapter 4 will focus on the concepts of organisational strategy development and planning. The chapter sets out the rationale for strategic management and discusses the need to prepare for the strategy development process. It then describes the four phases needed to develop and implement a strategic plan.

In Chapter 5 the issues and procedures involved in the effective management of staff (paid and unpaid) are considered. The chapter examines the topics of recruitment, selection, development and discipline in the context of people management. The chapter also considers the issues involved in managing and working with volunteers and discusses the 'paid/unpaid' barrier that affects many voluntary sport organisations.

Chapter 6 is concerned with providing readers with an overview of the key financial skills required to manage sport organisations. It will consider financial management conventions from a voluntary sport organisation perspective and present the principles of good financial management and define key terms. The chapter will then go on to address aspects of financial planning, budgeting and financial reporting.

Chapter 7 discusses the need for performance management and its role in the delivery of voluntary sport organisations. It will consider the terminology associated with performance management, methods of managing performance and will focus, in detail, on performance indicators as these are essential to voluntary sport organisations.

The multifaceted nature of change within voluntary sport organisations will be explored in Chapter 8. It will begin by considering what is meant by organisational change, presenting key approaches to the understanding and management of change. The chapter will also consider the barriers to change in these organisations and will end with a discussion of the methods of successfully introducing changes into the management of voluntary sport organisations.

Marketing of voluntary sport organisations has recently become significant as these organisations have looked for ways of decreasing their reliance on external funding. The purpose of Chapter 9 is to set out the principles of marketing and consider what can be marketed, how it can be marketed and strategies for communication and sponsorship.

At some stage all voluntary sport organisations stage an event, ranging from small club championships to the Olympic Games and World Championships. Chapter 10 sets out the operational principles that a voluntary sport organisation should use to successfully stage a sport event. It will consider the design of the event and then move on to look at how to develop the event to ensure successful implementation.

Finally, Part 3 will comprise four chapters that will consider specific issues that impact on, or are important to, the management of these organisations. The purpose of Chapter 11 is to provide a basic understanding and application of aspects of law and how it might apply to the voluntary sport sector. From a club perspective, it will examine a number of general legal principles affecting factors such as governance, employment, data protection and child safeguarding.

Chapter 12 sets out the principles associated with the management of risk within a sporting context. It begins by defining what risk is and how it can impact on voluntary sport organisations and then moves on to set out a risk management strategy. Finally, it discusses how VSOs can protect themselves from risk.

In Chapter 13, a review of information and communication technologies (ICT) as they apply or might apply to managing voluntary sport organisations is presented. The chapter discusses the use of information and how it might be communicated and then highlights several of the ICT solutions that have been used by voluntary sport organisations.

The final chapter, Chapter 14, will offer an overall evaluation of the usefulness to voluntary sport organisations of the techniques reviewed. It will discuss the key points and trends that emerge from the adaptation of best practice to the voluntary sector and will conclude with issues that are likely to impact on the future management of these organisations.

PART I

INTRODUCING THE VOLUNTARY SPORT SECTOR

CHAPTER 1

THE VOLUNTARY SPORT SECTOR

Leigh Robinson

The delivery of sporting opportunities tends to fall into three main sectors. The first sector is the public or state sector, which mainly encompasses the work of local authorities and schools. The second is the private or commercial sector primarily consisting of the health and fitness industry and professional sport leagues. The third, the focus of this book, is the voluntary sector, which, in the UK and many other countries, is primarily made up of clubs and national federations. It is, however, more complex than this as it is often difficult to determine what sector an organisation operates within. For example, many sport leagues operate on a commercial basis, although the teams that participate within them are usually part of the voluntary sector. The Olympic Games is a commercial event; however, some of the sports in the Games are professional, while others are still considered to be amateur. All athletes compete under the banner of their National Olympic Committee (NOC), which is part of the voluntary sector.

As a consequence, in order to make sense of this mixed economy of sport, it is necessary to be clear about the characteristics that lead an organisation to being part of a particular sector and thus this chapter begins with a definition of what a voluntary sport organisation (VSO) is, setting out the main organisations in this sector and the characteristics that they have in common. It then goes on to discuss the concept of managing within the voluntary sport sector and the skills associated with doing so.

DEFINING THE VOLUNTARY SPORT SECTOR

What is a voluntary sport organisation? Wilson and Butler (1986) have suggested two characteristics that characterise a VSO. These are that:

- a considerable proportion of the labour force is voluntary, rather than paid. Such organisations are still voluntary even if some of their members are paid, as is the case in many national federations, or if they receive financial aid from government agencies, such as Sport England
- the organisation does not seek profit from the selling of goods or services, although many set up profit-seeking subsidiary trading companies with the

purpose of providing funds for the organisation. For example, a number of national federations may sell achievement badges or team uniforms to participants and clubs.

These two points are important and go some way to highlight the diversity and complexity of organisations in the voluntary sport sector. First, organisations within the voluntary sport sector range from those that are large, professional and well resourced organisations, to those that are small, voluntary and often poorly resourced. The definition provides for organisations where the management of the organisation is not carried out by volunteers, rather the organisation is managed by paid staff. However, the delivery of grass-roots sport and events is carried out by clubs and the management of these organisations is carried out primarily by volunteers.

Second, it is possible for VSOs to make money. As will be demonstrated in Chapter 6, although most VSOs are driven by non-financial objectives, they can still generate revenue, and often a surplus of revenue over their expenditure. Alternatively, the Wilson and Butler definition allows for those small organisations that are created and managed entirely by volunteers, who come together to participate in sport with no interest in the generation of income. This great range of organisations is what makes the voluntary sport sector so flexible in its delivery of sport services. It is also what provides perhaps the greatest challenge to identifying what might be best practice in their management.

ORGANISATIONS OF THE VOLUNTARY SPORT SECTOR

There are a number of organisations that make up the voluntary sport sector. Most are hierarchically organised within the specific structure affecting each sport, which often reflects the structure set out in Figure 1.1, with organisations ranging from the local level to the global level. Others impact across a number of sport systems, or the sport system as a whole, such as the International Olympic Committee (IOC). The roles of key organisations are discussed below.

International federations

International federations (IFs) are the international non-governmental organisations that administer one or several sports at world level. They are responsible for maintaining and developing rules, promoting the sport on the world stage and organising world or continental championships. The membership of an IF is made up of the national federations (see below) found in each country that participates in the respective sport. IFs range from the very well known (Fédération Internationale de Football Association, FIFA) to the less well known (International Boot Throwing Association, IBTA).

4

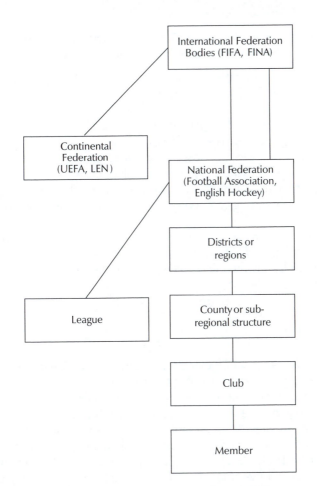

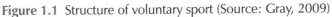

Figure 1.1 Structure of voluntary sport (Source: Gray, 2009)

National federations

Also known as national governing bodies (NGBs), national sport organisations or national sport associations, national federations (NFs) are responsible for planning and managing their sport at the national level. The IOC considers the role of an NF as being to 'exercise a specific, real and on-going sports activity, be affiliated to an IF recognised by the IOC and be governed by and comply in all aspects with both the Olympic Charter and the rules of its IF' (Article 30 of the Olympic Charter).

National federations have the same objectives as an international federation, but within the scope of one country, or even part of a country, as the name implies. They support local clubs and are often responsible for national teams. Sport

5

England currently recognises over 135 national federations of sport, although it is worth noting that ten of these are associated with bowling!

They have a number of roles of which the main one is to promote their sport within their country. They are also responsible for:

- managing the rules and regulations of their sport
- administering and developing officials
- maintaining links with their international federation
- encouraging participation in the sport at all levels
- developing talent and elite athletes to compete on the world stage
- organising and hosting competitions primarily at the national level.

The membership of an NF is made up of the participants of the sport in their country, who usually affiliate to the NF through clubs (see below). NFs range from the very well known (Volleyball England), to the less well known (Eton Fives Association).

Clubs

A sport club is an organisation that exists in order to provide the opportunity for people to take part in a sport and its sporting structures. In most countries, sport is organised into a system of sport clubs, and individuals who want to participate in competitions join clubs in order to do so. The most recent research into clubs showed that there were 106,400 affiliated clubs in England, with eight million members and that 60 per cent of young people belong to a sport club outside school (Sport England, 2002). Clubs, often through regional organisations, form the basis of NFs and therefore club members make up the membership of the NFs.

More importantly, sport clubs make a fundamentally positive contribution to society. They provide the opportunity for the expression of active citizenship through volunteering (Nichols et al, 2004) and opportunities for social interaction that enriches local communities. As noted by Taylor et al (2009: 7):

> in the broadest sense the ability of volunteers to come together and create something reflecting their shared values – in this case, their passion for sport – is a reflection of a society in which free expression of collective values is possible and encouraged, as a positive contribution to society.

6

leigh robinson

International Olympic Committee

The International Olympic Committee (IOC) is an international, non-profit, non-governmental organisation that promotes the Olympic values in accordance with the Olympic Charter. The mission of the IOC is to promote Olympism throughout the world and to lead the Olympic Movement. The goal of the Olympic Movement is to contribute to building a peaceful and better world by educating youth through sport practiced in accordance with Olympism and its values. The IOC owns the Olympic Games held in summer and winter, every four years. The membership of the IOC is complex. Each member of the IOC is elected for a period of eight years and may be re-elected. There are a number of categories of membership. These are:

- Members of the IOC who represent the IOC within their respective country (maximum 70). Their membership is not connected to any specific function.
- Active athletes who are elected by their peers during the Olympic Games (maximum 15).
- Executives or senior leaders within IFs, associations of IFs, or other organisations recognised by the IOC (maximum 15).
- Executives or senior leaders of NOCs, world or continental associations of NOCs (maximum 15). These people can not come from the same country as any of the members in the first category above.

National Olympic Committees

National Olympic Committees (NOCs) are the national organisations of the Olympic Movement. They are responsible for developing, promoting and protecting the Olympic Movement in their respective countries, in accordance with the Olympic Charter. The NOCs have the exclusive authority for the representation of their athletes at the Olympic Games, they can nominate cities within their respective areas as candidates for future Games and promote the development of sport within their country. Currently there are 205 NOCs whose membership is made up of their NFs.

Common characteristics

From this it is apparent that VSOs differ in size, complexity and shape. However, there are a number of features common to all as follows:

- They are all ultimately responsible to a voting membership, who has the power to determine the way the organisation is run. Members may be active in their club, or federation, or they may be passive; however, they have

7

the ultimate power to make decisions. This is why most decisions about an organisation have to be ratified at an annual general meeting, also known as an annual council or annual congress.

■ This membership usually establishes a governing board or a committee that is responsible for carrying out the wishes of the membership. In NOCs, IFs and NFs the board may be large and although most of the governing board will be elected, it may contain people who have been appointed. In addition, the board may contain people from outside the sport who bring specialist skills. For example, the Board of the Amateur Swimming Association contains eight elected regional representatives, four appointed independent specialists (appointed on the basis of their skills sets) and an appointed chair, who is in charge of the governing board. The elected president and forthcoming president are allowed to attend meetings, but have no vote.

■ In small NFs and nearly all clubs, the board or, as is often the case for clubs, the committee, will be small and will consist almost entirely of elected officials. There is likely to be a chair, or president, a secretary, treasurer and one or two other positions.

■ All voluntary sport organisations are guided by a set of rules known as statutes or a constitution. This will set out how the organisation must operate including rules regarding membership and the election of officials (see Chapter 3).

■ Voluntary sport organisations are always part of their country's sport system, and this will affect how they are structured and managed. As will be shown below, policies released by government can have an impact on VSOs from the largest NF to the smallest club.

THE MANAGEMENT OF VOLUNTARY SPORT ORGANISATIONS

Management is a formal process that occurs within organisations in order to direct and organise resources to meet stated objectives. Mullins (2004) regards management as activity that takes place within a structured organisational setting with prescribed roles that are directed towards the attainment of aims and objectives. This is achieved by managing the efforts of other people, using systems and procedures. From this it is apparent that management and managers are of importance to the voluntary sport sector, no matter their size, the resources available to them or their overall stage of development.

For some, managers and management are perceived to be unnecessary for voluntary sport organisations due to the implications of professionalism, commercialism and payment associated with the concepts. However, all VSOs have an organisational setting in which their sport occurs, for example, a pool, field, mountain or sport hall. They have a number of prescribed roles, many of them common across the sector such as president, secretary or coach and the people in these roles, whether paid or not, work towards achieving the objectives

leigh robinson

of the VSO. The success of voluntary sport organisations relies on the coordinated efforts of individuals following procedures, to be found in documents such as the constitution, coaching plans or risk assessments. Thus management occurs in voluntary sport organisations and is carried out by people who can be considered managers, whether they are paid or not. Therefore the term manager is used in this book to describe the person responsible for ensuring that tasks are carried out within the VSO in order for it to achieve its objectives, no matter whether they are paid or voluntary. Management is used to describe the activities and tasks required to achieve the VSO's objectives.

Management context

Within the UK, the way voluntary sport organisations are structured, organised and managed has changed significantly over the past decade, primarily as a result of a series of policy developments that have impacted greatly on the provision of sport in general. A key aim of these developments has been the modernisation of national federations, which has resulted in increasing prominence being placed on strategic planning, accountability, financial independence and good management. This modernisation drive was in part because of the contribution that sport is perceived to play in four key areas of society. These are:

■ *Health*: With a few exceptions sport makes people healthier as it compensates for the food and drink that they consume. With worldwide concerns about increasing obesity, especially among the young, increases in heart disease and an ageing population, sport has a key role in the government's agenda for health.

■ *Politics*: There is an increasing awareness of the political value of sport in terms of national prestige and the psychological benefits of sporting success to a nation, such as the 2008 Beijing Olympics and the 2003 Rugby World Cup victory. In addition, countries are increasingly using sporting events to 'show off' their culture, geography and heritage and to overcome adverse reputations. For example, both South Africa (2010 World Cup) and Brazil (2016 Olympics) will use these mega events to overcome concerns about the safety of the country as a destination for tourists.

■ *Social capital*: There are several arguments about the 'externalities' of sport participation (Gratton and Taylor, 2000) which suggest that participation is beneficial to society. Participation in sport, in addition to being intrinsically valuable, has also been identified as having social capital benefits such as creating social interaction, improving quality of life, improving educational standards and contributing towards lifelong learning (Nichols et al, 2004).

■ *Economics*: There is an increasing awareness of the contribution of hosting major sport events to urban regeneration, such as that which occurred in Manchester (Commonwealth Games 2002), is occurring in London (Olympics 2012) and will occur in Glasgow (Commonwealth Games 2014).

The 'modernisation agenda' has been set out, communicated and driven by two key policy documents. First, in 2002, the Department for Culture, Media and Sport (DCMS) released *A Sporting Future for All*, the Labour Government's strategy for sport in which the modernisation agenda for national federations was launched:

> This will mean sport bodies operate in a new environment. They will have to improve administration to be sure of meeting agreed targets, whilst at the same time becoming more accountable to lottery players, taxpayers and the public at large.

> (DCMS, 2000: 20)

This policy document set out the need for high standards of corporate governance and the modernisation of administration structures and practices, stating:

> Cups are not won in committee rooms, but we know from the experience of other countries that professional organisation and modern administration – supporting sport from primary schools right up to elite level – can increase the likelihood of international success.

> (DCMS, 2000: 19)

Sport clubs were also considered in the report, which stated 'that there is a need for a more systematic and structured development of sports clubs across the country' (DCMS, 2000: 40). The report also set out the proposed development of an accreditation scheme for junior sport clubs aiming to drive up their quality. This led to the subsequent development of Clubmark, which is built around a set of core criteria incorporated into a set of acceptable, minimum operating standards.

The second policy report of significance was released in 2003. The continuing need for change was clear within *Investing in Change – High Level Review of the Modernisation Programme for Governing Bodies of Sport*, which stated:

> Whatever their size or circumstances, NGBs need to anticipate, identify and respond to the numerous and varied changing needs of their stakeholders. NGBs are having to confront increasingly complicated external environments. To survive, NGBs need to have competent structures, people and policies to provide them with the ability and flexibility to adapt to the requirements of ever-changing circumstances.

> Deloitte and Touche (2003: 10)

The report set out a number of recommendations for the UK national federations that led to significant change in their management and governance. These were:

10

- *Financial independence should be a target for all NGBs*: Currently all UK national federations are reliant to a large extent on government funding through the sport councils, or UK Sport. There is a strong drive to reduce the proportion of funding that comes from government sources. This has implications for marketing, fund-raising, commercial activities and sponsorship – all of which will need to be more professional and successful.
- *Larger NGBs should professionalise their senior management*: The demands on larger NGBs are such that there is a need for full-time attention to be given to the management of the organisation. This is an unreasonable demand to place on a voluntary workforce and thus requires paid employees to focus on activities full-time.
- *Governance standards should be improved*: Governing boards are required to make increasingly complex decisions about larger amounts of funding, which affects increasing numbers of people. Thus, board involvement and strategic accountability needs to be developed to improve accountability and transparency.
- *Staff, board members and volunteers should be adequately trained*: Effective performance requires volunteers and paid staff with the right skills and knowledge to do their jobs properly. This will require induction, regular training audits and ongoing training.
- *Rationalisation of subgroups to minimise duplication*: Many sports have evolved in a piecemeal fashion, often leading to structures that duplicate roles, competition arrangements and voluntary activity. The way a sport is structured needs to be reviewed and there may be a need for the restructuring of the way the sport is organised.
- *Greater collaboration between home country and UK/GB NGBs*: Some sports have several NGBs responsible for different levels of the sport, or different territories. At times this creates gaps in sport provision and communication. Consequently, there is a need for greater communication between the various organisations responsible for the sport to ensure a smooth pathway from 'participation' to 'elite'.
- *More effective communication with and within stakeholders*: It is important that the management of NGBs is transparent and open. This will require much greater communication with stakeholders of the organisation.
- *Partnerships should be developed with delivery agents*: NGBs are not necessarily the best providers of all VSO services because of resource constraints, and they should look to the public and commercial sector for assistance where appropriate.
- *A customer focus on both members and participants*: There is a growing awareness of the need for NGBs to focus on the needs and satisfaction of key stakeholders. This will require active consultation with stakeholders and an increase in their participation in the management and operations of the NGB.

11

- *NGBs should measure their performance*: NGBs need to set objectives and work with performance indicators (see Chapter 7) to demonstrate the achievement of these objectives.

The impact of these policy reports has been far-reaching, substantial and diverse. The funding of national federations has been contingent on the development of a strategic plan and performance against key performance indicators, and some national federations have had their funding agreements cut substantially as a result of poor performance and poor governance. Indeed there have been instances of national federations going into receivership as a consequence of poor management arrangements. Clubs have not been immune from the modernisation agenda. Clubmark has led to the increasing formalisation of the operations of junior clubs. The UK national federations have placed an increasing emphasis on the delivery of their objectives via clubs, and an increased focus on professionalisation has required a greater commitment to training and development among volunteers.

In addition, there is a small but determined drive to encourage sport clubs down a social enterprise route, which are businesses that act for a social purpose. For a sport social enterprise, social aims could be making sport accessible to those on a low income, or by providing opportunities for learning through sport coaching or development, which is of particular interest for those clubs who raise income via junior academies. The impact of a business approach to the management of clubs on their voluntary nature is yet to be determined; however, it is possible to see how this might undermine the very nature of these voluntary organisations.

It is clear that management has become an essential and integral part of the voluntary sport sector. Although the UK policy context has been set out above, sport systems in many other countries are subject to the same pressures. For example, *The Canadian Sports Policy* released by Canadian Heritage (2002) called for a sport system that was more collaborative and coordinated, while the Crawford Report (2009: 101) sets out how 'the capacity of Australia's sporting organisations to expand the delivery of sport and physical activity needs urgent attention'. It is difficult to see how these policy intentions will be achieved without the coordination of the efforts of people towards the attainment of aims and objectives, and thus management of VSOs is intrinsic to policy success.

Management skills

This section considers the personal skills that are needed to be an effective manager of a voluntary sport organisation. It focuses on the key skills of decision making, problem solving, communicating, managing time and managing conflict, because these skills underpin all management activities.

leigh robinson

Decision making

The management of VSOs requires decision making. Managers need to make decisions about everything from the allocation of resources to the colour of team uniforms. Decision making is often difficult because of the turbulent environment within which sport organisations operate (see Chapter 2). Often managers cannot be sure of the exact consequences of the decisions they make and thus make few decisions about which they are certain. They also have to make risky decisions, which occur when there is some idea of the choices available but no definite idea of the outcomes. Thus, there is a risk to making decisions, which should be reduced by collecting additional information and relying on previous experience. For example, if a club's junior athletes have never travelled out of the country before, there is a risk that the situation will be so daunting that they fail to perform as expected. The likelihood of this happening can be assessed by considering the previous experiences of junior teams, or by asking the team how they feel about the trip.

Managers will make decisions where they have no clear idea of the alternatives and therefore the outcomes. This does not happen often, but it does arise in situations where there has been no precedent. Gathering additional information about the issue can help to reduce uncertainty, as can seeking help from others. The organisation may never have staged a major event, but seeking assistance and information from those who have will allow a more certain decision to be made.

Obviously, decisions about which managers are certain are the safest for the organisation. However, since there are few opportunities to make such decisions, the risk of decision making needs to be reduced, particularly for major decisions such as whether to invest in facilities, events or services. One way to reduce this risk is to adopt the problem solving process that is set out below. This will help to make decision making more rational. However, in order to make rational decisions, managers need to be clear about the choices available and the criteria against which they can select. Sufficient information in order to assess decisions against these criteria needs to be obtained. This information then should be used to come to a decision. This process is important when significant resources are involved. For example, a club with a limited budget may have to decide whether or not to enter a junior team into a competition that is being held in another country. There are four options: to enter them into the competition, to not enter them, to seek appropriate competition in the home country or to use the money for an alternative event for the team, such as a training camp.

There are costs and benefits associated with these options, such as the experience to be gained from the competition, the cost of travel, the experience to be gained from travelling to another country and the money to be saved by not going. The criteria used to make the decision might include monetary cost, other opportunities lost if the team is entered, how much schooling the team will miss, the benefits of exposing juniors to international competition, how this competition fits within the team's development plan and the level of competition expected. From these criteria, a decision can be made about entering the competition.

Problem solving

Problem solving is an important management skill and having a structured approach to problems will help the organisation become more effective, primarily by helping decision making to be more rational. First managers need to be aware that there is a problem, and this is not always as easy as it sounds. Volunteers and paid employees may hide the fact they are struggling with their work, or sponsors may be disappointed with the publicity they are getting but may say nothing. It is only when something goes wrong or when a sponsor withdraws support that the problem becomes apparent. Once the problem emerges, it can be dealt with; however, it is often easy to confuse the symptoms of the problem with the problem itself, for example, trying to raise money to deal with a loss of sponsorship rather than establishing why the sponsorship was lost.

Information on who perceives there to be a problem and on possible causes of the problem need to be gathered. This is best done in consultation with others since other people may have a different perspective on a problem and talking to them may allow the manager to identify a better solution. When the problem is one of sponsorship, those responsible for obtaining sponsorship should be consulted as should those who benefit from the sponsorship and, if possible, the sponsors themselves in order to identify why they have withdrawn their support.

Once the problem is identified and why it has arisen becomes clear, solutions need to be developed. If the problem involves sponsorship, alternative sponsors could be sought, or there could be an attempt to re-engage the lost sponsors. The VSO may not choose to seek new sponsorship, instead raising money from other sources, such as increased membership fees. The implications of these alternatives need to be considered because some decisions may solve the problem but may also cause greater problems. Raising membership fees is likely to be unpopular and lead to a decline in membership, and some available sponsors, such as tobacco companies, may not be considered appropriate by other sponsors, leading them to remove their sponsorship.

The next step is often the hardest. A decision has to be made and then communicated to all of those affected, such as funding bodies, athletes, members and other sponsors. The decision must be unambiguous, communicated appropriately and implemented well. Finally, a check needs to be made on whether the problem has been solved. For example, have funds increased as a result of the decision? Occasionally the decision may need to be changed in order to achieve the best result. It may even turn out to be a mistake and the process will have to start again.

14

This is clearly a lengthy process and is not likely to occur for all problem solving; indeed, it is not appropriate for all problems. It is important, however, to take a structured approach when the problems are so significant that they can fundamentally affect the organisation or the people working within it.

Communication

The ability to communicate is arguably the most important skill required of those responsible for managing people, and there are many advantages of good communication. Communication increases efficiency; the volunteers and paid staff make fewer mistakes because they know exactly what tasks have to be achieved, why they have to be completed and how to go about completing them. Not only is this motivating, it also reduces costs to the organisation since fewer errors are made. In addition, in order to engage stakeholders, managers need to establish what they want, which is particularly important for sponsors and funding agencies. Finally, the end result of greater motivation, involvement and reduced mistakes is better service to stakeholders.

Information can be communicated in written (paper or electronic) or verbal form and three factors affect the form of communication chosen. The purpose of the communication is important, and written information tends to be more formal than verbal information. For example, an offer of employment must be made in writing, while an offer of additional training could be made verbally. Although email is often used in an informal manner, it is important to realise that some people consider it to be a written form of communication and therefore it carries an element of formality.

The target audience also needs to be considered. It is appropriate to verbally pass information on to volunteers and paid staff; however, agreements with sponsors should be written. In addition, information needs to be communicated in an appropriate language and form. This may mean that information should be available in a foreign language, in large print or even in pictures if trying to communicate with children. Finally, the length of the communication is important. Verbal communication is appropriate for short messages, whilst lengthy and complex information is better disseminated in writing so that people can return to it to assist with understanding.

Time management

Managing time is one of the major problems facing those who work in voluntary sport organisations. The work that volunteers do is often in addition to other employment, or other responsibilities. It is often difficult to say no to additional work, particularly if it appears to be of value to the organisation. However, if time is not managed properly, there is a risk that work will not be completed to the proper standards. Alternatively, managers may become so overburdened that they cannot complete all their work. Therefore everyone who works with VSOs needs to be skilled at time management in order to manage themselves and the organisation's resources effectively.

A time management strategy is often required. First, however, managers should be aware of the activities that cause time to be lost, such as the following:

- *Lack of preparation*: Not spending enough time prioritising tasks or establishing what has to be achieved.
- *Procrastination*: Putting off tasks because they are too difficult or boring.
- *Poor prioritisation*: Working on tasks that are simple rather than important.
- *Confusing what is urgent with what is important:* Responding to the person who is the most persistent rather than doing the most important task.
- *Poor delegation*: Trying to do everything rather than getting someone to assist, or delegating so poorly that the staff member has to continually ask for help.
- *Poor communication*: Giving out incorrect or poorly expressed information so that time is wasted by having to provide more information or correct errors that have come about as a result of poor information.
- *Lengthy phone calls, meetings or conversations*: Taking a longer time with these than is required because the purpose is not clear or information is missing.
- *Taking work home after a full day*: Working inefficiently because of tiredness or conflicts with other demands.

A time management strategy is a useful way of handling these distractions. This requires:

- *Recording all commitments, including meetings, tasks to be completed and deadlines*: This record will allow regular work planning and ensure that plans are followed. Where this information is recorded is not important; it could be recorded on paper or electronically. What is important is that the record is kept.
- *Clarity about what has to be achieved*: It is not possible to do everything, so managers need to assess the tasks that are essential in terms of achieving the objectives of the organisation. It is more important to seek the information needed to complete a strategic plan than to respond to information about a social event, although the latter may be more enjoyable. This will allow the prioritising of tasks as it is easy to get sidetracked and to waste time on things that are interesting but not essential.
- *Structuring time*: Time should be divided into blocks and allocated to certain activities, such as writing reports, attending meetings, working with colleagues or performing administrative duties. Tasks requiring concentration and research should be allocated to the time when managers feel most alert, such as first thing in the morning. Alternatively, phone calls, paperwork and email can be left for times when it is more difficult to concentrate on work, such as after lunch. In addition, it is important to

16

leigh robinson

identify time periods when managers can and cannot be disturbed by those who work with them.

■ *Learning to say no*: The ability to turn down requests for work when overloaded or faced with other priorities is an indication of efficiency. If managers refuse to organise a team-building event because of workload, this will indicate to others that they have a large workload and are able to prioritise their tasks. If the team-building event cannot wait until the workload is reduced, managers should delegate the task to someone else.

Managers will have individual time management strategies that work best for them. Different techniques, such as delegation, using a 'to do' list or working from home, will suit different occupations, management styles and organisations. The key point is that once time has been lost, it is impossible to make it up.

Managing conflict

Conflict between individuals and teams is a part of every organisation. Individuals and teams compete for financial resources, time from managers, equipment and even customers. This competition will occasionally result in conflict within the organisation. Conflict within organisations is not always a bad thing, and constructive conflict can serve a variety of functions. Conflict can encourage people to work together to fight a common enemy. It can help define roles and increase understanding of others' feelings; for example, debate over who should be captain of a team will highlight what is important to those having the debate and the skills of those under consideration.

Constructive conflict can increase understanding of the problem, since conflict usually arises when individuals are not aware of the concerns of all involved. Thus, constructive conflict is to be welcomed in a voluntary sport organisation. Alternatively, destructive conflict is usually detrimental to the organisation because it tends to be based on personality differences or concerned with the preservation of power. It is necessary to identify destructive conflict and have a strategy for dealing with it.

There are several issues to consider before tackling conflict. The first question to address is whether it is worth intervening. If the conflict is not affecting the work of those involved and looks like it will resolve itself, intervention may inflame the situation. Managers will also need the personality characteristics and communication skills to be able to deal with the conflict in a calm, rational and fair manner. If they lack these skills, it is often better to have someone else deal with the situation.

Finally, the timing of the intervention is important. Intervention must come at a time when it can actually be of use, rather than too early or too late, when intervention may escalate the conflict or inflame it. For example, if a manager intervenes in an argument between a chief coach and an assistant coach, they may look ridiculous if the argument was over something minor or was unrelated to the job. Alternatively, if a number of arguments are ignored, team performance may be negatively affected. The skill is to intervene after the right number of arguments!

Once the decision has been made to intervene, a strategy to deal with the situation is required. This involves the following:

- *Identifying the problem*: It is necessary to identify who is involved in the conflict, why the conflict has arisen and the issues involved.
- *Examining the relationships that the protagonists have within the organisation*: This will allow the identification of other people who may help resolve the problem.
- *Identifying the problems and the costs of the behaviour*: This may be in terms of time wasted, the demotivating effect on others in the team or an unpalatable atmosphere.
- *Approaching those involved in the conflict*: All involved need to work together to search for a solution.
- *Implementing the solution and then evaluating the situation*: After implementation, evaluate the situation on an ongoing basis until the conflict has been resolved.

Although handling conflict is often an unpleasant task, if it is ignored there are likely to be negative consequences for the organisation. The best strategy is to be aware of where conflict may arise and to develop plans to prevent it from arising. This strategy can be facilitated by the fair allocation of resources, equitable and fair treatment of all involved with the organisation, and awareness of relationships and tensions that may be occurring within the organisation. Preventing conflict is not always possible, however, and once conflict is identified, it needs to be managed efficiently and effectively.

All of these skills are necessary for the effective management of voluntary sport organisations. The ability to make decisions and communicate these and to organise and complete a full workload is essential in order for objectives to be met. Fortunately all of these skills can be developed or improved by personal development activities, such as training courses. Therefore it is important for managers to evaluate their level of skill in the above areas and then improve on this if necessary.

leigh robinson

CHAPTER 2

THE OPERATING ENVIRONMENT OF VOLUNTARY SPORT ORGANISATIONS

Leigh Robinson

In order for voluntary sport organisations to be effective, managers need to understand the internal and external operating environments affecting the organisation. This includes having an understanding of where the organisation fits into the country's sport system. This will allow managers to understand who they need to work with in order to be the most successful for their sport and their organisation. This is the purpose of this chapter, which will first set out the nature of organisations and then present and discuss factors in the operating environments that need to be taken into account when managing a voluntary sport organisation.

THE SPORT SYSTEM

The sport system of a country is made up of the various organisations that have an impact on sport either through policy, funding or delivery. The system will consist of organisations that are directly related to sport, such as clubs and leagues, and organisations that are not directly related to sport, but have an impact on sport, such as sponsors and government departments. In addition, as set out in Chapter 1, each VSO will have a structure that is directly related to their sport.

Within each sport system, managers need to know which organisations and people they should work directly with in order to promote and deliver their sport, and which they should be aware of, periodically checking to see if their activities might have a more direct impact on the VSO. The organisations and people that directly impact on the organisation should be considered in any management activity.

19

What is an organisation?

An organisation is a group of people working together to achieve an end goal. A voluntary sport organisation is therefore a group of people working together to achieve goals related to sport. There are four core elements that make up an organisation:

- *People*: How people are identified within an organisation depends on the context, but identification falls principally into one or more of three categories:
  - individual identity, or who they are
  - role and formal position, or their principal duties in the organisation
  - type of stakeholder (see below), or type of interest or group they represent.
- *Rules*: These define formal and informal tasks, roles and responsibilities; principles of good corporate governance; patterns of communication; authority relationships; and the nature of power in organisations. Organisations invariably work by certain rules. These may be formally stated or they may be agreed upon informally. Similarly, the roles and responsibilities of a particular post can be formally stated in a job description (see Chapter 5), informally agreed upon or even simply implicit in the title of a job, such as team manager.
- *Goals and purposes*: Every organisation can be characterised by its goals and purposes. For example, the purpose of an NOC is to promote Olympism. The goals used to achieve this purpose can vary from providing recreational opportunities at the grass-roots level to sending athletes to the Olympic Games.
- *Resources*: Without these, it would be impossible for an organisation to function. The resources that are available come in many forms, such as revenue, people, services and time.

When trying to identify how the organisation might function more effectively, these elements need to be addressed. However, it is also necessary to remember that the external context will have a significant impact on the way the organisation can be managed. For example, the Olympic Movement will significantly influence the goals that national federations can pursue. It also has a large influence on the rules by which most voluntary sport organisations operate as even the most commercial national federation is likely to have an elected board made up of volunteers. Finally, the context allows the organisation to access people who are prepared to give up their time without pay because of their belief in the value of sport. Very few other operating contexts provide such access to volunteers.

Stakeholders

A stakeholder is anyone who has a stake or interest in the organisation. That interest may not be material or financial, it could be emotional, such as the interest that the general public has in the performance of their country at the Olympic Games. This means that stakeholders include everyone who is affected by the organisation. For example, the stakeholders of a sports club could be:

■ members: athletes and officials
■ parents
■ schools
■ the national federation
■ sponsors
■ volunteers
■ board members
■ paid staff (if applicable)
■ government
■ the general public/community.

Managers need to know who the organisation's stakeholders are as these people will have expectations of the organisation. They may impact on strategy (see Chapter 4) and may provide opportunities to set up partnerships to expand the work the organisation can do. Not only must managers be clear about who the VSO's stakeholders are, but they also need to know who is the most important so that their expectations, objectives and needs are met.

Impact of government

Government is a key player in the sport system of most countries as it sets objectives for national organisations and provides funding for VSOs at all levels. Therefore it needs to be considered as a stakeholder due to the role it will play in developing policy and providing funding. Both of these will affect voluntary sport organisations, no matter how small or their perceived importance in the sport system.

In particular, the attitude of politicians towards sport, the prominence of sport in policy and as a policy tool, and the relationships amongst the organisations responsible for sport in the country will all have a big impact on sport organisations. For example, if government policy values sport as a means of increasing health or decreasing crime, it is likely to be easier to access funds for services. If the relationship between sport organisations and government departments is poor, it may be more difficult to promote and deliver sport. The stability of governments and key politicians will also affect a manager's ability to plan and fund activities.

21

Perhaps most crucially, the value that government policies place on physical education for children will dictate whether the country values sport or not.

The impact of government can be significant for many sport organisations as governments dictate what policy is important and this dictates where funding goes. Therefore, managers have a responsibility to understand their government's approach to sport, how it impacts on voluntary sport organisations and what might be done, if anything, to help shape policy.

ENVIRONMENTAL AUDITING

Although VSOs operate within the country's sport system and within the structure of its sport, each organisation in this system operates in a unique environment. A number of factors within the organisation's environment will offer opportunities, but others will pose challenges for the organisation. All organisations exist and operate within an external environment that determines its success, offers opportunities, presents threats and shapes strategy. As a result, it is essential that managers carry out an appraisal of this environment. In addition, it is important that managers are aware of the capability of the internal environment – the organisation itself. This will allow managers to identify strengths of the service, such as staff, or weaknesses, such as ageing facilities. Understanding the environment requires auditing.

Two main factors affect the success of environmental auditing. First, the accuracy of the audit will only be as good as the information upon which the audit is based. It is therefore important to have access to current and relevant information on trends and changes that may affect the organisation. Second, the success of environmental analysis relies on a structured approach to the review. This ensures that all key aspects of the environment are addressed in a comprehensive manner. The danger is that without a structured approach, important changes in the environments may be missed. This is particularly vital when auditing the external environment, given its size and the number of features to consider. A commonly used structure for carrying out external analysis is presented below.

Auditing the external environment

Managers should audit and evaluate the dimensions that impact on the business environment in which they operate (Sloman and Sutcliffe, 2001). Analysis of these dimensions is referred to by the acronym PESTLE, which stands for the Political, Economic, Social, Technological, Legal and Environmental dimensions of the external environment.

leigh robinson

Political factors

Political factors primarily come from government initiatives or the initiatives of significant organisations in the sport system. This includes policies, such as those issued by the IOC or World Anti-Doping Agency (WADA), a government's 'health agenda' and the political values expressed by government, such as 'sport for all'. For example, the release of the *Investing in Change* report (Deloitte and Touche, 2003) in the UK in 2003 and the Crawford Report (Crawford, 2009) in Australia in 2009 had a fundamental impact on the voluntary sport organisations in those countries, requiring a change in the structure, objectives and management of their respective voluntary sport systems. Political influence is not necessarily limited to the country in which the organisation is situated; many VSOs operate internationally and are therefore affected by the political factors present wherever they are providing services.

Economic factors

Economic factors are features such as the strength of the economy, unemployment levels, how much people are prepared to pay for services and whether people can afford to be volunteers. Because there is no requirement for people to use voluntary sport organisations, such organisations must compete for income that is left over after people have met their basic needs for shelter, food and clothing. Factors such as the inflation rate, unemployment rate, level of disposable income and cost of living all determine how much money people have to spend on sport services. Indeed, in a number of countries the economic factors are such that it is not possible for sport organisations to charge for their services, which affects the type and extent of services offered.

A significant economic factor is the level of competition an organisation faces, and VSOs operate in a highly competitive industry. As mentioned, voluntary sport organisations compete for the money left over after basic needs are met, but so do many other organisations. Although competition can be for money, for most VSOs it is likely to be for people. If football is the most popular sport in a country, it is often difficult for other sports to attract large numbers of participants. If religious or cultural events are an essential part of society, people will spend more of their leisure time taking part in these events rather than sport.

Perhaps most importantly, the value that a government places on sport will have a significant economic impact because of funding. It dictates whether the economic context is good, poor or even changing. In addition, managers need to know how the government funds sport. For example, funding could go directly to regional level organisations, or even straight to clubs, or it could be given only to large VSOs, such as the NOC, to be distributed to member organisations. This information will influence the process for accessing funding, accountability and how the organisation will be evaluated.

Social factors

Social factors are a result of the way that a society is structured and behaves. Social factors include demographic features such as an ageing population, smaller households, changing lifestyles, a trend towards watching sport rather than taking part and a trend towards team sport rather than individual sport. Factors such as the gender and age make-up of the population, family structure, income distribution, levels of education and social mobility will affect who is attracted to your organisation. More importantly, however, cultural factors such as attitudes towards sport participation, including parental attitudes towards children's participation and attitudes towards work and leisure, will affect the role that VSOs can play in society.

Technological factors

Technological factors come from an increasingly diverse range of sources and are those that relate to advances in technology, engineering or technical skills. For example, changes in information and communication technology (see Chapter 13) means that information can be created, sorted and disseminated rapidly by all voluntary sport organisations. The use of 'third' officials has become common in sports, such as rugby and cricket. The Hawk-Eye technology used in tennis overrules human decision making, and improvements in fabric technology has meant that the international body for swimming – Fédération Internationale de Natation (FINA) – has had to rule on whether certain swimsuits are legal or not. Perhaps most interestingly, technology is becoming a competitor to VSOs, as for example video games, such as the Wii Sport system, allow people to be active in their own homes.

Legal factors

There are no sports without rules. Sports are regulated by rules and standards of conduct established within the organisation to ensure the survival of the sport's basic principles and the permanence of the sport organisations. These rules fulfil the following functions:

- Establish standards of play (technical rules) for the specific sport or athletic discipline.
- Establish standards for competition.
- Establish standards of conduct that participants in the sport must follow.
- Establish rules governing the relationships (membership or participation) of the bodies and people comprising the athletics movement.

Thus, sport can be said to be self-regulating and to exist within its own internal legal system. Therefore the organisation must change as the rules of the sport change. In addition, all voluntary sport organisations have some form of statutes or constitution that guide and regulate the way that the organisation can operate. These form the internal legal framework, which is the basis for all other considerations facing the organisation.

In addition, no sport organisation operates in a vacuum separate from the rest of society, and in its interaction with its stakeholders, it will be affected by the legal rules of that wider environment. As a result, managers should have some awareness of the following areas of law (see also Chapter 11):

■ *Delict or tort*: This is the failure to perform a duty of care to the required standard. A particular type of delictual or tort action relates to negligence, perhaps the most likely cause of legal liability for a sport organisation. What is considered to be negligence may differ amongst countries and therefore managers need to understand how a country's legal system defines negligence.
■ *Employment law*: Each country is likely to have laws that affect the employment and treatment of staff. For example, the Bosman ruling requires free movement of workers amongst countries of the European Union (EU).
■ *Drugs and doping*: Laws regarding the use of banned substances must be understood.
■ *Intellectual property*: These laws ensure protection of the organisation's brand.
■ *Health and safety*: These laws are important for risk management, which will be discussed in Chapter 12.
■ *Defamation, slander and libel*: These laws involve protection of a person's reputation.

There may be a perception within some countries that such legal concerns are more applicable to a jurisdiction with a sophisticated and litigious legal environment. However, it is still important that everyone responsible for the management of a voluntary sport organisation fully understands the legal framework within which the organisation operates, and in particular it is important for the board and its members to be aware of the potential liability they face.

Environmental factors

Environmental factors are those which occur in the wider operating environment of an organisation. Factors such as climate change, carbon offsetting, recycling, chemical disposal and planning regulations impact on the way VSOs can plan their activities. For example, a national federation may choose to send their athletes to competition by train, rather than plane, in order to reduce carbon emissions. Sports, such as triathlon, which use the natural environment, may be limited in where they can compete due to environmental restrictions designed to protect the countryside.

25

Auditing the internal environment

Johnson et al (2008) have proposed that the auditing of the internal environment should focus on four basic areas:

■ *Physical resources*: The actual items at the disposal of the service, such as equipment or facilities, the age and condition of these items and the potential to use these items to enhance *services or benefits*.
■ *Human resources*: The service's staff in terms of the roles required, the skills and experience available and the ability of staff to adapt to potential changes.
■ *Financial resources*: How the organisation is financed and funded, the management of income and expenditure and the relationship with key financial stakeholders, such as Sport England, commercial partners or banks.
■ *Operational resources*: Such as how the service operates, where it operates, the resources required by different services and how the services are perceived.

Within these areas managers need to examine and evaluate past performance. The purpose of this is to try to account for why the service has had its past successes and failures. It is not enough to just be aware of the success and/or failure of service strategies, managers must be able to explain or account for these in order to learn from the past.

Next there must be an evaluation of current practices within the organisation. There are a number of approaches for doing the evaluation; however, the Towards an Excellent Service (TAES) or Quest frameworks outlined in Chapter 7 are appropriate for this activity. This should focus on what is actually happening, not what policies or strategic documents say should happen. This will ensure that the audit actually reflects the existing internal environment.

Impact of the operating context

From the previous discussion it is clear that managers need to have a good understanding of the operating context of their organisation. Each country, each region and each town or village is likely to have different factors that influence the management of the organisation. In addition, it is unlikely that the factors in the operating environment will remain constant. For this reason, it may be necessary to change the way the organisation is managed and the direction of the organisation. A review of the operating contexts of a UK national governing body in Table 2.1 sets out features in the operating context that may impact on management of the organisation.

Table 2.1 Contextual influences on a UK National Governing Body

External environment	Central policy initiatives to:
	    improve the health of the nation
	    to tackle childhood obesity
	    to increase accountability
	    to continuously improve governance
	    to make people more active
	
	Increases in health and safety legislation
	Data Protection
	Increases in child safeguarding legislation
	Changes to employment law
	
	Increasing expectations
	Ageing of the population
	Trend towards spectating
	Trend towards team sports
	London 2012
	
	Decreases in budgets
	Changes in funding
	    lottery
	    European Union
	Recession
	Increases in competition for customers
	Increasing need for transparency and accountability
	
	Improvements in data storage, transfer and retrieval
	Improvements in leisure technology
	Improvements in broadcasting

Internal environment	Need for improved governance Increasing professionalism Need for commercial practices Pressure to generate revenue or decrease reliance on government subsidy Lack of control over facilities Decreases in staff numbers

MATCHING INTERNAL CAPABILITIES WITH EXTERNAL OPPORTUNITIES

Essential to the effective management of VSOs is the concept of matching capabilities of the internal environment with opportunities available in the external environment (Finlay, 2000; Johnson et al, 2008; Adcroft and Teckman, 2009). This encourages organisations to follow strategies that are appropriate for the needs of their organisation and within its resources, to be competitive and to develop competencies for future development. In order to do this, managers must be very clear about the capabilities that the organisation has in relation to the opportunities on offer in the external environment. This is frequently a problem for VSOs, particularly small organisations, such as clubs, or voluntary sport organisations in developing sport systems, which are heavily reliant on external funding that is often made available for predetermined activities, such as coach education. As this is the major, if not only, source of external funding for these organisations, this 'ring-fencing' of funding encourages managers to follow strategies that may not be appropriate for their size, level of development, or other resources.

In an attempt to address this, Minikin (2009) has developed an internal analytical framework, which amongst its many purposes evaluates the capability of a sport organisation in relation to the sport programme it wants to deliver. From his research, carried out with voluntary sport organisations in the Pacific region, Minikin identified seven dimensions of performance within VSOs, defined as follows:

- *Governance*: Including rules and regulations, policies and strategic planning.
- *Management*: Including organisational structure, role development.
- *Physical resources*: Including equipment (sport and administrative), facilities access and availability.
- *Human resources*: Including type and diversity as well as planning and management practices.
- *Finance*: Including record keeping, marketing and planning.
- *Communication*: Including methods used, responsiveness and technology available.
- *Sport activity*: Including competition or preparing for competition, development programmes, training.

Each of these dimensions is made up of a number of elements that become increasingly complex as the organisation becomes increasingly developed and thus more capable. Figure 2.1 sets out the performance dimensions and their associated elements.

In addition to establishing the performance dimensions and the hierarchical order of elements that make these up, the research established what organisational capability was required for a number of externally funded programmes. This allows a manager to assess the organisation's capabilities against the requirements of an external programme in order to identify first, whether they have the capability to deliver the programme and second, where they need to develop the organisation in order to achieve the required levels of capability.

An assessment of a VSO's status against the elements is carried out through consultation with the key internal and external stakeholders. This analysis is then plotted against the organisational requirements that have been determined for the programme. Figure 2.2 sets this out for a VSO wishing to run a level 1

leigh robinson

Governance	Management	Sport Activity	Communication	Finance	Physical Resource	Human Resources
Business contracts	Established partnerships	Hosting international events	Web platform for all members	Financial independence	Own headquarters	Full professional HR management
Annual congress held	Sophisticated event management	Success in WC/OG	Organisation social networking established	Diverse income streams	Vehicles	Full time national team personnel
Franchise infrastructure	Formal evaluation procedures	Attend WC/OG	Mass media advertising	Investment accounts/ assets	Reliable sponsor support	Education specialist
Independent office	Comprehensive risk management	Regional championships	Own magazine	Sponsorship at commercial level	Supporting amenities	CEO deployed
Long-term strategic plan	Event management manual	International competitions	TV announcements	Dedicated programme funding	Investment assets	Elite athletes
Executive board has portfolio	Advanced operational procedure	Sub-regional championship	Media events	Fund-raising now effective	Regular training venue	Specialist coaches/TOs
Adoption of international rules	Established competition management	Selection criteria for international events	Mass email	Maximum solidarity programme support	IF regulated uniforms	Sport science support
Detailed constitution	Operational procedures	National championships	Basic web site	Significant IF funding support	Office or headquarters	Graded officials
Membership through districts	Specific project administration	Year around competitions	Individual social networking	Solidarity world funding	Shared club facility	Facility managers
Formal governance document exists	Event management strategies	Qualifying championships	Communicate high responsiveness	Regular sponsorship support	Membership-based club	National team coordinators
Annual general meetings	Specialist departments	Calendar of events	Press conferences	Some IF funding support	Internet access	Specialised officials
Membership through clubs	Implement IF rules and regulations	Consistent competition management	Regular media releases	Sustainable member fees	Computer and printer/ office equipment	Coaches/coach training
Basic strategic plan in place	Coordinated risk management	Inter-state/inter-district	Email	Budgeting	Tracksuits and kit for players	Specialised athletes
Affiliation to IF/NOC	Implement IOC rules and regulations	Junior/senior/open competitions	Radio announcement	Event revenue	Standard sport equipment	Referees
Elected committee	Regular meetings held	Established competition seasons	Newsletter	Olympic solidarity basic support	Standard venue	Basic training for administrators
Standard rules and regulations	Simple operational plan	Regular formal competition	Advertising	Government support	Access to office facilities	Basic training for officials
Generic development planning	Clubs are formed	Introduction to schools/ programmes	Notice board - sport specific	Consistent member fees	Standard uniform	Competition managers
Basic constitution in place	Basic risk management	Graded competitions	Text messaging	Basic financial reporting	Uniforms	Athlete training
Governing committee forms	Competition committee forms	Hosting tournaments	Media releases	Fund raising activity	Fax and phone	Specialised volunteers
Basic sport rules	Ad hoc competition management	Inter village competition	Posters	Basic record keeping	Simple sport equipment	Casual event organisers
Ad hoc planning	Natural leadership	Formal competitions	Contact person	Bank account	Playground	Equipment officers
Casual membership base	Organising teams	Regular informal competitions	Written notices	Basic book-keeping	Personal resources	Volunteer administrators
Informal policies	Volunteer administration	Social activities	Bulletin board - public	Inconsistent membership fees	Donated equipment	Village groups
Basic regulations	Peer pressure	Irregular competitions	Group network	Word of mouth marketing	Simple prepared sport area	All-round athletes (play other sports)
Non regulated	Casual following	Play	Coconut wireless	Inconsistent competition registration fees	In-kind sponsor	Friends

Figure 2.1 Dimensions of performance of Olympic sport organisations

Governance	Management	Sport Activity	Communication	Finance	Physical Resource	Human Resources
Business contracts	Established partnerships	Hosting international events	Web platform for all members	Financial independence	Own headquarters	Full professional HR management
Annual congress held	Sophisticated event management	Success in WC/OG	Organisation social networking established	Diverse income streams	Vehicles	Full time national team personnel.
Franchise infrastructure	Formal evaluation procedures	Attend WC/OG	Mass media advertising	Investment accounts/assets	Reliable sponsor support	Education specialist
Independent office	Comprehensive risk management	Regional championships	Own magazine	Sponsorship at commercial level	Supporting amenities	CEO deployed
Long-term strategic plan	Event management manual	International competitions	TV announcements	Dedicated programme funding	Investment assets	Elite athletes
Executive board has portfolio	Advanced operational procedure	Sub-regional championship	Media events	Fund-raising now effective	Regular training venue	Specialist coaches/TOs
Adoption of international rules	Established competition management	Selection criteria for international events	Mass email	Maximum solidarity programme support	IF regulated uniforms	Sport science support
Detailed constitution	Operational procedures	National championships	Basic web site	Significant IF funding support	Office or headquarters	Graded officials
Membership through districts	Specific project administration	Year around competitions	Individual social networking	Solidarity world funding	Shared club facility	Facility managers
Formal governance document exists	Event management strategies	Qualifying championships	Communicate high responsiveness	Regular sponsorship support	Membership-based club	National team coordinators	Level 1 coach course
Annual general meetings	Specialist departments	Calendar of events	Press conferences	Some IF funding support	Internet access	Specialised officials
Membership through clubs	Implement IF rules and regulations.	Consistent competition management	Regular media releases	Sustainable member fees	Computer and printer/office equipment	Coaches/coach training
Basic strategic plan in place	O Coordinated risk management	Inter-state/inter-district	X Email	X Budgeting	X Tracksuits and kit for players	Specialised athletes
Affiliation to IF/NOC	X Implement IOC rules and regulations	Junior/senior/open competitions	Radio announcement	O Event revenue	X Standard sport equipment	X Referees
Elected committee	Regular meetings held	X Established competition ...	Newsletter	Olympic solidarity basic support	Standard venue	Basic training for administrators
Standard rules and regulations	Simple operational plan	X Regular formal competition	X Advertising	Government support	Access to office facilities	O Basic training for officials
Generic development planning	Clubs are formed	O Introduction to schools/programmes	Notice board - sport specific	Consistent member fees	Standard uniform	Competition managers
Basic constitution in place	Basic risk management	Graded competitions	Text messaging	Basic financial reporting	Uniforms	Athlete training
Governing committee forms	Competition committee forms	Hosting tournaments	O Media releases	Fund raising activity	O Fax and phone	Specialised volunteers
Basic sport rules	Ad hoc competition management	Inter village competition	Posters	Basic record-keeping	Simple sport equipment	Casual event organisers
Ad hoc planning	Natural leadership	Formal competitions	Contact person	Bank account	Playground	Equipment officers
Casual membership base	Organising teams	Regular informal competitions	Written notices	Basic book-keeping	Personal resources	Volunteer administrators
Informal policies	Volunteer administration	Social activities	Bulletin board - public	Inconsistent membership fees	Donated equipment	Village groups
Basic regulations	Peer pressure	Irregular competitions	Group network	Word of mouth marketing	Simple prepared sport area	All-round athletes (play other sports)
Non regulated	Casual following	Play	Coconut wireless	Inconsistent comp reg fees	In-kind sponsor	Friends

Figure 2.2 Assessment of capability to run level one coaching course

International coaching programme. In this example, an 'X' is put against those elements that are considered necessary for level one coaching to proceed. The 'O' is placed next to the highest element already established for this organisation.

An analysis of the gap between what the organisation has in place and what is required for successful delivery of the programme will enable the manager to determine their capability to take on a level one coaching programme offered by an external funder. By identifying those elements that are not in place, managers can address these before proceeding with a programme that is being offered. Using Figure 2.2 as an example of a national federation, it could identify the list of elements that might need to be addressed before a decision is made to proceed with the coaching programme offered. These might include:

■ *Governance*: Governance elements appear to be adequate; however, planning the establishment of a formal governance document, annual general meetings and current membership status might be considered.
■ *Management*: Need to establish and implement a simple operational plan and conduct more regular meetings. In the longer term the organisation may wish to address its rules and regulations and review its operating structure to include specialist departments, in the first instance coach or human resources development, leading to a review of event management strategies.
■ *Sport activity*: This organisation would appear to need to establish a better competition infrastructure around regular formal competition that might include a school-based competition and graded competitions beyond the hosting of regular tournaments. The organisation might also look ahead in its planning to the elements listed in the range from establishing a calendar of events to the establishment of competition seasons.
■ *Communication*: The elements required appear to be in place, but for planning purposes the establishment of email contact and the implementation of regular media releases and press conferences as steps towards improving the responsiveness of members appear desirable.
■ *Finance*: This organisation appears to urgently need to address its budgeting procedures and look at its income from government, external funders and member fees and, as well, establish a basic financial reporting system, before the international coaching course is held. At this point, it will then be able to address more sustainable membership fees, regular international federation and sponsorship support.
■ *Physical resources*: Before the course can go ahead the organisation will need to establish access to a standard venue and have at its disposal standard sport equipment. It may then wish to address the elements leading up to membership-based clubs as part of its medium- to long-term planning.
■ *Human resources*: The organisation appears to lack the human resources to proceed towards conducting an international coaching programme and so will need to urgently address training programmes for athletes, competition

31

managers, officials, referees and even establish some specialised athletes in the organisation.

This research has created a diagnostic tool to help analyse the internal state of voluntary sport organisations in terms of their development across the seven key performance dimensions. The intention is that this analysis will help these organisations to make more informed decisions about whether its internal capabilities match up with external opportunities. The advantage of this tool is that it can immediately provide feedback to a VSO on its overall development. This then feeds into the strategic plan and improves organisational capacity.

SUMMARY

Understanding the operating context is a fundamental management activity. It is necessary for the development of organisational strategies (Chapter 4) and allows managers to identify potential areas of change (Chapter 8). It is important to note that these techniques do not tell the manager what to do, they are simply techniques for arranging information in order to make sense of complex environments. They should be used to monitor trends in the sport system, identify change and determine what the organisation is capable of. Managers then use this information to make decisions about improving the effectiveness of their voluntary sport organisation.

leigh robinson

CHAPTER 3

GOVERNANCE OF VOLUNTARY SPORT ORGANISATIONS

Dick Palmer

> You'll never get lost on a straight road.
> (Sir Denis Follows, Chairman BOA 1977–1983)

Governance can be difficult to define but is perhaps easier to recognise in practice. It involves the use of power to direct, control and regulate activities within an organisation. It deals with the high-level issues of strategy and policy direction, transparency and accountability and is not concerned with daily operations, which are the responsibility of management. Corporate governance refers to the systems and processes for ensuring proper accountability, probity and openness in the conduct of an organisation. This might include the processes by which committees are selected, monitored and replaced; the capacity of committees to effectively formulate and implement sound policies; and the respect of members for the structures and the procedures that govern economic and social interactions amongst them.

This chapter sets out the principles by which organisations should be governed, focusing specifically on the role of the elected board. Good governance is applicable to all VSOs. Although the principles set out below may appear more applicable to bigger, more complex VSOs, the committee of the smallest local clubs should consider these important and follow them to the best of their ability, making appropriate changes to fit the circumstances of the club. In the discussion below, the term 'board' will be used to describe the elected body that is responsible for governing the organisation. As mentioned in Chapter 1, this may be also known as the board of directors, executive board, or committee. The chapter concludes with a discussion of features of organisations that impact on governance.

The word 'governance' was hardly part of common coinage amongst sport organisations until the early 1990s. However, around that time a series of issues affecting sporting organisations and a number of high profile cases in the corporate world brought governance to the attention of all those involved in the management and direction of sport bodies. The role of funding organisations, such as sport councils anxious and concerned about the use to which public funds were

33

being put, caused them to pay greater attention to the governance aspects of the organisations that were the beneficiaries of public funds. They demanded better governance from these bodies and set about giving guidance and direction as to how this should be achieved. The consequence of all this has led to a vast amount of information emanating from public bodies, academic institutions, management consultants, legal bodies and others, all seeking to provide guidance and support regarding governance and how good governance is achieved.

The IOC, itself subject to a serious breach of acceptable good governance by a number of its members, has now taken a firm stance on this matter. Jacques Rogge, speaking at a 'Rules of the Games' conference in 2002, stated, 'Because sport is based on ethics and fair competition, the governance of sport should fulfil the highest standards in terms of transparency, democracy and accountability.' More recently, Thomas Bach, Vice President of the IOC, speaking at the 2009 Olympic Congress in Copenhagen, posed the question: 'How can the Olympic Movement best co-operate with different governments and supranational governmental organisations?' He went on to say:

> If their autonomy is to be respected, sporting organisations in the Olympic Movement need to ensure that they apply principles of 'good governance' to their everyday work. They must hold themselves to stringent ethical standards and ensure a high degree of transparency and accountability. To this end there is a need to invest more in the training and professional development of sports administrators. Only by enhancing and solidifying our internal structures and functioning can we demand the full respect of governments.

Good governance should lead to the efficient, effective and ethical management of sport. Although good governance will not solve all of the problems faced by an organisation, it will create the conditions necessary for success by enabling managers to make the most effective use of their resources and allow them to consider fully the interests of stakeholders. When evaluating the governance of voluntary sport organisations, the following need considering:

- *A clear delineation of roles*: A clear organisational structure is needed, with no overlap of the powers of any two individuals or bodies. There needs to be separation between the board (strategic direction) and the executive (management) and a documented delineation of the roles of each.
- *Effective governance processes*: There should be clear, documented governance policies and processes, reflecting best practice to record meeting processes, decision making, agenda and minute taking, committee and commission purposes, authority and scope, and executive delegation authority.
- *Effective governance controls*: There should be agreement about organisational values, vision, mission, goals, strategic plan, operational objectives and key

34

performance measures, risk management, legal compliance, accounting and auditing, reporting and evaluation systems, and performance-review processes. This may include a self-assurance process, which is becoming an increasing expectation of funding agencies. For example, the Sports Council for Wales self-assurance process is a self-checking list that is required to be backed up by the appropriate documentation and lodged periodically with the Sports Council. The areas covered by the process are governance, strategic planning, financial management, organisational policy, risk management and capital policy. It is therefore a comprehensive process and gives an indication of how the organisation is operating.

■ *Governance improvement*: Systems of governance need to include regular performance review and induction training and regular development training for all board members and staff.

■ *Member responsiveness*: Good member–stakeholder relationships are important and will develop from transparency and accountability, good internal and external communication, feedback and prompt responsiveness to concerns, and preparation of a public annual report covering all aspects of governance, finance and sport performance.

BARRIERS TO GOVERNANCE IN VOLUNTARY SPORT ORGANISATIONS

The move towards good governance has not been achieved lightly or easily. There have been a number of inherent difficulties that voluntary sport organisations have had to overcome in order to achieve the better governance of their organisations. Some of these are listed as follows:

■ traditional and outdated governance and management practices
■ a resistance to change within organisations
■ the professionalisation of sport leading to higher expectations from stakeholders
■ tensions between paid staff and volunteers
■ the inability to confront and manage risk
■ outdated technology
■ unclear definition of roles within organisations
■ lack of knowledge or understanding of governance and management roles and responsibilities.

Many of these factors are present in many voluntary sport organisations and have had to be overcome in order for governance practices to improve. Intrinsic to this is a belief that good governance is important. Once this has been established it facilitates the practices of good governance set out in this chapter.

THE DOCUMENTS OF GOVERNANCE: STATUTES

All sport organisations have as their basis a set of rules known as the statutes or constitution and this directs how the institution should conduct its affairs. Key elements of most statutes are:

- aims and objectives of the organisation
- who constitutes its membership and therefore who are eligible to vote at general meetings
- the regularity of meetings
- the business of the general meetings such as:
    - the elections and their regularity
    - the annual report for the proceeding year
    - the annual accounts for the proceeding year
    - the appointment of auditors
- the roles and responsibilities of the main committee including the general meeting and the executive board and those of the officers and chief executive officer (CEO)
- importantly, how the statutes may be amended or changed.

Invariably the statutes require the organisation to hold a general meeting at which the members elect the officers (i.e. the president/chairperson) and elect a board. It is this board, together with the elected officers, that is legally responsible for the conduct, activities and direction of the organisation.

Thus the statutes form the cornerstone of the proper governance of the organisation. Many organisations have statutes that have been drafted decades previously and may, for a number of reasons, such as changes in legislations circumstances of the organisation, and the environment in which the organisation operates, have become out of date and not 'fit for purpose'. It follows therefore that it is the responsibility of the board to ensure that the statutes are regularly assessed (at least every 4–5 years) to ensure that they are relevant to the current circumstances of the organisation. Invariably it is advisable to seek appropriate legal advice to ensure that all aspects of the organisation's responsibilities are covered by any changes contemplated and are compliant with relevant current legislation.

THE ROLE OF THE BOARD

As outlined previously, good governance requires a clear separation between the board, which is the highest decision-making body, and the operating staff of the organisation. The day-to-day management of the organisation is not a board function, and the authority for this should be delegated to the volunteers or paid staff who are responsible for delivering the board's decisions. Large VSOs are

36

likely to have a CEO or equivalent, as well as specialist administrative support, such as financial or legal support, to provide assistance both to the board and the CEO.

It is essential that the board has a clear understanding of their legal duties, responsibilities and liabilities (Chapter 11) and a good working knowledge of the many ways in which governance of their organisation can be improved in order to manage and reduce risk in their daily operations and decision making. Therefore, those who make up the board need to have the necessary skills and abilities to make strategic decisions about the organisation. This means that board members should be appointed because of ability rather than time served in the organisation or political favour.

Many new board members have little understanding of their legal duties, the potential liability their position places upon them or the governance mechanisms operating within the organisation. Newly elected board members may have little experience of governance or management of an organisation, and the statutes of their organisation may provide them with little guidance as to their daily responsibilities. Therefore board members need the same induction as all new members of staff, and training needs should be assessed on a regular basis.

Democracy underpins voluntary sport organisations, and the rules determining who can be admitted or removed from the register of members must be clear. In addition, members must be able to choose representatives by democratic elections. In order to ensure good governance, the process by which members of the board are elected should be set in writing and communicated to all those who are entitled to vote. The process for nominating candidates should be fair and transparent, and the organisation should make reasonable attempts to promote elections and voting levels. The results of elections should be widely communicated to all members. Board members should be appointed for a specified period of time and reappointment should not be automatic.

The role of office holders

A board will have a number of 'officers' such as a chairperson, president, secretary and treasurer. These roles make up the executive of the governing board and each serve a critical role in the good governance of a VSO. The roles that these officers perform are very briefly described below.

President/chairperson

The president or chairperson (the title will depend on the organisation) is the senior *elected* member of the organisation. Their responsibilities will include:

■ providing the ultimate leadership role to the organisation

- ensuring the board fulfils its respective responsibilities for the governance of the organisation
- working in partnership with senior managers (if applicable) to assist them in achieving the objectives set for the organisation;
- ensuring that there are effective relationships between the board, the membership, staff, volunteers and all other stakeholders.

If applicable, they have a crucial role in the organisation in providing the day-to-day link with the professional staff; in most cases through the CEO. The president/chairman may represent the organisation to other key organisations or they may delegate such responsibilities to other members of the board or senior staff. In addition, they need to be sensitive to the outside environment and to external agencies, government, sports councils, international and national federations.

Role of the secretary

In general, the secretary is responsible for administration and for preparation of meetings, agendas and minutes. In addition, the secretary should know:

- what is happening in the organisation
- what decisions are needed and by what time
- the most effective order to place items on the agenda
- the timing of agendas.

There will be a significant difference in the responsibilities of the secretary depending on whether the post is part-time or full-time, paid or unpaid.

Role of the treasurer

The treasurer is responsible for keeping the accounts and establishing appropriate financial procedures. The treasurer should:

- have the ability to keep straight, clear records and accounts
- be familiar with money at the level at which the association deals
- be skilled in financial management
- present financial reports and accounts
- submit estimates of expenditure for approval
- make comments on the financial viability of projects
- present the annual accounts in draft to the executive committee
- forward the accounts from the executive committee to the auditors
- present the audited accounts to the annual general meeting for approval.

Responsibilities of the board

The board of a voluntary sport organisation has the ultimate responsibility for the overall conduct of the organisation and, as stated earlier, are legally liable in many cases for the organisation. Therefore there are two key responsibilities facing the board. First, the board has a legal responsibility to ensure that the activities and business of the organisation are conducted to the highest possible standards. Second, governance by the board is an individual and collective behaviour, meaning that the board as a whole and board members as individuals must work to maintain and improve the governance of the VSO. The question therefore arises as to how the board conducts itself to ensure that it discharges its governance duties.

The Organisation for Economic Co-operation and Development proposes that a board should:

- act on a fully informed basis, in good faith in the best interests of organisation
- act fairly
- comply with law and in the interests of stakeholders
- exercise objective judgement on corporate affairs – independent from management
- devote sufficient time
- have access to accurate, relevant and timely information
- act in good faith.

This therefore sets the tone for the conduct of the board, its integrity, objectivity and responsibility. In addition, the Board should attempt to achieve a 'no surprise' organisation, meaning that the board should not be surprised by what happens in the VSO. If they are, it means that communication is poor and therefore good governance may have been compromised. For example, the board should not be surprised to learn that the CEO is resigning as a result of months of bad relations with the president. The board should have been made aware of the difficulties much earlier.

Conduct of board members

Having been elected to the board, members must, individually and collectively, conduct themselves to ensure the highest standards of integrity and stewardship are maintained. Figure 3.1 sets out the personal commitments that people taking public roles should adhere to and board members have a responsibility to:

- Act with probity, due prudence and take and consider professional advice on matters where they do not themselves have sufficient expertise.

- Ensure that the organisation is administered in the interests of the current, potential and future stakeholders.
- Hold themselves responsible to the stakeholders of the organisation for the board's decisions, the performance of the board, the staff and the overall performance of the organisation.
- With the assistance of the management, ensure that the organisation complies with regulatory and statutory requirements and exercises overall control over the organisation's financial affairs.
- Have a commitment to good practice to improve the working of the governance and management of the organisation.
- Be aware of the need to have a balanced, competent board and of the need for arrangements to be made for the appointment or election of future key office holders in the organisation, such as the chair, CEO, finance director or board member.
- Ensure that there is clear understanding of the scope of authority delegated to those responsible for managing the organisation, such as the CEO or secretary.
- Policies agreed by the board should be expressed in unambiguous and practical terms so that those responsible for the policies are clear about what they need to do.
- The board must understand and respect the different roles between the board, the president or chair and the senior staff to ensure that all work together as a cohesive whole for the benefit of the organisation, developing mutually supportive and loyal relationships. This is discussed in more detail below.

THE TOOLS OF GOOD GOVERNANCE

Governance is a process that should be guided by the highest standards of public life. In order to carry out this function the board and its elected officers have a number of management tools at their disposal. Indeed modern management practice provides the board with a set of management tools to help ensure that it discharges its responsibilities with regard to its governance duties and thereby be in control of the business of the organisation. Table 3.1 sets out the responsibilities of the board and the management function that may provide them with the appropriate tools. It is important to note that the board should not use these tools to run the organisation; rather they should be used to help the board carry out its strategic, governance function. (For further information on the management functions see Part 2 of this book.)

40

The following principles set out the behaviours that board members should commit to.

- They should conduct themselves according to the Nolan Principles Seven Principles of Public Life as defined by Nolan (1995). These are:
  - Selflessness: Board members should take decisions solely in terms of public interest, not in order to gain benefits for themselves, their family or their friends
  - Integrity: Board members should not place themselves under any obligation to outside individuals that might influence them in the performance of their duties
  - Objectivity: Decisions must be made on the basis of merit
  - Accountability: Board members must be accountable for the decisions they make and subject themselves to whatever scrutiny is appropriate
  - Openness: Board members should be as open as possible about the decisions they make
  - Honesty: Board members must declare private interests and resolve conflicts of interests (see Chapter 12)
  - Leadership: Board members should promote and support these principles by leadership and example.
- They must take decisions jointly and take joint responsibility for them.
- They must acknowledge that, having accepted a seat on the Board, their responsibility is to the organisation and not to a body they may represent or to any other outside interest.
- They should attend all meetings and ensure that decisions are made in the organisation's best interests.
- They must adhere to a code of practice in respect of conflicts of interest.
- Confidential information must remain confidential and within the confines of the Board.
- Having delegated authority, Board members should be careful to ensure that this authority is not undermined either by word or action.

Figure 3.1 The personal commitments of a board member

THE RELATIONSHIP BETWEEN GOVERNANCE AND MANAGEMENT

The traditional view of the governance interface in an organisation is that the CEO and staff are the servants of the organisation and that all power, authority and responsibility for the organisation rests with the elected officers, executive board and ultimately with the membership. However, the operational reality is that, in many voluntary sport organisations nowadays, the various functions

Table 3.1 The management areas associated with good governance

Functional area	Board responsibility
Strategic management	Regularly reviewing the values of the organisation and how it discharges its business in the light of these values.
	Regularly reviewing the aims and objectives of the organisation in the light of its current circumstance and the organisational environment
	Developing and controlling a strategic plan for the organisation
Human resources management	Selecting and compensating key executives
	Succession planning including that of the Board
	Ensuring equality and inclusion
Financial management	Reviewing budgets and business plans
	Ensuring the integrity of the accounting system
Performance management	Auditing the outcomes of the strategic plan, generally by using Key Performance Indicators (KPIs)
	Monitoring the effectiveness of its own governance practices
Risk management	Developing an effective risk management process
	Monitoring risk
Legal management	Ensuring compliance with current legislation and with the rules and regulations of the overarching organisation

carried out by the paid staff are so complex, so involved, require such expert knowledge that effectively the operation of the organisation is in the hands of the president or chair, CEO, the finance director and other members of staff.

Most VSOs, particularly national organisations, will employ staff in order to carry through the day-to-day work of the organisation. The paid staff, headed and led by a chief executive officer or general secretary, become an important element in the organisation's dynamics. Invariably the day-to-day activities of the organisation pass through the hands of the paid staff, the management of activities becomes their responsibility and the proper management of the finances and other activities passes into their domain. How then does the board interact with the management?

It is fundamental for the board to ensure that they have a clear understanding of what is happening within the organisation and how this is impacting on its overall strategic direction. For example:

■ Do all departments of the organisation give a regular report to the board as to what they are doing in the name of the organisation?
■ Are the accounts presented simply and clearly?
■ Does the risk register (Chapter 12) reflect the major risks currently facing the organisation?

42

- Is the management able to present good and bad news?
- Do the agendas of the board meetings allow the board to consider the full range of its responsibilities on a regular basis?

Answers to these questions will highlight whether the board has a full understanding of the organisation and control over its strategic direction. If the answer to any of the above is 'no', then the board needs to put in place mechanisms to ensure that they get the information they need.

The partnership model of governance

Although the elected board is responsible for the ultimate governance of the VSO, good practice is a wholesome partnership between the board, led by the chair/president and the team who run the organisation. In a professionally managed organisation, the CEO and senior management are responsible for the running of the organisation and the board should refrain from interfering in the operational management whilst ensuring clear lines of accountability and a framework within which the chief executive and the staff can operate and manage. This relationship is set out in Figure 3.2, which shows that the leadership of the organisation is carried out by both the governance function and the management function, with communication between both.

Of key importance is the relationship between the chair and the person responsible for managing the organisation – the secretary general or the CEO, depending on the organisation. The relationship must be based on:

- Mutual trust and a communality of aims between the two individuals.
- Total transparency in the working relationship.
- A complete understanding of the respective roles of both, and a commitment to work within those roles and to discuss and work through the 'blurred edges'.
- Regular, frequent and open communication so that every nuance relating to the work of the organisation is understood by both parties.

Figure 3.2 A partnership model of governance

This essentially reflects a partnership model where governance and management operate in a flexible, interactive way, each supportive of the other's role. Key to the success of this is the need to review, on a continuous basis, the roles and direction of the organisation. But it is important also that the management take on not only the efficient running of the organisation's affairs, but also the intellectual process of contributing to the future strategy of the organisation. Whilst this partnership model represents an ideal, the reality will invariably reflect the personalities, egos and efficiency of the people concerned. In practice it is easy to find organisations where either the president or the CEO takes up a dominant position in the running of the organisation and this is often determined by personality or the amount of time the president is able to devote to the organisation.

Some final thoughts on the relationship between governance and management:

■ All parties in the organisation must make a conscious effort to recognise their own role and ensure that others recognise and accept what that is.
■ There must be an acknowledgement by all parties that ultimately the organisation must proceed on the basis of consensus and partnership.
■ Professional staff must accept that their role is not only the effective and efficient running of the organisation, but also in the intellectual process of contributing to the future strategy. In addition they must:
    ■ implement mechanisms to develop future strategy
    ■ communicate the strategic direction across all areas of the organisation
    ■ ensure, together with the board, that clear, transparent policies and plans are accepted across the organisation.
■ Both the board and management have a responsibility to ensure the integrity of the organisation. Whilst the board must ensure that the staff and volunteers conform to the rules of integrity and good practice, by the same token staff cannot stand by if members of the board behave in a manner that does not conform to the highest standards of public life (see Figure 3.1).

ISSUES RELATING TO SMALL VOLUNTARY SPORT ORGANISATIONS

Much of the above has been predicated on VSOs that are able to appoint professional staff to carry out day-to-day management duties, as well as major functions and projects. However, there are many small sporting organisations, such as clubs, that do not have the luxury of being able to employ people to 'do the work'. This places an added burden on the board who, in many cases, will have to rely on themselves or other willing volunteers to carry out the duties and tasks that would otherwise have been undertaken by professional staff. This makes the task of governance by the board fraught with difficulty as the line between governance and management becomes unclear and roles become confused.

44

Nevertheless, the task of proper oversight and governance does not go away and the board must be incisive in ensuring basic governance duties are properly discharged. An honorary treasurer must deal with the organisation's finances in an acceptable and competent manner; membership needs to know the organisation is running well and athletes and coaches deserve good administrative backup. Although this is difficult it is not impossible, and the backbone of the voluntary sport sector, clubs, survive and flourish thanks to the dedication of competent people, giving their labour and professional expertise free and in the cause of sport.

ORGANISATIONAL EFFECTS ON GOVERNANCE

The discussion above set out the principles of good governance. However, it is important to realise the VSO's effectiveness will be best improved by applying the principles of governance in a way that is acceptable to the culture, power and political systems within the organisation.

Organisational culture

Organisational culture refers to members' assumptions and beliefs about an organisation and the way these assumptions and beliefs affect members' behaviour. The ways that the members of an organisation value volunteers, address board members and believe in the value of sport are all examples of organisational culture.

Organisational culture shapes the organisation's goals and objectives because it leads members to make assumptions about what the organisation values. For example, objectives regarding drug testing are based on the assumption that the organisation values drug-free sport. Organisational culture also affects the relationships that exist within the organisation because it dictates who and what is important. For example, the secretary of a club may be perceived as being more important than the president or chair because the secretary controls information in the organisation. In addition, organisational culture outlines the accepted ways of working, behaving and even dressing. It is the way things are done in an organisation, and therefore it has a significant impact on governance.

Although it can be difficult to understand organisational culture because it is often hard to see, it is possible to create a picture of what it might be by considering the following:

■ stories about the behaviour of members at general assemblies or about the value of decisions made by elected members
■ choice of spokespeople for the organisation

45

- use of logos on all posters, pamphlets and advertising, which suggests professionalism and a corporate image
- use of first names even when addressing seniors
- use of acronyms such as IOC and WADA, which indicates that some issues are so well known that they can be referred to in shorthand
- club Christmas parties, social events for volunteers and the announcement of teams for major events
- office layout, decoration and age of the building
- uniforms, trophies and mascots.

These factors make it possible to identify the unwritten rules of the organisation and what it considers to be important.

Culture affects governance by affecting how resources are allocated. It provides an explanation for why certain decisions are made, why some groups appear to be more important to the organisation than others, and why some staff members are promoted and others are not. A successful chief coach may be able to behave towards the board in a manner that would not be acceptable from the chief executive. Funding may be diverted from development programmes to elite teams if the board considers elite sport to be the *raison d'être* for the organisation. Therefore culture determines who is powerful and what is important to the people in the organisation. It is necessary to understand culture and use this understanding as a framework for governance activities.

Power

Governance of organisations will be affected by the exercise of power because the influence of individuals and groups upon decision making depends on the relative power that they are perceived to have in the organisation. Elected members can insist that paid staff implement decisions made by the board since elected members are ultimately responsible for decision making. However, if those decisions are contrary to the wishes of funding bodies, the funding body can veto the decision.

Power comes from six main sources:

- *Physical size*: This power comes from physical characteristics such as size. For example, members may vote en bloc to force a policy change even if it is against the advice of the elected board.
- *Position in the organisation*: The chief executive is more powerful than administrative staff, and the elected board should be more powerful than the executive staff. Some less obvious positions can also be considered powerful, such as the personal assistant to the chief executive, who controls access to the chief executive.

- *Personality of individuals*: Some people are powerful in organisations simply because of who they are.
- *Control of resources*: Some power arises from control of resources such as money, volunteers, equipment and facilities.
- *Expert skills*: This power comes from knowledge or abilities that are limited within an organisation. For example, the person who knows how to set up a new piece of equipment has expert power; however, this power only exists for as long as there is a need for the expertise.
- *Ability to prevent things from happening*: An organisation relies on the goodwill of volunteers and staff to follow decisions and guidelines. The volunteers and staff can exert power by refusing to do what is asked.

Power affects governance in a number of ways. First, those people or groups with the greatest power can determine the strategic direction of the organisation by influencing the planning process. For example, the general assembly can effectively block the introduction of good governance into the organisation by voting against proposed changes. As outlined previously, those with power can determine who and what gets resources and thus what activities and programmes can be followed. For example, Sport England has forced the introduction of good governance principle into NGBs by tying this to funding (see Chapter 7). Power affects who is involved in decision making even to the extent of influencing who is elected to the board. Finally, people with power determine what behaviours are considered acceptable to the organisation. If the chief executive and the president are openly in conflict with each other, it signals to others that such behaviour is acceptable. Therefore it is necessary to understand who has power within the organisation and why they have that power. In many organisations, this requires an awareness of organisational politics, which is the third factor affecting the governance of organisations.

Politics

All organisations have an internal political system, which is difficult to describe because it is often hard to see. Organisational politics can be thought of as the manifestation of power, and it occurs whenever an individual or group seeks to influence the thoughts, attitudes or behaviours of another individual or group. The most obvious example of politics is seen in meetings where attendees know that the major decisions have already been taken outside of the meeting and that the meeting is a mere formality. This is because politics determines who makes the decisions (usually the most powerful groups or individuals) and even what will be discussed. This is clearly contrary to the principles of good governance; however, it would be naive to think that this type of organisational behaviour does not occur.

47

Organisational politics has both benefits and drawbacks for VSOs. The politics of an organisation assists with team building, ensures communication and coordination, and helps provide a framework for decision making. Conversely, politics may lead to misuse of resources, create conflict and distract attention from the objectives of the organisation. Despite these serious drawbacks, all organisations have an internal political system that will influence decision making and determine who controls the resources. Thus, in order for governance to be effective, board members need to be aware of the organisation's politics and then find a way of working with the system.

SUMMARY

The principles of good governance provide a framework for the management of voluntary sport organisations that ensures that the organisation is effective, transparent and, above all, ethical. This is clearly of key importance in an industry that provides role models for children, offers worldwide entertainment and utilises public monies. However, it is not an end in itself. It should be remembered that the business of a sport organisation is to run sport for the benefit of those involved, such as athletes, coaches, administrators, members, spectators and the media and to be on the cutting edge of 'doing things better'. Ticking the boxes in the governance checklist is of course important but it is not the ultimate outcome. The ultimate outcomes of good governance are to deliver better sport, which is enjoyed by all those touched by the experience, and to involve more and more people.

PART II

THE MANAGEMENT OF VOLUNTARY SPORT ORGANISATIONS

CHAPTER 4

STRATEGIC MANAGEMENT AND PLANNING

Jean-Loup Chappelet

This chapter presents the strategic management process and the phases required to develop and implement strategy within voluntary sport organisations. The chapter sets out the rationale for strategic management and discusses the need to prepare for the strategy development process. It then describes the four phases needed to develop and implement a strategic plan. These processes are illustrated by the case of a major sport organisation: the International Olympic Committee.

THE RATIONALE FOR STRATEGIC MANAGEMENT IN VOLUNTARY SPORT ORGANISATIONS

The concept of strategic management began to emerge in the 1960s as a result of the increasing competition that was beginning to affect a number of commercial industries. Consequently, customers became more demanding requiring management to move away from setting objectives to suit themselves to setting objectives that could be considered strategic in that they permitted an organisation win the commercial war that was being waged.

For some considerable time sport organisations were spared from this competitive environment. During the 1970s, however, a number of new sports and disciplines were 'invented', such as surfing, windsurfing, snowboarding, mountain biking, roller-skating and sport climbing, thus creating increasing competition for traditional sport providers. Linked to leisure activity rather than competition, they met the needs of those who enjoyed physical activity and sport, but did not necessary want to be competitive or in a structured club environment. As a result, these new consumers of sport either became more demanding of traditional sports or ignored them completely. In return, many of the relevant international federations ignored the new sports, such as jogging and road racing for athletics, or underestimated them, such as snowboarding for skiing. Many who took part in the new sports did so outside traditional sport organisations such as a club, league, or federation or within commercial organisations, such as fitness clubs, racquet sport centres and leisure facilities.

The IOC was created in 1894 and developed over a century to a point where, at its 1994 centenary, it was recognised as the leading international sports organisation. For example, the United Nations declared 1994 the Year of Sport and the Olympic Ideal. The IOC's development took on particular impetus during the presidency of Juan Antonio Samaranch from 1980 until 2001. After this period of strong growth, Jacques Rogge – the new President elected in July 2001 – aimed to consolidate the organisation after its highly rapid expansion under his predecessor.

Immediately after his arrival, he began a process of full examination of the IOC administration's mission, structures, working methods and other procedures. This involved both internal and external audits in eight areas with the help of seven external consultants or consulting companies. The audits notably resulted in a new organisation chart, adopted by the IOC Executive board at the end of 2002 and including two new structures: 1) an Olympic Games department to handle the strategic and operational aspects of the IOC's main "product" and intended to work in cross-discipline way with all the other departments of the administration (marketing, legal affairs, communication, sports, etc.; and 2) a strategic planning unit later renamed to become Corporate Development, under the Director General and notably responsible for drawing up a (strategic) Corporate Plan for the organisation and to monitor its implementation by the IOC administration's 13 departments. The unit started its operation in 2003. Three individuals work in the unit in 2009.

The previous budget planning system was progressively replaced by proactive strategic planning worthy of a major service organisation, drawing inspiration from methods that had proved their worth in private companies, notably an Olympic sponsor in the information technology services sector. The size and importance of the IOC meant that it could no longer be satisfied with an intuitive approach to management that had many successes but had also led to near-disaster on several occasions in the 1990s (corruption on the part of members in relation to the awarding of the Olympic Games, poor organisation of the Centenary Games in Atlanta, headquarters expenses poorly controlled, absence of financial reserves in the case of cancelled Games). Moreover, it was no longer sufficient for the over 300 members of staff at the IOC Administration to have the overall goal of supervising the Games and the Olympic movement: it was necessary to define clear objectives for each department, approved by the President – taking on the role of Chief Executive Officer – and have the Director General – taking on the role of Chief Operating officer – monitor their achievement over the four-year Olympiad. The IOC had entered the era of strategic management, just as other Olympic sport organisations had done before.

Figure 4.1 The IOC's approach to strategic planning (Source: IOC, 2002; Kübler and Chappelet, 2007)

In parallel, sport began to attract more and more media attention and became an important vehicle for sponsorship. Television networks fought to obtain broadcasting rights for major sport events such as the Olympic Games, the Football World Cup or the Tour de France. The rights to market the image of these events, the organisations behind them, and the athletes taking part in them were also sold at a high price to organisations wishing to benefit from the image and media impact associated with these events.

International sport organisations such as the IOC, the international federations and even national federations or leagues took on greater importance and consequently had major resources become available that they had to manage. Public organisations and some private companies turned their interests towards sport, notably via the construction of sport facilities or through the promotion of sport tourism. Sport competitions that competed with those of traditional organisations were launched by private groups, such as attempts by the G14 group to replace the Union of European Football Associations (UEFA) Champions League in football.

The diversification of sport practice and the commercialisation of sport inevitably led to greater competition between the traditional and new sports in terms of gaining or retaining athletes, fans, television viewers and/or sponsors. In response to this, voluntary sport organisations have had to move towards a process of strategic management, just as many commercial organisations were forced to do in the 1960s. The need for strategic management in VSOs was initially identified in Europe but spread quickly to all continents as a consequence of the globalisation of sport, and many NOCs, IFs and NFs have had strategic planning processes in place for some time (Chappelet and Bayle, 2005). In the Olympic Movement, strategic planning greater gained momentum in 2002 when the IOC created a Strategic Planning Unit. The IOC considers that developing a strategy at the highest level of an organisation, aligned with its vision, is the first among the 'basic universal principles of good governance of the Olympic and sports movement' (IOC, 2008) and it has requested that those IFs wishing to remain within the Olympic programme, or to be included therein, must have a 'four-year strategic planning process' (Criterion 26, Olympic Programme Commission, 2005). Figure 4.1 sets out the IOC's recent approach to strategic planning.

THE PHASES OF STRATEGIC MANAGEMENT

Strategic management can be illustrated simply by means of a four-phase process focused around the stated vision and mission of the organisation that underpin the whole process (see Figure 4.2).

Simple yet fundamental questions correspond to each of the four phases of Figure 4.2. They must be addressed by a VSO in its strategy development process:

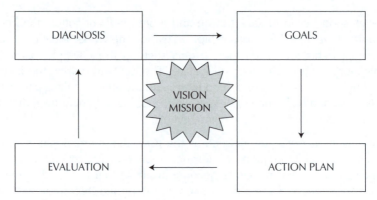

Figure 4.2 Strategic management process

■ *Phase one: Diagnosis*: Where are we now? What is our situation?
■ *Phase two: Goals*: Where do we want to go? What are our goals?
■ *Phase three: Action plan*: How do we go about it? How can we achieve these goals?
■ *Phase four: Evaluation*: Have we achieved these goals? Are we succeeding in reaching them?

Each of these four phases will be described in detail below. However, first it is necessary to consider the role of the vision, mission and values of an organisation in strategy development.

Vision, mission and values

The vision, mission and values of a VSO underpin the strategy development process as they set out the rationale for, and direction of, the organisation. The vision is the very long-term goal that the organisation wishes to achieve and can even be so idealistic that it can never be completely achieved. The mission is a short summary of the main ways in which the VSO will achieve its vision. For example, the vision of the World Anti-Doping Agency is: 'A world that values and fosters doping-free sport.' Its mission is: 'To promote, coordinate and monitor, on an international basis, the campaign against doping in sport in all its forms' (WADA, 2007).

Many voluntary sport organisations over-focus their vision and/or mission on sport performance, such as winning medals, increasing the number of participants and staying in a specific league. These are, however, more like operational objectives and their vision and mission should include a humanist dimension that reflects their social responsibility and their status as a voluntary, non-profit organisation. For example, Figure 4.3 sets out the vision and mission of the IOC as stated in

54

IOC vision:

Olympism is a philosophy of life, exalting and combining in a balanced whole the qualities of body, will and mind. Blending sport with culture and education, Olympism seeks to create a way of life based on the joy of effort, the educational value of good example and respect for universal fundamental principles. The goal of Olympism is to place everywhere sport at the service of the harmonious development of man, with a view to promoting a peaceful society concerned with the preservation of human dignity. (Olympic Charter, Fundamental Principles 1 and 2)

IOC mission:

The mission of the IOC is to promote Olympism throughout the world and to lead the Olympic Movement. The IOC's role is:

1. to encourage and support the promotion of ethics in sport as well as education of youth through sport and to dedicate its efforts to ensuring that, in sport, the spirit of fair play prevails and violence is banned;

2. to encourage and support the organisation, development and coordination of sports competitions;

3. to ensure the regular celebration of the Olympic Games;

[...13 other roles are mentioned in article 2 of the Olympic Charter].

Figure 4.3 The vision and mission of the IOC (Source: IOC, 2007)

the Olympic Charter. It is interesting to see that through these official statements, the IOC positions itself as an organisation with an ideal goal that is wider in scope than simply the regular organisation of the Games.

It is often useful to identify the values to which the organisation subscribes. The values are the underpinning beliefs that the organisation wants to promote and these must be shared by the elected officials and paid and unpaid staff. They should also resonate with stakeholders and therefore it is important to make the values clear in order that they can be easily communicated. The values must be in line with the organisation's vision. Figure 4.4 presents the IOC's three core values and six principles, which were outlined in 2007.

Excellence

Giving one's best, on the field of play or in the professional arena. It is not only about winning, but also participating, making progress against personal goals, striving to be and to do our best in our daily lives and benefiting from the healthy combination of a strong body, mind and will.

Friendship

Considering sport as a tool for mutual understanding among individuals and people from all over the world. The Olympic Games inspire humanity to overcome political, economic, gender, racial or religious differences and forge friendships in spite of those differences.

Respect

For oneself, one's body, for others, for the rules and regulations, for sport and the environment. Related to sport, respect stands for fair play and fight against doping and any other unethical behaviour.

Six principles: non-discrimination; sustainability; humanism; universality; solidarity; alliance between sport, education and culture.

Figure 4.4 The core values and principles of the IOC (Source: Mass, 2007)

Preparation for planning

If a VSO is embarking on the planning process for the first time, there is a fifth *preparatory* phase that must be carried out. During this preparatory phase, five questions must be answered:

■ *What are the reasons for such an exercise?* Developing a strategic approach takes time and resources. It may therefore be necessary to justify the undertaking of such an exercise to those in charge of the organisation. Internal reasons can be cited, such as a lack of cohesion or common objectives, or the absence of a clear definition of the various roles within the organisation. However, it is usually external reasons that present the best rationale. For example, a sport organisation is losing members, its services are not attractive, loss of interest on the part of fans, financial difficulties, or even increased competition from similar organisations or new entrants to its market.
■ *What methodology for strategic planning should be used?* A four-phase method is proposed here although other, more sophisticated, approaches also exist. It would be helpful to establish whether a specific method has been used by similar organisations, or whether one is being used by a major

entity within the same environment, such as Sport England or the British Olympic Association in the UK.

- *Who is going to be involved?* Those that should be involved in the strategy development process are the board members, volunteers and staff of a sport organisation. If many people are to be involved, it is useful to create a working group made up of representatives of the main responsibilities within the organisation. It is also wise to involve stakeholders as much as possible. The decision to embark on the planning process should be made by the governing board, and the general assembly of its members should be kept fully abreast of the strategic plan and its results as the process moves forward.

- *How much time is there to carry out the work?* Drawing up the first strategic plan should not take less than 3 months or more than 12 months. The idea is that the preparation of this first plan should not be endless, and nor should it be a rapidly completed, superficial exercise. Time should be taken for the plan to be widely discussed within the organisation and approved by its governing body. Finally, the plan must be implemented and its effects evaluated.

- *What is the budget?* In addition to budgeting for the time and human resource required, it is also essential to draw up a financial budget for developing the first plan in order to finance the cost of necessary studies, to collect information, and possibly to bring in consultants. Some funding could be set aside for brainstorming sessions or in order to cover meals or other incentives for those contributing to the process, whether volunteers or employees. If no such budget is possible, the strategy development process runs the risk of being seen as unimportant. Once launched, strategic management falls within the organisation's normal administrative costs.

Phase one: Diagnosis

Diagnosis is the first step within the strategic management process of a voluntary sport organisation. Its purpose is to determine where the organisation is situated with regard to its immediate and wider operating environment (see Chapter 2). Such a diagnosis can be drawn up by a person who knows the organisation well, but it is preferable for it to be carried out by a group familiar with the organisation, including representatives of all those who work there and, if possible, those who are stakeholders.

At the beginning of the diagnosis, it is important to have a clear view of the organisational environment in which the organisation is situated. One way of exploring this environment is by identifying the stakeholders of the organisation. The stakeholders of an organisation are the individuals, groups or organisations that can affect its current or future situation, either directly or indirectly. In a commercial company, the owners or shareholders are the dominant group within the stakeholders. For the managers and employees of such a company, the primary goal is to increase profits and the shareholder value. In a voluntary sport organisation, however, the situation is more complex. The stakeholders are numerous and many are important. For example, in a voluntary sport context, typical stakeholders are:

- the organisation's board and executives (elected or employed)
- members
- the staff and volunteers
- others who benefit from the services provided
- public authorities who often provide subsidies and expect sport to provide benefits such as health, education and social integration
- sponsors, suppliers and donors
- the media who report on the organisation's activities and at times pay broadcasting rights for competitions
- fans and spectators

A distinction can be made between internal stakeholders, such as members, the board and staff, and external ones, such as funding agencies and sponsors. A voluntary sport organisation should maintain its autonomy with regard to its external stakeholders, notably the sponsors and the public authorities. This is one of the 'basic universal principles of good governance' for organisations within the Olympic Movement (cf. principle 7 in IOC, 2008).

It is essential to identify all the stakeholders of the organisation as this provides a better analysis of the environment in which it is situated and allows the extent to which they can support (or not) the strategy to be developed. Identifying those stakeholders that can provide assistance to the organisation and to communicate with them at the earliest possible stage in order to gain a sound understanding of their point of view and possibly to integrate their feedback is also very important. Similarly, by identifying the stakeholders who might oppose any future strategy, it is possible to anticipate their reactions and thus be in a position to handle them more effectively.

Identifying stakeholders is mainly carried out by brainstorming with people who know the organisation well. It is possible to concentrate, initially, on those with direct and regular contact with the organisation and then to involve those who have less contact. It is often useful to have a 'map' of all the identified stakeholders with the sport organisation at its centre. Figure 4.5 shows the map of the IOC Administration Department's shareholders, drawn up following an internal process aimed at identifying the services provided by the IOC Administration to its stakeholders (BOOST, 2005).

A power–interest matrix of the stakeholders (Table 4.1) makes it possible to classify them depending on the attention that the organisation must pay to them. There are four priorities that correspond to the four quadrants of the matrix:

58

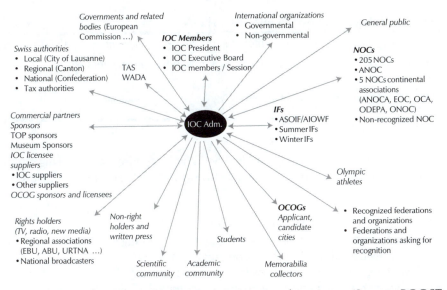

Figure 4.5 Stakeholders of the IOC administration department (Source: BOOST 2005)

- *Priority 1 High power, interested stakeholders*: These are the stakeholders that should be fully engaged in the strategy development process, and who need to be satisfied.
- *Priority 2 High power, less interested stakeholders*: These stakeholders should be involved in order to keep them satisfied, but not so much that they become bored with the process.
- *Priority 3 Low power, interested stakeholders*: Keep these stakeholders adequately informed, and consult with them to ensure that no major issues arise. These stakeholders can often be very helpful with the detail of the plan.
- Priority 4 *Low power, less interested stakeholders*: Monitor these stakeholders.

Priority 1 stakeholders are of key importance for the organisation's strategy. It is essential to understand their strategies and, if they are individuals, their motivation for involvement. Among the stakeholders of the IOC Administration the most important ones (priority 1) are the IOC members, international sport federations, national Olympic committees and Olympic organising committees (OCOGs: Organising Committees for the Olympic Games), which are emboldened in Figure 4.5. In addition to these priority 1 stakeholders, others are linked to the IOC Administration by two-way arrows showing that they are priorities 2 and 3. The others, including the academic community, are priority 4 for the IOC Administration.

Table 4.1 Power-interest matrix for stakeholders

Stakeholders with	Low interest in the strategy	High interest in the strategy
Low power over the strategy	Monitor (minimum effort)	Keep informed
High power over the strategy	Keep satisfied	Manage closely

Once the stakeholders have been identified and categorised, the working group set up to diagnose the current situation of the organisation can tackle the following questions:

- What is our history? Where do we come from?
- What are our current vision and/or mission? Are they well formulated? Are our activities adapted to this vision and this mission?
- What are the urgent questions that we need to face?
- Who are our competitors? Who are our potential allies?
- What are the opportunities and threats for our organisation?
- What are the strengths and weaknesses of our organisation?

The two last questions on this list are particularly important as they allow the development of a diagnostic tool known as a SWOT analysis (Strengths, Weaknesses, Opportunities and Threats). This technique consists of identifying and setting out, in a matrix with four quadrants, the organisation's internal strengths and weaknesses, notably in relation to its own resources, and the external opportunities and threats that it faces within its environment. A SWOT analysis should cover:

- *Strengths*: Skills, distinctive competencies, capabilities, competitive advantages or resources that the organisation can draw on in selecting a strategy. The strengths must be maintained or developed by means of good strategic management.
- *Weaknesses*: Lack of skills, distinctive competencies, competitive advantages or resources. Weaknesses can and must be corrected by better management.
- *Opportunities*: Situations in which benefits are fairly clear and likely to be realised if certain actions are taken. The opportunities are beyond the control of the organisation but it can use them to its benefit for good strategic management.
- *Threats*: Situations that give rise to potentially harmful events and outcomes if action is not taken in the immediate future; they must be actively confronted to prevent trouble. Threats and risks are beyond the control of the organisation, but they must nevertheless be overcome by good strategic management.

60

STRENGTHS	OPPORTUNITIES
1. The Olympic rings (the world's best-known brand) 2. Olympic values well appreciated 3. Universality of the Olympic movement 4. Considerable financial resources available 5. Olympic Solidarity programme	1. Sport is still a growth sector 2. Athletes are motivated by the Games 3. Many candidate cities 4. New broadcasting techniques 5. Many sports wishing to join the Olympic Games
WEAKNESSES	THREATS
1. Gigantism and high cost of the Games 2. Olympic programme somewhat obsolete (few new, fun sports) 3. Internal changes are slow and difficult 4. Revenues are stagnant 5. Few women IOC members	1. Doping is rampant 2. Politicisation of the Games, terrorism 3. Corruption of officials and athletes 4. Sport is too commercialised 5. Young people somewhat disinterested in sport and the Games

Figure 4.6 2009 IOC SWOT Matrix

A SWOT analysis can be applied to all types of organisations, whatever their size, as long as the focus is on the organisation itself. It must be said, however, that it is not always easy to distinguish internal and external factors or even strengths and weaknesses from opportunities and threats, as difficulties (weaknesses or threats) can be seen as reasons to act positively and thus become a strength or an opportunity. For example, the crisis or threat that the IOC underwent following actions on the part of some of its members surrounding the selection of Salt Lake City to host the 2002 Winter Games permitted it to revisit its governance in depth (opportunity) and regain its reputation (Kübler and Chappelet, 2007).

In case of doubt, it is always possible to place factors at the borders within the matrix. There is no particular order in which the analysis should be carried out, but it is recommended to begin with the positive factors even though it is often those factors that are seen as negative that trigger the need for strategic analysis. Once brainstorming is completed, the SWOT matrix is a good way of presenting the strategic diagnosis before moving onto the next stage (see Figure 4.6). It is wise to concentrate on three to six of the most important factors only.

Phase two: Goals

The work of identifying strategic goals might begin with a revision of the organisation's vision and mission if they do not reflect clearly the organisation's overall goal. In principle, the vision and mission statements are so closely linked to the organisation's reason for existence that they should remain as stable as possible, although clarifications and improvements are always possible. For example, the mission of the WADA, when it was first created in 2000, was: 'To promote and coordinate, on an international basis, the fight against doping in sport in all its forms.' It has since become: 'To promote, coordinate *and monitor* on an international basis, the *campaign* against doping in sport in all its forms' (WADA, 2007; emphasis added).

Visions, missions and values are, however, not enough to manage an organisation strategically. In order to do this, it is necessary to develop the organisation's strategic goals, by taking the SWOT analysis into consideration. In short, goals should focus on maintaining strengths, correcting weaknesses, seizing opportunities and blocking threats to the organisation. Goals that make it possible to tackle several factors at once are those that can be considered as strategic. For example, by improving its competition structure, a sport organisation decreases the risk of not having athletes who qualify for the Olympic Games, thereby increasing its chances of gaining sponsorship.

In principle, a VSO should have between three and nine goals and they should be what the organisation aspires to in the long term. They should be linked to the major milestones of the organisation, such as a major event and to major client-oriented processes, such as membership. They should remain constant throughout the life of the strategic plan. In short, they set out what it is essential for the organisation to achieve in order to ensure its success, its legitimacy and its sustainability in the long term. Generally speaking, at least one of the goals identified should focus on improving the internal functioning of the organisation (see goal four in Figure 4.7). It is worth noting that in the strategic plans of many organisations the terms objectives, targets, outcomes, fundamental duties or key result/focus areas are also used in the same sense as 'goal' (see for instance FIVB, 2002; USOC, 2004; WADA, 2007; FITA, 2007). Although the language might change, the purpose remains the same, which is to guide the activities of the organisation throughout the life of the strategic plan. Figure 4.7 sets out the medium-term goals for the IOC.

Once multi-year goals have been established, it is then necessary to define annual objectives. These should be 'SMART':

- Significant: They should be important to the organisation and contribute to its overall end goals.
- Measurable: It must be possible to evaluate whether they have been achieved.
- Action-oriented: They should enable plans to be developed.
- Realistic: The VSO should be able to achieve the objective.
- Time-bound: The objective must be achieved within a certain time period.

The IOC's four medium-term goals are linked to client-oriented processes that it calls 'activity streams'. Each focuses on a specific group of clients:

- *Goal 1*: The athletes and Olympic fans.
- *Goal 2*: The beneficiaries (NOCs, IFs and OCOGs) and providers (sponsors, media rights holders, suppliers) of Olympic revenues.

Activity Streams	Goals
Celebration of Olympic Games	1. Keep Olympic Games unique and manageable
Financing and support of the Olympic Movement	2. Ensure stability of revenues for redistribution and improve services offered
Promotion of sport and Olympic values in society	3. Leverage the IOC's role as an opinion leader to bring to life Olympic values through specific programmes and promote sport in society, particularly grassroots sport, paying special attention to younger generations
Performance of the organisation	4. Be recognised as a state-of-the-art service organisation

Figure 4.7 Medium-term goals for the IOC (2009–2012)

- *Goal 3*: Sportsmen and women in general and young people in particular.
- *Goal 4*: Internal clients (members, employees) and indirect clients (media, general public).

The goals can also be linked to the SWOT set out in Figure 4.6. For example, goal 1 aims to correct weaknesses 1 and 2, to tackle threats 2 and 5, while seizing opportunities 3 and 5 that are identified in the IOC's SWOT matrix, while maintaining the IOC's brand (strength 1).

It is also worth noting that the IOC's medium-term goals are all linked to the four-year period from 2009–2012. They are also significant, action-oriented and realistic. However, it is not clear how they can be easily measured. Such general goals should be clarified by including more detailed, more operational objectives that can then be measured with the help of performance indicators (see phase four).

Phase three: Action plan

Once the strategic goals have been established it is necessary to break each strategic goal down into operational objectives and concrete annual actions. These elements, when broken down, can be called activities, projects, programmes, tasks, initiatives or even strategies. Although the terms vary, the technique is to break down overall and medium- to long-term goals into concrete, short-term objectives and actions. Certain plans may run for a period of years or be linked to a precise date, such as a general assembly or a sport event. The operational objectives, with relevant details and with the resources that are allocated to them, constitute a strategic action plan.

At the IOC, the action plan is called the Corporate Plan and the four goals for 2009–2012 will be achieved by means of corporate programmes (see

63

Figure 4.8). In addition to these programmes, the IOC Administration handles recurring activities linked to its organisational function, notably the evaluation of candidatures by cities, supervision of the organisation of the Games, meetings of the statutory commissions and the IOC General Assembly. All of these are important objectives or actions but limited in time because of their predefined cycles.

It is again possible to use the SMART mnemonic for the objectives identified in the action plan. The two most important adjectives in this case are that plans must be measurable (M) and time-bound (T). It is also important, for each action to be allocated a person or department responsible, and to have a budget in terms of human resources (by identifying the persons involved by name) and of finance (by indicating the corresponding budget line or account). Partnerships of a strategic kind must be developed in order to achieve the objectives if the internal resources are not sufficient.

This exercise of allocating responsibilities and resources was carried out by the IOC for each corporate programme. For example, Figure 4.9 sets this out for programme 1.1 of Figure 4.8: Olympic Games Knowledge Management, a

Goals	Corporate programmes 2009–2012 (objectives)
1. Keep Olympic Games unique and manageable	1.1. Olympic Games Knowledge Management (OGKM) 1.2. Games Management Strategy (360° System) 1.3. Youth Olympic Games
2. Ensure stability of revenues for redistribution and improve services offered	2.1. Olympic Solidarity Quadrennial Programmes 2.2. Athletes' Education and Career Management 2.3. Protection of Athletes' Health
3. Leverage the IOC's role as an opinion leader to bring to life Olympic values through specific programmes and promote sport in society, particularly grassroots sport, paying special attention to younger generations	3.1. Promotional Campaign 3.2. Olympic Values Education Programme 3.3. Social Responsibility Platform 3.4. Olympic Sports for Hope 3.5. Olympic Day
4. Be recognised as a state-of-the-art service organisation	4.1. Olympic Museum 2020 4.2. Patrimonial Assets Management 4.3. Intellectual Property 4.4. 3net (corporate intranet, extranet and internet) 4.5. Contract Management 4.6. Financial Information System (SAP-SADD) 4.7. Record and Archive Information Management 4.8. Olympic Congress Preparation (to be dropped after 2009)

Figure 4.8 The corporate programmes to meet IOC goals (Source: IOC, 2009)

64

programme dedicated to passing information and knowledge from past Olympic organising committees to current and candidature committees.

Once an action plan has been formulated, it must be implemented by the organisation's managers. The organisation and its members must operate according to the plan, and the stated objectives and actions must be achieved progressively throughout the period of the plan. This is what can be called operational management as opposed to strategic management. The need of a champion to drive the process is essential. This champion must be backed by the board and be able to rely on a proper evaluation process (see below). If commitment to the implementation or execution of the plan is superficial, the evaluation of the plan is likely to be cursory because the evaluation is likely to reflect badly on individuals and departments whereas effective implementation provides positive and encouraging feedback.

Phase four: Evaluation

Evaluation is the final phase in the strategic management process. Without evaluation, a strategic plan, no matter how elaborate, will remain a case of wishful thinking. The aim of evaluation is to compare the objectives and strategic actions defined in the plan with the results obtained. Not only will this allow the correction of existing action plans but it will also allow future strategic planning cycles to be based on a realistic diagnosis of the situation that takes non-achieved objectives and the underlying reasons for this into account.

This evaluation must be carried out at each level of management in relation to the objectives defined for that particular level, and must then be consolidated for the organisation as a whole. The governing body of the sport organisation should request and review these evaluations on a regular basis. The review process that is followed by the IOC is set out in Figure 4.10.

To assist with evaluation, performance indicators (PIs) should be developed when action plans are drawn up, to facilitate the evaluation process. The evaluation will be based on these indicators, which should be both quantitative and qualitative. In addition, they should not be too numerous or complicated to collect. In the IOC, the indicators are expressed in the form of expected deliverables (see Figure 4.9). See Chapter 7 for a fuller discussion of performance indicators.

Many organisations develop a strategic approach but nevertheless neglect the evaluation phase for several reasons. For example:

- it takes time and resources
- management prefers looking to the future rather than at the present and the past
- necessary information is not readily available

Programme	Corporate Plan objectives (actions)	Annual objectives	Expected deliverable	Lead Dept.	Impacted Department
1.1. OGKM	- Consolidate the OGKM programme by optimising the quality of the services offered, broadening the user base and strengthening the image of the programme among all internal and external users - Develop a '2.0' philosophy around the OGKM products and services (new extranet, new formula for workshops and seminars): greater interaction with users, listen more to clients' needs, more intense exchanges with our partners, more dynamic tools and pay more attention to context and cultures - Deploy a new information-gathering process and adapt content to suit the different target audiences	Activate the measures accepted by the steering committee: - Put in place tools and quality processes for each of the products and services offered by OGKM - Put in place a new format for preparing, running and following up the workshops and seminars - Put in place training modules for internal and external users (running and facilitation, inter-cultural management, etc.) - Optimise the information-gathering process - Successfully implement a new extranet on a CMS basis	- Greater visibility for the OGKM programme within OCOGs and enlarged user base - High level of satisfaction among OGKM clients (measured regularly using questionnaires) - Successful implementation of a new information-gathering process and a full assessment procedure (definition, gathering, analysis, change management) - Successful logistics and operations supporting the organisation of the observers' programme and official debriefing	Olympic Games	Technology, Information management

Figure 4.9 Breakdown of the OGKM Corporate Programme objective (Source: IOC, 2009)

In 2004 a yearly corporate plan was drawn up for the first time in order to provide the IOC President and the Director General with a better understanding of what was to be delivered by the whole IOC Administration in a specific year. The objective was to provide a consolidated overview and ensure a proper decision-making process on priorities. The process evolved over time and by 2006 the corporate plan included departmental objectives (including means and criteria to achieve them) as well as a description of recurring activities and programmes, and was aligned with the budget. Since the establishment of a corporate plan, everyone within the IOC administration could see at a glance what would be the corporate priorities for the next year.

From 2007, an annual process was established with four reviews, occurring at the end of each quarter. By the middle of each year, the IOC Administration departments must submit their departmental plan, which is studied by the Corporate Development Unit and Director General. After the third quarterly review and further to the IOC President's choices, the individual plans are consolidated into the corporate plan for the next year, aligned with the next annual budget. In 2008, the IOC President agreed, for the first time, to a corporate plan for the next four years (2009 to 2012), moving from corporate annual planning to mid-term strategic planning aligned with the Olympic four-year cycle ending after the Games in London in 2012.

Figure 4.10 The review process followed by the IOC (Source: Marchand, 2008; IOC, 2009)

■ the evaluation does not seem to be as fruitful a task as others
■ it can lead to difficult situations with superiors or staff.

However, failing to carry out an evaluation prevents the organisation from being able to benefit from the lessons of experience and thus improving. Moreover, evaluation makes it possible to establish a sport organisation's contribution to society and this evaluation of the global impact of an organisation can be of use when seeking funds from sponsors, donors or public authorities, or more generally from stakeholders.

The evaluation phase can be formalised by publishing an annual internal report for the officers of an organisation. The report can also serve as the basis for publishing a public report. For example, for several years, the Olympic Solidarity department has been publishing an annual report presenting the indicators for its activities, such as number of courses, grants, seminars, amount of subsidies. It also publishes a report on the four years following an edition of the Olympic

strategic management and planning

Summer Games (for example, Olympic Solidarity, 2005). The annual reports serve to prepare the four-year plan by Olympic Solidarity for the following period.

SUMMARY

The strategic management process presented in this chapter should facilitate the work of those in charge of voluntary sport organisations in that it sets out the four phases to be accomplished in order to develop and implement a strategy. First of all, it is necessary to analyse the organisation's situation from the point of view of its internal resources and external environment, and to identify its stakeholders. From this, it is then possible to define major goals for the organisation, which should be linked to its vision and mission that, like the values shared by its internal stakeholders, must be clearly stated. The main goals can then be operationalised by an action plan. The execution of the plan must be regularly evaluated by the VSO's governing body and a regular status report to the organisation's governing body shows how the plan is being executed and serves as a basis for updating it.

Such a systematic approach offers those in charge of organisations better control. It makes it possible to move from a culture whereby the resources available are simply consumed, to one of results and performance. It is not only a case of being efficient by using the means available to the organisation sensibly, but also of being effective in spending or deploying the resources according to deliberately chosen objectives that fully reflect the organisation's vision and mission. In other words, doing the right things, not only doing the things right!

ADDITIONAL ACTIVITIES

■ Obtain a strategic plan of a VSO and evaluate it against the principles outlined in this chapter.

Consider the following:

■ Why do so many voluntary sport organisations carry out strategic management?
■ What are the pitfalls of strategic management in VSOs?
■ What role should the governing board play in the strategic management process?

FURTHER READING

Bryson, J. M. (2004) *Creating and Implementing Your Strategic Plan: A Workbook for Public and Nonprofit Organizations*. San Francisco: Jossey Bass.

jean-loup chappelet

Chappelet, J.-L. and Bayle, E. (2005) *Strategic and Performance Management of Olympic Sport Organisations*. Champaign, IL: Human Kinetics.

Leach, R., Robson, S., Simpson, K. and Tucker, L. (eds) (2010) *Strategic Sports Development*. London: Routledge.

WADA (2007) *Strategic Plan 2007–2012*. Version 4 May 2007. Montreal: WADA. Available from WADA website: www.wada-ama.org

CHAPTER 5

MANAGING HUMAN RESOURCES

Tracy Taylor and Peter McGraw

Key considerations in the effective management of paid employees and volunteers are presented in this chapter. The chapter examines the topics of recruitment, selection, orientation, training and development, and performance management in the overall context of attracting and retaining the best possible staff and providing an environment where they can perform to their highest potential. Matters associated with managing and working within a voluntary sport organisation and related to the 'paid/unpaid' dichotomy of many such organisations are also discussed.

Contemporary sport organisations operate in intensively competitive and dynamic environments. In this context, the ability of VSOs to achieve their mission is inevitably tied to a clear and vigilant approach to operations and a strategic focus on human resource management (HRM). Effective HR planning and management are vital components in the positioning and development of human resources for any organisation. Although most HRM operates from a common or generic basis, the unique context of VSOs' governance structure, incentive structure and use of volunteers requires a somewhat different approach. In essence, VSOs are governed by a volunteer board of directors, and are reliant on substantial volunteer contributions in addition to the work of salaried staff. Therefore, VSOs must recognise and build HR systems for both paid and volunteer workers, and the merging of these roles, in managing their operations (Leisure Industries Research Centre, 2003).

HRM is fundamentally the overall philosophy and process of managing people so that they are motivated and able to perform to their potential within the context of the organisation's strategy. Consequently, HRM should provide an integrated framework for making decisions about all people-related decisions within an organisation: who to appoint, how to manage performance, both good and bad, how to reward people and provide incentives for them to perform to their full capacity, how to determine training and development needs, and when and how to let people go (Taylor et al, 2008). In a VSO, effective HRM will need to distinguish between the role that employees play and that which volunteers play in contributing to the organisation's success.

70

THE PAID STAFF – VOLUNTEER CONTEXT

Volunteers are the backbone of VSOs and the effective management of volunteers requires the development of policies and procedures to assist with the integration of volunteers into the operations of the organisation. Effective volunteer HRM programmes establish the parameters of volunteer involvement and provide tangible expression to the implicit and explicit expectations of both the volunteers and the organisation.

Effective differentiation of the respective roles of volunteers and staff can be achieved through clear and up front communication of expectations, how to carry out respective tasks, and knowledge of performance outcomes. Research has found that sport administrators who understand what they are expected to do in their role (scope of responsibilities) will experience more enjoyment and satisfaction in that role, and are more likely to feel a greater sense of attachment to the organisation (Taylor et al, 2008). Any uncertainty may be intensified with the introduction of paid staff where changes in the structure and nature of voluntary organisations subsequent to hiring may lead to a blurring of the roles and responsibilities of both paid staff and volunteer board members (Kikulis, 2000). Furthermore, having a clear understanding of the consequences of role performance (performance outcomes), and how to carry out role responsibilities (means–ends knowledge), are meaningful determinants of how much effort VSO administrators will exert on the job.

THE ROLE OF THE BOARD

The legal responsibility of the VSO board will vary by country, and within countries, e.g. by state/region, as different governance systems exist. The most common system is the unitary board or single tiered; however, some countries require a dual board or two-tier system for non-profit sport organisations (Yeh et al, 2009). Two-tier board systems found in countries such as China, Germany, Japan and The Netherlands comprise a board of directors and a board of supervisors elected by the VSO's members. The board of directors has the principal responsibility for fulfilment of the organisation's mission and the legal accountability for its operations. The board of supervisors are primarily responsible for performing monitoring roles, particularly in regard to financial accounts and resource decisions made by directors.

Boards are fully responsible to their stakeholders, including members, local communities, service recipients, sponsors and government, for the conduct of the organisation. In order to deliver the VSO's mission, the board should develop a strategic plan to accomplish the mission, monitor and evaluate the plan's success, provide supervision and support to any executive staff hired by the VSO, ensure financial viability and have a system of policies and procedures for HRM. In some cases, the law imposes specific fiduciary duties of care, loyalty and obedience to the law on these directors. In most situations the board will delegate the oversight and management of HR to a paid chief executive officer or an administrative officer, where these positions exist. If there are no paid employees in the organisation the board may constitute an HR committee to deal with such matters. In the latter case it would be preferable that the chair of the committee had relevant HR expertise and/or experience.

In relation to HR matters, the board should approve written policies and procedures governing its employees and volunteers. HR polices and procedures should cover: working conditions; evaluation and grievance procedures; confidentiality of member, employee, volunteer and organisation records and information; and employee and volunteer induction, training and development.

Meinhard (2006) has suggested that boards should ensure that four key HR areas are covered in the course of executing their duties and responsibilities. First, the board must ensure compliance with all legal requirements pertaining to employment relationships, including volunteers. Second, the workplace and working conditions must be adequate for them to perform their duties: a safe environment with appropriate resources, free from risks, and volunteers and staff must be provided equitable treatment and conditions. Third, the board should monitor the performance evaluation and feedback mechanisms used to support and develop employees and volunteers. Fourth, the board should ensure that the organisation adheres to its stated values and ethics. Although it is not usually required by regulatory bodies, training and development for board members should be a component of every VSOs HRM programme.

KEY COMPONENTS OF HRM

The main elements of the HRM process can be represented via a six-phase model (Figure 5.1) with the main activities of HR occurring in a sequential order that can be replicated for the different activity cycles of the organisation.

The phases are:

- *HR planning*: Which involves aligning organisational people management policies and processes to overall organisational strategy.
- *Recruitment and selection*: Activities that are undertaken to provide the VSO with the human resources necessary to achieve its projected goals.
- *Orientation and induction*: The process of assisting new recruits to adapt to the organisation, its processes, procedures, regulations and culture, as well as their particular role in the VSO.
- *Performance management*: An evaluation system that provides feedback to employees/volunteers on their performance, sets future goals and determines rewards.

72

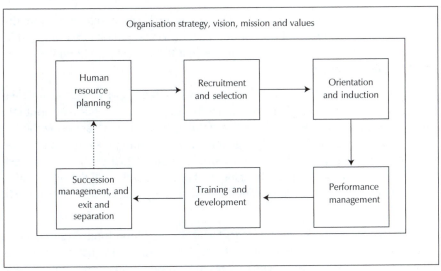

Figure 5.1 The human resources management model

- *Training and development*: A strategic system of development that aims to improve performance, develops new skills and enhances workforce flexibility. Training and development needs can be diagnosed and implemented at the level of the task, the individual and the organisation.
- *Succession management, and exit and separation*: All aspects of the continued adjustment of the organisation to its environment over time taking into account information and feedback from all other phases.

HR planning

HR planning aims to ensure that the right people, with the right skills and knowledge are in the right positions to fulfil the organisation's mission. Strategic HRM planning is central to any organisation's overall strategic planning process, but is particularly important for member organisations, such as VSOs, where the 'value' created by the organisation is determined by human interaction. The HR planning process encompasses supply and demand forecasting, goal setting and strategic planning, identification of gaps between current and forecast requirements, development and implementation of 'downstream' HR programmes and evaluation. The integration of strategic planning with HR functions provides the basis for a congruent approach to the organisation's day-to-day operations and the organisation's long-term vision.

There are at least three levels of conceptualising the role of HR in the strategic planning process of the organisation. First, HR may be viewed as implementation activities that are distinct from the strategy set by the board of directors. From this perspective HR planning is simply about reacting to the staffing needs implied by the separate and primary analysis of mainstream VSO activity. Therefore, in this role HR follows strategy.

A second way of conceptualising HR's role in strategy is to view it as a linked process with overall strategic planning. From this perspective, HR has input into the overall strategy process as an active partner, particularly in assessing the HR strengths and weaknesses of the organisation and crafting a strategy that takes them into account alongside any new general strategic plans. This role is more concerned with 'alignment' or changing the HR configuration of the organisation so that it can successfully implement the new strategy. Therefore, in this role HR partners strategy.

The classic SWOT analysis (Strengths, Weaknesses, Opportunities and Threats – Chapter 4) is a central component of this approach and is used to generate information from which the organisation's new strategic direction is determined.

Third, more contemporary views of strategy such as the 'resource-based view' suggest that HR can actually be an enabler of strategic capability through, for example, developing a unique culture in an organisation that provides a difficult to replicate source of competitive advantage. From this perspective HR processes are central to the overall competitive positioning of the organisation and are therefore at least at some level facilitative or leaders of strategy. In this model the human resources team would form part of the governance team of the organisation, which might also include the functional areas of marketing, finance, IT and legal. Due to size, resource constraints and the largely voluntary basis of the workforce, in most VSOs the approach to HR would be located in the first or second domains listed above.

The planning process requires an assessment of the organisation's internal and external environment and mapping of the HR requirements to meet current needs and future projections. An evaluation should be made as to whether the current knowledge, skills, attitudes, attributes and capabilities of the workforce are sufficient to meet the organisation's strategic goals and priorities.

HR planning is about ensuring that the organisation has the right people in the right jobs at the right time. It is therefore necessary to identity the critical success factors that will facilitate organisational effectiveness and sustainable organisational performance. These factors are then built into recruitment strategies, performance appraisal systems, reward and promotion structures, training and development programmes, and separation/exit processes. In many VSOs volunteer management is incorporated into the organisation's overall HRM system. However, some VSOs may have separate HR strategies for their volunteers and specific policies that address the interaction of volunteers and the organisation.

The process of HR planning is illustrated in the following example. A large member-based sport club developed a strategy of managing its youth league through the use of a new customer relationship management database system. An internal skills audit of current volunteers found that few had the technological skills or training to establish, operate and maintain the planned new system. In response, the sport club developed an HR plan to emphasise greater technology oriented customer focus and used this for recruitment, selection and volunteer training programmes.

VSO's HR planning should also take into consideration the demographic context of its current and potential membership. Many sports are now finding that their traditional member base, for participants, volunteers and staff, is either decreasing in absolute size or has become more difficult to draw into the sport. Therefore, attracting a more diverse population, often including non-traditional sport participants, can become an important consideration for the continued viability of many VSOs. In this instance, diversity refers to differences in culture, ethnicity, race, gender, age, religion, social economic status, sexual orientation and physical ability. The benefits of strategically planning for effective management of diversity can be found in the notion that an inclusive and non-threatening work and sport environment can maximise HR potential, lower turnover rates and create a tangible competitive advantage. Planning to implement strategic HR practices and processes to ensure appropriate diversity management is one way of capitalising on such opportunities. Case study 5.1 illustrates such an initiative.

Case study 5.1 United States Tennis Association diversity goals

The United States Tennis Association are committed to enhancing the diversity of the workplace through recruitment, hiring, retention, training and professional development of a diverse group of employees. To this end they have articulated a number of diversity initiative goals that aim to increase the number of people from different cultures in the organisational leadership and staff in both the professional and volunteer ranks.

Goals set in the 2006–2008 Diversity Plan:

- Establish accountability for volunteers to ensure timely achievement of increasing multicultural participation amongst volunteers, committee and council leadership, and the USTA board of directors.
- Establish accountability for national committees to accomplish greater outreach and inclusion in keeping with the committee charge.
- Determine key motivators or incentives to encourage sections to establish multicultural participation goals and hold their staff and volunteers accountable for the results.
- Provide job-function diversity training for all national divisions and sections to ensure maximum efficiency and eliminate fundamental barriers that are currently preventing focused outreach efforts. (USTA, 2006)

The template below provides some ideas for the type of skills and duties that can be included on a job description for a Coach. The duties should be amended, improved, added to or deleted to suit the circumstances of the club, but in particular to suit the person taking on the job, e.g. their current commitments, skills, time constraints, etc.

JOB TITLE: Head Coach/ Coach/ Assistant Coach. (It is suggested that separate job descriptions are written for each coach)

RESPONSIBLE FOR: (Junior section/ ladies/ male/ 1st, 2nd team)

RESPONSIBLE TO: The Club Management Committee

RECOMMENDED QUALIFICATIONS: It is recommended that the club contact their National Governing Body for advice on the minimum qualifications required for coaching, i.e. Level 1 Coach Award and First Aid Qualifications.

SKILLS REQUIRED: The Coach should be able to:
■ Motivate performers and volunteers, and communicate effectively with them
■ Make things FUN
■ Use time efficiently and effectively
■ Provide structured planning and make best use of time available
■ Show an appropriate level of technical knowledge
■ Break skills down if appropriate, analyse skills and make improvements
■ Make use of appropriate equipment and adapt if necessary
■ Provide advice on sports science and lifestyle guidance.

MAIN DUTIES:
1   Consult with team captain/ manager/ organiser about the aims of the sessions
2   (Head Coach) Co-ordinate the coaches and coaching for the XX section
3   (Head Coach) Provide support and advice to the assistant coaches and helpers within the coaching team
4   Be prepared to delegate organisational jobs which do not need your coaching skills, e.g. keeping the register, equipment and venue hire
5   Brief all helpers and assistant coaches on the aims of the session and the purpose of each activity. Involve all helpers and make sure they are made aware of the value of their input
6   Liaise with the club management committee to ensure there are regular, appropriate, competitive opportunities for members

Figure 5.2 Coach Job Description Template

7 Ensure that you are well briefed about any special needs of the participants involved, i.e. levels of fitness, significant medical conditions, physical impairments or disabilities

8 Plan and deliver coaching sessions appropriate to the ability of participants

9 Make participants aware of their progress

10 Identify and recruit, in line with club procedures, additional volunteers to assist in the running of club activities, e.g. parents

11 Ensure the Management Committee is aware of all club activities and ensure strong links and communication between each team throughout the season

12 Provide information on where the participant can continue in the sport, and liaise with NGB to access county and national structure for talented performers

13 Abide by and promote sound ethics and club policy; child protection, fair play and equal opportunities to all members

14 Ensure that all coaching staff qualifications are kept up to date

15 Take responsibility for ensuring that the equipment is correct and is kept in good working order

16 Be aware of and follow the procedures for recording accidents

17 The coach should be aware of the club's Health & Safety policy and Emergency Procedures and take their own responsibility for Health & Safety

18 Ensure that there is an accessible, well stocked first aid kit at the venue and a telephone nearby.

TIME COMMITMENT:

This will be different for each club – dependent on size of club, level of players, more during the peak playing
season etc.

SIGNATURES: Coach ....Date ....

Chair Person ....Date ....

Secretary ....Date ....

Recruitment and selection

Recruitment and selection are separate but related processes. Recruitment refers to the activities and processes undertaken by an organisation in order to define its employee or volunteer needs and generate a suitably qualified pool of candidates for various positions. Selection refers to the techniques and methods of choosing the best candidate from the pool that has been generated by recruitment (Taylor et al, 2008).

Selecting the right people is arguably one of the most important components of HRM since the costs associated with poor recruitment and selection practices are very high both directly and indirectly. According to the UK Cost of Recruitment Calculator the average cost associated with recruiting a new employee is more than £5,000, which includes advertising, responding to enquiries, time to read resumés, interview, advising unsuccessful applicants, use of technology and facilities, the cost of 'empty chair' time – the impact of hiring delays on turnover, the costs of losing embedded knowledge and lost promotional potential. The selection decision associated with the new employee or volunteer will have an impact on the performance and reputation of the VSO, positive or negative. It is important that appointment processes are transparent, consistent and fair (Barbeito, 2004). Important components of the recruitment and selection process are job analysis, job specification and job description. See Figure 5.2 for a Coach job description template.

Job analysis

An analysis of what skills, knowledge, experience and capabilities the organisation requires for the job is undertaken before effective recruitment can occur for a specific position. This *job needs analysis* is a systematic process of collecting data for determining the knowledge, skills, abilities and other characteristics that are needed to perform a job successfully (Pynes, 2004). The competencies required for the role are identified by an analysis of the specific requirements of the role together with organisation's culture and strategy. The skills required may be precise and technical, such as related to the capabilities of coaches or referees (specific accreditation required) or capability-based (critical thinking, interpersonal communication, teamwork skills) for management positions. Voluntary positions are typically described in more general terms (e.g. enthusiastic to work with adolescents) and the aim is to appeal to a broad range of potential applicants, although there may be technical positions that require specific skills from volunteers, such as a coach.

Examples of situations that require a job analysis to be conducted are:

■ A non-profit sport association intends to implement a performance management system for staff and volunteers. In order to develop measures for each job the key dimensions of the position need to be identified.

78

- In recruiting volunteer drivers for a sport event there is a need to identify legal and insurance requirements for the drivers, e.g. valid licence at appropriate level, clean driving record and so forth.

Data collection techniques used in job analysis typically use two or more methods to collect information that is required for a valid analysis. Some commonly used techniques include:

- direct observation of employees – for example noting the various interactions of an athlete and coach
- task diaries/logs completed by employees and volunteers
- critical incident identification – critical incidents are the abilities that define success or failure in a job. For example, how a coach responds to complaints from parents
- work samples – such as a completed annual budget
- individual or group interviews
- focus groups or seminars
- questionnaire surveys.

The information gathered in the analysis provides the basis for the *job description* and *job specifications* that list the knowledge, skills and abilities required. The job description focuses on the tasks that are to be performed and includes reporting relationships, working conditions, accountabilities and responsibilities. The job specification concentrates on the type of person required and their skills, knowledge, personal qualities, qualifications and experience. An example of how a job specification might be written is shown in Figure 5.3.

Job analysis for volunteer positions should be approached using the same basic principles as for paid staff positions. The first step is to identify all critical priority areas, e.g. membership recruitment, fund-raising, event organisation. The second step is to prepare a task brief to identify all opportunities for volunteer involvement and to determine the number of volunteers and the skill requirements.

Position:	Sport events manager
Education:	Degree or equivalent qualification in sport or event management. Financial and risk management skills.
Experience:	Minimum of 5 years including at least 2 years in a position with financial accountability.
Essential skills:	Demonstrable capacity in project management, oral and written communication, negotiation and conflict resolution, staff supervision, volunteer management, leadership, teamwork.

Figure 5.3 Job Specification for a sport events manager

Sourcing candidates

Once the specifications have been articulated, the next step is to recruit candidates for the position. The recruitment of personnel can be achieved from a range of options. There are several matters that should be considered before choosing the recruitment medium and these are set out in Table 5.1.

Personal contact with potential volunteers through friends, family or individuals already involved in an organisation is one of the most common ways that sport volunteers first became involved with VSOs. While the most successful strategy for recruiting volunteers is the direct one-to-one approach, other methods of recruiting should not be dismissed, e.g. local radio/newspapers, noticeboards, newsletters, email. A well thought out combination of all methods that are relevant to the membership should be used. When recruiting volunteers it is important to emphasise the benefits for the volunteer rather than the needs of the organisation. The main reasons people volunteer will vary between VSOs and by position type. However, research has found that core reasons for volunteering will include: contribution to community, personal enrichment, ability to contribute required skills, and to be associated with the sport (Doherty, 2003); and the Australian Bureau of Statistics (2008) found the main reasons for volunteering

Table 5.1 Sourcing considerations

Source	Suitability for recruitment
Internal candidates	There is sufficient talent in the organisation Familiarity with the organisation is desired Less expensive option
Newspaper/professional and Trade publications	Skills needed are not present in current employees Wide canvassing of candidates is required Need to achieve diversity in employee base
Internet lists, databases and e-recruiting	Can target specific internet group memberships Easy to get worldwide coverage Low cost option Can be used to complement other methods
Outsourcing to employment agencies, search firms, external agents	High levels of confidentiality and discretion are needed May fill temporary needs Short supply of talent
Graduate recruitment from educational institutions	Useful when substantial experience is not essential For entry level positions or traineeships

80

in sport in Australia were firstly, for personal and family involvement; secondly, helping others in the community; and thirdly, 'doing something worthwhile'.

Selection techniques

Selection of the most appropriate techniques to choose the best candidate for a position underpins a robust selection process and reduces the possibility of selection error. Techniques such as cognitive ability and aptitude tests, achievement tests, personality inventories, work samples, in-basket exercises, interviews and other techniques may be used singularly or in combination in the selection process to provide the highest possible validity and reliability. To have *validity* these techniques should have a proven relationship with effective performance of the job and the capacity to predict likely performance. Selection techniques should also be *reliable*, that is, they should measure the same thing accurately each time they are used. Table 5.2 presents information about the reliability and validity of some of the main selection techniques. As can be seen, some techniques are more useful than others but it should be noted that none are infallible and some of the better techniques are expensive, time-consuming and may be deemed inappropriate for certain staff. To reduce error in selection it is advisable to use a variety of techniques in combination but this may not always be possible from a practical perspective.

The most frequently used selection technique is the interview. To be effective an interview must be well structured and gather pertinent information for decision making about the applicant's abilities to meet the job requirements. This involves collecting all relevant information and allows for direct comparison between candidates (Stone, 1998). The techniques outlined in Table 5.2 are of varying cost to implement, and given the expense associated with more extensive approaches such as assessment centres it is unlikely that VSOs would use these. Therefore, as *interviews* are a commonly used technique used in candidate selection in VSOs, more detail on these is provided below.

Table 5.2 Selection techniques

Technique	Overall reliability and validity rating
Application form	Low
Behavioural based interviews	Moderate – High
Traditional interviews	Low
Ability tests	Moderate – High
Assessment Centres	High
Modern personality tests	Moderate

Source: Taylor et al. 2008

The structure and quality of interviews can vary enormously. *Unstructured interviews* are unplanned, non-directed, unformatted and flexible and require the interviewer to have good skills in questioning and probing. *Semi-structured interviews* are predetermined, with directed but flexible questions within key topic areas. *Structured interviews* are formally structured, have specific questions, are interviewer directed, standardised and not very flexible. In most cases, a semi-structured interview is more appropriate.

The four most common types of selection interviews are:

■ *Job-related interviews*, which ask the applicant about their past behaviour on jobs. These interviews are typically conducted by HR or managers.
■ *Situational interviews*, which involve questions based on the job together with hypothetical situations. This type of interviewing is typically used by psychologists or HR recruitment specialists.
■ *Psychological interviews*, which are used to assess the candidate's personality and are usually conducted by organisational psychologists or persons trained in the administration of the instrument being used.
■ *Competency interviews*, which are broader than psychological interviews and encompass competencies such as communication, confidence and other such characteristics.

Interviews may involve one interviewer or more. The benefits of having more than one interviewer are primarily to offset the subjectivity inherent in conducting one-on-one interviews. Different people will provide varying perspectives and interpretations, and the non-questioning interview panel members can look at body language and other subtleties that the interviewer undertaking the questioning may miss. Regardless of the number of interviewers, each should have undertaken some training in interview techniques and relevant laws and regulations that apply to issues such as gender and age.

A method of interviewing that has particularly good reliability and validity is *behavioural-based interviews* (McGraw, 2001). These interviews are structured to find out about the applicant's behaviour, and do not focus on feelings, opinions, inferences or generalisations. Clusters of behaviours, motivations and knowledge related to job success or failure are determined and questions are structured to elicit past experiences that demonstrate these. The underlying principle of this type of interview is that past behaviour predicts future behaviour. It provides a more objective set of facts to make employment decisions than other interviewing methods. The interview questions are developed from a job analysis and critical incident assessment of effective and ineffective performance. While traditional interview questions typically ask general questions such as, 'Tell me what you would bring to the position', the process of behavioural interviewing is much more probing.

In a behavioural-based interview the questions are asked to obtain explicit and comprehensive descriptions that relate to the context, what the applicant did specifically, and the result or outcome. This is framed within a three-step process:

1   situation
2   action
3   result/outcome.

For example, in a behavioural-based interview with a volunteer coordinator the question might be, 'Tell me about a time when you specifically worked to improve the positive experiences of volunteers.' The three-step answer would be:

1   Situation/task: I was working with a sport association and I instigated a volunteer involvement programme (VIP).
2   Action: I met with all the clubs at the beginning of each year to go through their volunteer training, recognition and reward schemes for the forthcoming season.
3   Result: Over the course of the 3 years I was working with the association the volunteer retention rates showed significant improvement.

Some typical behavioural-based questions are:

■   Could you please provide a specific example of a time when you were able to implement an effective conflict resolution process?
■   Describe a time on any job that you held in which you were faced with problems or stresses that tested your ability to cope. How did you deal with these this situation?

The selection process that is best for a particular organisation will depend on its policies, resources, the level of the position and the number of applications anticipated. In situations where there are a large number of applicants it may be appropriate to screen them prior to the formal application process. Screening is commonly done via telephone contact or with an online application form that has set essential requirements that have to be met (e.g. particular educational qualification) for the candidate to be able to lodge their application. In these cases only applicants that meet these essential requirements can apply for the position.

Before making an offer of employment, or confirming a volunteer appointment, referees reports or personal/professional references that were requested in the application process should be checked. The VSO should also determine the amount of risk it will accept in relation to its appointment policies and criminal background checks (Barbeito, 2004). The VSO has a responsibility to protect its membership and service recipients from harm. For example, in many countries

I certify that the above information is accurate and understand that if I have provided false or misleading information it may result in a decision not to employ me, or, if already employed, may lead to my dismissal.

I am aware that if considered for child-related employment, several checks will be undertaken to ascertain my suitability, including:

1   a national criminal record check for charges and/or convictions (including spent convictions) for:

   ■   any sexual offence (including but not limited to, sexual assault, acts of indecency, child pornography, child prostitution and carnal knowledge);
   ■   any child-related personal violence offence;
   ■   any assault, ill treatment or neglect of, or psychological harm to a child and any registrable offence; punishable by imprisonment for 12 months or more.

   I understand that this check includes convictions or charges that:

   ■   may have not been heard or finalised by a court; or
   ■   are proven but have not led to a conviction; or
   ■   have been dismissed, withdrawn or discharged by a court.

2   a check for relevant Apprehended Violence Orders taken out by a police officer or other public official for the protection of a child; and

3   a check for relevant employment proceedings involving an act of violence committed in the course of employment and in the presence of children or reportable conduct. Reportable conduct means any sexual offence, or sexual misconduct committed against, with or in the presence of a child (including a child pornography offence), any child-related personal violence offence, or any assault, ill treatment or neglect of a child, or any behaviour that causes psychological harm to a child.

I understand that a conviction for a serious sex offence (including, but not limited to, sexual assault, acts of indecency, child pornography, child prostitution and carnal knowledge) or child-related personal violence offence (including but not limited to, intentionally wounding or causing grievous bodily harm to a child) will automatically prohibit me from child-related employment. This includes a charge that is proven in court but

Figure 5.4 Working with children background check consent form. Note that his example is taken from an organisation operating within the Australian legal system. Other countries may have different laws relating to this issue.

84

does not proceed to a conviction. I am aware that if I am a "Registrable Person" under the Child Protection (Registrable Offenders) Act, 2000, I am prohibited from child-related employment.

I consent to these checks being conducted and am aware that if any relevant record is identified, additional information relating to that record may be sought by an Approved Screening Agency from sources such as courts, police, prosecutors and past employers to enable a full and informed estimate of risk.

I acknowledge that:

- the above information and any information obtained during the Working With Children background check may be collected and used by/or disclosed to the Commission for Children and Young People or any Approved Screening Agency for the purposes of the Working With Children Check;
- the Commission for Children and Young People or any Approved Screening Agency may share the information obtained during the Working With Children background check with each other to support further estimates of risk arising from additional Working With Children background checks;
- the outcome of an estimate of risk conducted with information obtained through the Working with Children Check by the Approved Screening Agency may be provided to my current or prospective employers or an employer-related body (where applicable) only for background checking purposes;
- details of my relevant records will not be released to my current or prospective employers;
- any information obtained as part of this process may be used by Australian Police Services for law enforcement purposes, including the investigation of any outstanding criminal offences; and
- the information provided may be referred to the Commission for Children and Young People and/or to NSW Police for law enforcement purposes and for monitoring and auditing compliance with the procedures and standards for the Working With Children Check in accordance with Section 36 (1) (f) of the Commission for Children and Young People Act 1998.

(Source: NSW Department of the Arts, Sport and Recreation http://www.dlg.nsw.gov.au/Files/Information/DLG_Background_Check_Form.pdf accessed May 2008)

sporting and recreation organisations work with children and young people and have an obligation to provide a safe environment for them. In these situations criminal and background checks are required to help determine whether a person is suitable to work with children. It helps to ensure, as far as possible, that people who may pose a risk to children are not employed in roles where they have direct, unsupervised contact with children (see Figure 5.4 for an example).

Upon completion of all the selection process requirements a letter of offer is sent to the preferred candidate, starting salary (if applicable), conditions and associated employment details. In the case of volunteers, contact is made with a notification of their acceptance and an invitation to attend a volunteer briefing or induction session. The volunteer would typically sign a declaration to abide by the VSO's code of conduct and any other relevant legislative requirements.

Selection decisions should be carefully planned and executed. The cost of a poor appointment decision is not only job underperformance, but also the negative impacts it can have on other staff, difficulties that may arise in termination and the opportunity cost of a poor or incorrect hire. On the other hand, a good choice contributes to productivity and profitability, and can also positively affect morale. An appropriate selection can strengthen an organisation's strategic capability by adding to the pool of well skilled and committed people from which future managers and leaders can emerge. These outcomes are equally relevant to paid and volunteer selection decisions.

Orientation and induction

A good orientation and induction programme will provide new recruits with the information that they require to feel comfortable and perform effectively. This process is an important step in establishing a good relationship between the new board member, employee or volunteer, and the VSO. An orientation for new board members would typically be presented by a combination of staff and existing board members. New board members should be provided with the code of conduct for the board and its committees, and any other relevant materials about the organisation's current and recent activities, as well as any information that will be useful in their position.

Employee orientation should cover: general information about values, mission, daily operational matters and how to operate around the office, e.g. how to use the telephone system, how to login to the intranet, emergency procedures; the new recruit's role; precise details on organisational procedures, work conditions and employee benefits; the policy manual; and the current organisation structure, the role of the board of directors and its committee and, where relevant, the role of the membership of the VSO. The induction should clearly set out organisational expectations and answer any questions that might arise.

tracy taylor and peter mcgraw

Volunteers:

- Have the right to know as much about the organisation as possible
- Have the right to receive training for the job
- Have the right to receive sound guidance and direction
- Have the right to participate across all facets of the organisation
- Have the right to be heard and consulted
- Have the right to work in a safe and supportive environment
- Have the right to be re-imbursed for approved out of pocket expenses.
- Have the right to have their contributions recognised and respected.

Volunteers will be expected to:

- Make realistic commitments, in terms of both time and areas of involvement, and the organisation will expect these commitments to be filled.
- Keep all details of recipients, other volunteers and members confidential and private unless prior consent has been obtained from the individual and/or the volunteer manager.
- Value and support all recipients, volunteers, and others in a way that is non-judgemental and non-discriminatory.

Figure 5.5 Volunteers rights

Volunteer induction and orientation will vary depending on the duration and role of the volunteer. Many VSOs produce volunteer induction kits, and these typically include position descriptions, rights and responsibilities/codes of conduct, grievance and conflict resolution policies, confidentiality arrangements and relevant technical information. An example of a rights and responsibilities policy is set out in Figure 5.5.

The orientation process should increase the likelihood of role clarity, workgroup integration and understanding of the politics of the organisation; factors that are ultimately important in their job satisfaction, commitment and retention (Taylor et al, 2008). The expectations for success and the ways in which the newcomer's performance is to be evaluated should also be made clear.

Performance management

The increasing demands for accountability made by stakeholders of sport organisations mean that greater emphasis is now placed on evaluating the performance of the individuals who work for it. The information gained from performance appraisals can be used to inform a range of decisions such as monetary rewards, promotions, transfers, termination and training and development needs (Bratton and Gold, 1999) and are used to assist the VSO to determine whether HRM systems are working effectively to deliver on the organisation's mission. However, the recent trend to evaluate people more closely in organisations needs to be balanced against the other major element of managing performance, that of developing staff. Most modern performance systems attempt to reconcile the, sometimes conflicting, needs between evaluation (or judging) and developing, which aim to ensure staff maximise their potential contribution to an organisation. The tension between these two aims of performance management needs to be carefully balanced by organisational leaders, and in some cases one might need to be subordinated to the other, more important, goal.

Performance management provides a link between career planning and training and development, and can be used to support job analysis and recruitment. Consider the example of the volunteer club event organiser who was commended for her excellent outcomes and conscientious performance over a three-year period. The chair of the board recommended her for a service award and she was subsequently supported by the national sport body to complete an Executive Certificate in Event Management.

The performance review should be based on the job description, together with any other nominated performance objectives and targets. There should also be clarity about the standards that will be used to judge effectiveness. Performance reviews are typically undertaken at designated intervals during the initial period of tenure and then annually. The formal review process should be complemented with regular feedback sessions.

The performance review should be a formal requirement that is fully documented, signed by the employee and supervisor and kept on the employee's file. The aim of the review is to assess performance, identify strengths and development opportunities and provide the employee with a means to discuss their work environment, career plans and goals for the upcoming year. Performance review methods vary but may include:

- *Rating systems* that involve ranking job performance on a standardised set of criteria.
- *Instruments* such as 360 feedback surveys (where the employee and their manager, direct reports and peers and relevant others respond to questions about the employee's work behaviours).
- *Behaviour reviews*, which can be highly specified using detailed job scales or may involve observational techniques.
- *Management by objectives*, which is a results-focused assessment based on set objectives where employees are assessed against a set of predefined goals.

88

tracy taylor and peter mcgraw

- *Critical incidents* where actual incidents are recorded of successful or unsuccessful performance or work actions. The supervisor uses these to evaluate performance.

The choice of system should be made carefully keeping the primary goal of the performance review in mind since all the systems have strengths and weaknesses that make them more suited to one purpose or another. For full-time employees it is common for sport organisations to use systems such as those noted above. Boards of VSOs should conduct self-evaluations and regularly review their own composition to ensure constituent representation, and board expertise and commitment. The board should also hire, set the compensation for, and annually evaluate the performance of the executive director of the organisation. For volunteers a less formal system based around informal developmental feedback is likely to be used.

Given volunteers often work in groups or teams it is also worth considering the development of measures of team performance outcomes to use in planning performance and reward and recognition schemes.

In the difficult situation where a volunteer is not performing effectively, McCurley (1993) recommends the following actions are taken:

- *Re-supervise.* You may have a volunteer who doesn't understand the rules that have to be followed. This is a common problem for organisations who utilise youth volunteers, some of whom automatically 'test' the rules as part of their self-expression. Re-enforcement may end the problem.
- *Re-assign.* Transfer the volunteer to a new position. You may, on the basis of a short interview, have misread their skills or inclinations. They may simply not be getting along with the staff or other volunteers with whom they are working. Try them in a new setting and see what happens.
- *Re-train.* Send them back for training a second time. Some people take longer than others to learn new techniques. Some may require a different training approach, such as one-on-one mentoring rather than classroom lectures. If the problem is lack of knowledge rather than lack of motivation, then work to provide the knowledge.
- *Re-vitalise.* If a long-time volunteer has started to malfunction, they may just need a rest. This is particularly true with volunteers who have intense jobs, such as one-time work with troubled clients. The volunteer may not realise or admit that they're burned out. Give them a sabbatical and let them recharge. Practice 'crop rotation' and transfer them temporarily to something that is less emotionally draining.
- *Refer.* Maybe they just need a whole new outlook of life, one they can only get by volunteering in an entirely different agency. Refer them to the volunteer centre or set up an exchange programme with a sister agency. Swap your volunteers for a few months and let them learn a few new tricks.

- *Retire.* Recognise that some volunteers may simply reach a diminished capacity in which they can no longer do the work they once did and may even be a danger to themselves and to others. Give them the honour they deserve and ensure that they don't end their volunteer careers in a way they will regret.

Performance management is a key tool in diagnosing the training and development requirements of both the individual and the organisation.

Training and development

The demands placed on VSOs are multifaceted and resources are often very tight, yet stakeholder expectations seem to be continually increasing. Within this context the VSO's mission must be the determinant of all training and development initiatives. These initiatives need to improve the skills of employees and volunteers and enhance their capacity to deal with the demands of a changing sport environment.

An example of this is in the area of legal issues (Chapter 11) and risk management (Chapter 12). The increasing attention on legal matters requires sport organisations to identify areas of potential legal risk. Training programmes in this area highlight:

- the role a constitution plays in a sport organisation and the areas a constitution should cover
- the application of specific legal principles in the sport environment
- considerations relevant to the liability for injury
- the advantages of risk management and insurance.

It could also cover contractual obligations, copyright issues and specific legislation, e.g. child protection.

The first step in a training process is to determine specific training needs. As noted earlier these needs may be evaluated at the level of the task, the individual or at an organisational level. Needs analysis might be done via surveys and interviews with employees, volunteers and board members; performance evaluations that identify areas to target (as discussed in the previous section); comments from stakeholder groups; changes in regulations or operating procedures; or specific requests by individuals or groups. Typically, *training* will be based around technical, job-related skills and abilities. Programmes may comprise on the job or off the job training. *Development* is concerned with more generic interpersonal or managerial/leadership skill development.

On the job training might include:

tracy taylor and peter mcgraw

- *Training positions* where individuals in the organisation are given specific responsibilities to perform that are outside their normal position and/or are allocated a senior person to work with and learn from.
- *Planned work activities* where work assignments are given to develop skills, experience and contacts. These are typically used to give the trainee insights into how the organisation functions at a functional and cultural level.
- *Job rotation*, which involves moving an individual between jobs to broaden experience and exposure in a variety of the organisation's operational areas.
- *Coaching* (or mentoring) is an increasingly popular method used by managers to train and develop subordinates. Coaching involves setting performance objectives and holding constant discussions about these dimensions.

Off the job training removes the person involved in the training from the workplace and can be individual or group based. Organisations using off the job training should ensure that it is tied to strategic goals (see example below). It is also essential that mechanisms are put in place for the transfer of learning back to the workplace. Examples of programme types are on or off site classroom sessions, and technical or professional courses that provide accreditation or upgrade skills. There is an increasing use of online training packages and programmes that target the development of specific skill areas in a self-paced approach.

Consider this example of how training is linked to strategy. A community sport association has a strategy to arrest membership decline, which is diagnosed as being related to member dissatisfaction with employee service performance. The employee development strategies for accomplishing better member satisfaction levels include sending employees to off the job training with a hospitality training organisation. The training focuses on instructing managers and employees in how to better interact with members and ensure that in the future members feel more highly valued by the organisation.

Training opportunities for volunteers to enhance existing technical and interpersonal skills, develop new skills and develop confidence in the role should be provided. Gaps between the level of skill and knowledge required for the role and the abilities of the volunteer are identified and access to the appropriate level of support and/or training provided.

Development activities include programmes that target interpersonal aspects such as improving communication skills, managerial skill development and growing leadership capacity. Other approaches could include coaching, and mentoring where less experienced employees work with more experienced employees to provide advice on career decisions, development and ways to operate effectively in the VSO. Mentors can gain valuable insight from their protégés and become better managers.

All training and development should be evaluated to determine whether the objectives set for the programme were met. Kirkpatrick (1994) suggested that there are four levels of evaluation:

- *Participant's reactions:* Were attitudes changed, knowledge improved or skills developed?
- *Did learning occur as part of the programme:* This requires longer term assessment of the impact of the training.
- The extent to which actual work performance has changed.
- *The final results of the training*: In terms of the impact of the training on the organisation and its ability to deliver its mission.

Succession management, and exit and separation

Succession management

Succession management is a process through which an organisation ensures that it has a supply of appropriately skilled employees and managers to replace those who leave or are promoted within the organisation. A robust succession system is vital for the sustained operations of a VSO. The result of a steadily ageing workforce and a tight job market is that many VSOs may struggle to attract, retain and develop appropriately skilled employees in sufficient numbers. In this context, VSOs may need to consider how to fully develop career planning and succession management systems. An effective system will guard against talented staff leaving; allow support staff and volunteers to reach their potential; and balance the competing needs of promotion versus recruitment. Succession management ensures continuity in key positions through the retention and development of knowledge and human capital for the future. This process usually involves identifying critical positions (e.g. level one coach) and/or employees and growing leadership capacity (e.g. identifying and mentoring a junior coach with high potential and supporting them to attain relevant qualifications and experience).

Effective succession management systems should involve the board, CEO/managing director and other executive staff, be supported by senior management, involve line management in identifying candidates; use developmental assignments; and link succession management plans to the mission and strategic plan. Case study 5.2 outlines British Cycling's succession management strategy for the CEO position.

British Cycling appoints new CEO

Nov 17 2008

Peter King is to stand down at the end of the year, with current deputy chief executive Ian Drake taking his place. The news was revealed at British Cycling's annual National Council meeting on 15 November, where President Brian Cookson OBE announced the board's appointment of Ian Drake as chief executive from 1 January 2009 as part of a succession management plan developed over the past year. Peter will continue to work with British Cycling as an executive director and focus on external projects linked to London 2012 and other stakeholders.

Cookson said: 'It is no exaggeration to say that Peter has been pivotal in transforming British Cycling from near-bankruptcy to a world-leading governing body with a reputation for consistently delivering on its objectives. Thanks to Peter, British Cycling is recognised at the highest levels of government as a sound, effective, and reliable body, and the benefits of this can be seen in the achievements and developments in our sport over the past 12 years.'

Drake has worked with British Cycling since 1996, when he worked as a consultant on the development of young people's programmes in schools and clubs. This laid the foundations for British Cycling's successful Go-Ride youth coaching programme. From 1998, Drake led the development and funding submission for the World Class Start and Potential programmes to support British Cycling's vision of becoming the world's number one cycling nation by 2012. This led to the creation of British Cycling's renowned talent identification and development programmes.

In 2000, Drake continued this work when he was appointed as national talent co-ordinator and implemented the Talent Team programme. This has nurtured the likes of Beijing medallists Ed Clancy and Steven Burke along with riders such as Lizzie Armitstead, David Daniel and Anna Blythe who are now emerging as athletes with the potential to win medals at London 2012.

Since 2004 Drake has had responsibility for all British Cycling's Sports Council funding submissions and has been the driving force behind the current 2005 to 2009 'UK Wide One Stop Plan', which has brought unprecedented growth in the sport at all levels. Over the past 18 months he has increasingly taken on more responsibilities as deputy chief executive to allow King to become more externally focused.

Cookson said: 'I am particularly pleased that Peter's expertise will not be lost by British Cycling as he continues as an executive director. It is my intention that we will retain his services in this role for some time to come.

'In Ian Drake, I am convinced that we have found a worthy successor. Ian's knowledge and experience within the organisation on the participation, governance and excellence aspects of our business is second to none and his proven track record on delivery against our UK Wide One Stop Plan key performance indicators stands out amongst all national governing bodies.'

Source:www.bikebiz.com

Disciplinary policies

Organisations should have a disciplinary policy that outlines the steps that indicate the likely circumstances where disciplinary action can be invoked against employees or volunteers who breach an organisation's rules or code of conduct. Usually a disciplinary procedure outlines a process to be followed where breaches of discipline are relatively minor and a second procedure for use when the breach is severe and warrants immediate suspension or dismissal from duty. The different categories are informed by local law in relation to employees and in some instances to volunteers although the latter may be less well defined overall. The following procedure is typically used when breaches of discipline are relatively minor.

A verbal notification of the need to improve/modify behaviour is used as the first step in disciplinary action. This warning can be noted in the employee/volunteer's file or the supervisor may choose to informally record the action in their own records for reference. The next step is a formal written warning, which identifies the problem/issue and notes expectations for change and the disciplinary measures that will occur should the matter persist (e.g. termination, demotion and/or reduction in compensation). This written warning should be signed by the supervisor and the employee/volunteer and kept on file. The final step in a progressive disciplinary process is termination. When the employee/volunteer continually fails to meet performance requirements or standards or when they commit a serious offence they should be dismissed with appropriate reference to their rights and entitlements as specified in the legal framework governing the jurisdiction within which the organisation operates.

Exit/separation

Termination of an employee's or volunteer's services may be required when a breach of the employment contract has occurred, if volunteer responsibilities have been neglected, if performance is not satisfactory, or if the position becomes redundant. The legal requirement associated with such terminations should be clearly understood by all parties. These conditions will vary depending on the type of employment contract, union stipulations and relevant legislation. These conditions will usually require a notice of termination, although in some cases summary termination (i.e. without notice and other normal entitlements) can be enacted, usually when there has been a serious misconduct or breach of contract. In situations where there is strong evidence but no immediate proof of serious wrongdoing, it is normal to suspend staff while an investigation occurs.

Exit strategies can include the provision of references, assistance with job-seeking or outplacements and retraining opportunities. Exit interviews can be valuable to determine the person's reasons for leaving and identify workplace improvements, although in some cases there can be doubt about the accuracy of data collected at such a time. Many departures from an organisation are understandable and are for reasons related to family matters, age, ill health, relocation and other personal circumstances. Reasons for departures should not be assumed, but rather need to be fully understood particularly if a reoccurrence of a negative situation is to be avoided. This process will act as a debriefing for the departing employee/volunteer.

McCurley (1993) offers the following suggestions if there is a need to end the services of a volunteer:

■ Conduct the meeting in a private setting. This will preserve the dignity of the volunteer and perhaps of you.
■ Be quick, direct and absolute. Don't beat around the bush. It is quite embarrassing to have the volunteer show up for work the next day because they didn't get the hint.
■ Practise the exact words you will use in telling the volunteer, and make sure they are unequivocal. Do not back down from them even if you want to preserve your image as a 'nice' person.
■ Announce, don't argue. The purpose of the meeting is simply, and only, to communicate to the volunteer that they are being separated from the organisation. This meeting is not to discuss and argue the decision, because, if you followed the system, all the arguments have already been heard. You should also avoid arguing to make sure you don't put your foot in your mouth while venting your feelings. Expect the volunteer to vent, but you need to keep quiet.
■ Don't attempt to counsel. If counselling were an option, you would not be having this meeting. Face reality, at this point you are not the friend of this former volunteer and any attempt to appear so is misguided and insulting.
■ Follow up the meeting with a letter to the volunteer reiterating the decision and informing them of any departure details. Make sure you also follow up with others. Inform staff and clients of the change in status, although you do not need to inform them of the reasons behind the change.

95

MANAGING VOLUNTEER AND PAID STAFF RELATIONSHIPS

The working relationship between paid staff and volunteers is influenced by the expectations of each and needs to be managed with understanding and collaboration. Paid staff and volunteers, including board members, should all be working together to achieve the goals of the organisation. As reiterated throughout this chapter, a VSO's personnel should receive appropriate support, training and feedback; know what is expected of them, how their contribution will be valued, and be provided with precise job descriptions. Unambiguous boundaries between paid work and voluntary work, good communication processes and regular opportunities to discuss issues and interact can facilitate good relationships between paid staff and volunteers.

Tensions between paid and unpaid staff can be present for a number of reasons, and are often associated with issues of control, power and trust, as related to roles and expectations. For example, when paid workers are assigned to roles previously considered the domain of volunteers, such as a club coach, the volunteers who gladly accepted the responsibility of the role in the past may have developed a sense of ownership and thus may feel disenfranchised when a paid appointment is made.

Other common areas of conflict can occur when long-term volunteers can no longer handle the required duties as well as they used to, or may not have the new skills needed. For example, contemporary sponsorship and public relations requirements may require high level technology skills, or the culture of the VSO changes and no longer aligns with the values and beliefs of the volunteer.

There can also be times when paid staff are hesitant about working with volunteers. This reluctance can be related to belief that the volunteer will:

- create an increased workload related to training and/or supervising the volunteer
- be a burden rather than a help
- not be subject to the same performance standards
- not be dependable
- possibly compromise confidentiality.

Therefore, it is important to ascertain any paid staff concerns and address these through policy and practice.

Volunteers may also have concerns about working with paid staff. These may be related to personal perceptions that:

- I am better qualified than the paid staff member
- the organisation should be thankful they have me to assist
- I am never asked about my good ideas for improving the VSO

96

- I only get the work that no one else wants to do
- staff should be subordinate to the board members (volunteers).

There are a number of ways to facilitate effective working relationships such as:

- including objectives related to working with volunteers as an integral part of the job descriptions of paid staff
- ensuring that staff are supported in this endeavour and that performance appraisals evaluate outcomes
- including volunteering information in staff induction and ongoing training
- involving staff in the development of new or revised volunteering roles, and in the selection and induction of volunteers
- recognising paid staff who work well with volunteers.

For volunteers it is important to have a staff policy that outlines why different types of paid staff are employed by the organisation and how this relates to the work of volunteers, have effective staff relationships included in volunteer role descriptions and provide volunteers with an appropriate participatory role in the organisation.

In summary, good volunteer and staff relationships are characterised by:

- articulation of all the roles in the organisation and the associated expectations
- good communication channels and outlets
- involving all personnel, where appropriate, in planning and decision-making forums
- transparent evaluation of job performance of both paid staff and volunteers
- public and private recognition of the accomplishments of volunteers and paid staff, especially the acknowledgement of joint achievements
- dealing with problems and people who persistently fail to work together, through appropriate management, disciplinary and election procedures. The ultimate focus should be on your organisation achieving its mission – the human resources are there to make that happen.

SUMMARY

HRM provides you with the framework to achieve the 'best mix' of people to allow the VSO to meet its strategic objectives now and into the future. Effective HRM polices and practices will facilitate the recruitment, development and maintenance of a productive, committed, motivated and fulfilled workforce of paid and unpaid staff.

In this chapter HRM was presented as an integrated management strategy that is applied to board members, paid employees and volunteers using a six-phase HR process: HR planning; recruitment and selection; orientation and induction; performance management; training and development; and succession management, and exit and separation. HRM strategies, policies and practices should support and facilitate the organisation to run effectively and meet its goals and objectives.

Increased professionalisation, demographic shifts such as an ageing workforce, advances in technology, legal and regulatory legislation, and changes in the global financial markets will impact HR policies and practices of the future. Changes to the VSO sector will impact stakeholder demands, consumer relationships and organisational strategy. Aspects of organisational performance and HRM are inextricably linked and HR practices will need to respond accordingly to facilitate and develop employees and volunteers to achieve organisational success.

Changes in volunteer demographics, attitudes of different generations, imprecise boundaries on reward and recognition structures, welfare to work schemes, public liability issues and mandatory volunteer contracts all contribute to obscuring of the volunteer–employee distinction. The HRM challenge is to establish an attractive environment for volunteers that rewards, recognises and empowers individuals for their contributions to the VSO.

ADDITIONAL ACTIVITIES

- Discuss the similarities and differences involved in recruiting and selecting volunteers and paid employees for voluntary sport organisations.
- Write a job advertisement and description for the position of general manager of a sport association.
- Identify the types of training and development programmes that an employee might undertake if they worked as a sport development officer for community football.

FURTHER READING

Braithwaite, T. (2004) 'Human resources management in sport', in Beech, J. and Chadwick, S. (eds) *The Business of Sport Management*. Harlow: Pearson Education Ltd.

Minten, S. and Foster, W. (2009) 'Human resource management', in Bill, K. (ed) *Sport Management*. Exeter: Learning Matters.

tracy taylor and peter mcgraw

CHAPTER 6

MANAGING FINANCES

Simon Shibli

There is often some confusion over the importance of financial management to voluntary sport organisations. To some extent this confusion is caused by terminology describing the sector, such as 'non-profit making' or 'non-profit distributing'. Whilst it is true that voluntary sector organisations do not exist primarily to make a profit, there are no rules that prevent them from actually doing so. In many sport clubs it is by making profits from bars, catering and fruit machines that funds are obtained to invest in the maintenance of club houses, new playing equipment and the payment of professional staff. For clubs without premises, it is profitable fund-raising from social events that is used to support the costs of playing sport.

So, in brief, voluntary sport organisations can make a profit. However, the distinctive feature of the voluntary sector is that organisations are not allowed to distribute any of the profits amongst the membership. Whilst it is acceptable for a sport club to pay professional coaches for their services, it would not be acceptable for a committee to share out any profits amongst its members. Profits should be retained within the organisation and should be used for the collective benefit of the membership. This point holds true whether talking about an international governing body of sport such as the International Association of Athletics Federations (IAAF), or a group of like-minded people who come together once a week as a club for a game of netball.

The scale of financial transactions in the voluntary sector should not be underestimated. For example, in a typical golf club there will be around 500 members who each pay around £600 per year in subscriptions yielding £300,000 in membership income alone. Total income will also include golf lessons, green fees from non-members, bar and catering revenues as well as fund-raising activities, which could easily increase the club's revenue to around £750,000+ per annum. On the expenditure side there will be professional staff to pay as well as a club house and golf course to maintain. All of this financial activity points to a golf club being in effect a small business, which in turn requires a good grasp of the principles of financial management. Even at the level of an informal club with one team somebody needs to be responsible for collecting subscriptions and match fees from members and for paying expenses to facility providers and match officials.

Throughout this chapter the case study of the ASA, the national governing body for swimming in England, is used to illustrate the points being made about the importance of financial management to voluntary sport organisations. This national federation has income and expenditure of more than £10m and can accurately be described as a small to medium size enterprise (SME). It is not possible to run a £10m business like the ASA effectively without appropriate financial management. This chapter is concerned with providing readers with an overview of the key financial skills required to manage sport organisations.

KEY TERMS AND THE RELEVANCE OF FINANCIAL MANAGEMENT

The field of financial management is divided into two distinct disciplines, namely: financial accounting and management accounting. A helpful starting point is to define the two disciplines and to explain how managers of sport organisations might encounter them.

Financial accounting is information, in financial terms, that is consistent with the principles outlined in publications such Generally Accepted Accounting Practice (GAAP). Financial accounting involves the recording and summary of business transactions and events. It is concerned with the preparation of financial statements, in a recognised format, for external users such as creditors, investors, and suppliers. An organisation's financial statements include:

- the balance sheet,
- the income statement (or profit and loss account), and;
- the statement of changes in financial position (or cash flow statement).

There are three points worth highlighting in the above definition of financial accounting. First, financial accounting is concerned with the activity of recording and summarising financial transactions. This can be viewed as a starting point because the real value of both financial and management accounting is how the data that has been recorded and summarised is used. Second, financial accounting is governed by a series of prescribed rules and procedures known as Generally Accepted Accounting Principles. The important point of note is that for many organisations it is a legal requirement to undertake financial accounting. Third, the presentation of the results of financial accounting is in a specified form, i.e. the income and expenditure statement for voluntary organisations (more commonly known as the profit and loss account), the balance sheet and the cash flow statement. Collectively, these three specified forms are known as an organisation's 'financial statements' and it is essential that managers know what these are and how to interpret or 'read' them. Later in the chapter the ASA's financial statements will be examined and an explanation will be provided about what they are, what they mean and how they relate to one another.

Management accounting is the process of identification, measurement, accumulation, analysis, preparation, interpretation, and communication of financial information that is used by management to plan, evaluate, make decisions and control an organisation. Managerial accounting is concerned with providing information to internal managers who are charged with directing, planning and controlling operations and making a variety of management decisions.

There are two points worth highlighting from the above definition of management accounting. First, management accounting involves being proactive with the use of financial data by using it for planning, decision-making and control purposes. By contrast, financial accounting data is used for reporting financial performance on a historical basis. Second, management accounting information is compiled and reported in a way which best suits the needs of an organisation, rather than in the prescribed formats used in financial accounting. Unlike financial accounting data, which is in the public domain, there are no legal requirements to give external users access to management accounting data. It is good practice to regard financial accounting and management accounting as two sides of the same coin. Businesses are required by law to record their financial transactions according to the rules of financial accounting.

However, no credible manager will plan to record financial transactions and wait to see what happens at the end of the year. Good managers plan their operations in order to achieve a desired outcome and take corrective action to ensure a close match between what was planned to happen and what happened in reality. The only way to achieve a desired outcome is by taking steps to plan and control the performance of a business. Planning and control is achieved by techniques such as budgeting, which is one of the disciplines found within management accounting. The term 'financial management' can be defined as 'the application of financial accounting and management accounting techniques to the management of an organisation'. It is in this sense that the term 'financial management' is used throughout the chapter. Other key terms that are important are:

- *Assets*: Something of value that the organisation owns or has the use of. These can be current assets, which are only owned for a short time, such as cash, or fixed or long-term assets, such as a building.
- *Liability*: Something owed to someone else; liabilities are the debts of the organisation. Again, these can be current liabilities, which must be paid within a fairly short time, such as the money owed to travel agencies, or long-term liabilities, such as the money owed to a bank for a mortgage on headquarters.
- *Overheads*: Costs needed to run daily operations. These include the cost of heating, electricity and financial staff.
- *Surplus*: An excess of income over expenditure.
- *Deficit*: An excess of expenditure over income.

- *Liquidity*: The amount of money that can be accessed immediately to pay debts.
- *Reserves*: The amount of unspent funds at any given point.
- *Balance sheet*: A list of all assets owned and liabilities owed by the organisation at a given date.
- *Income and expenditure statement*: A record of income generated and expenditure incurred over a given period. This statement shows whether the organisation has a surplus or a deficit.
- *Capital expenditure*: Expenditure that results in the acquisition of, or improvements to, fixed assets, such as a building.
- *Revenue expenditure*: Expenditure incurred in the operation of the organisation or on maintaining the earning capacity of fixed assets, such as maintenance on a building that is hired out.

FINANCIAL STATEMENTS

One of the useful features of financial statements is that they are presented in a standardised format. This means that if one set of financial statements can be read, any can be read. However, before considering how to analyse and interpret accounts it is important to take stock of what they are and how they relate to each other. There are two main financial statements that are readily available for a voluntary sport organisation: the income and expenditure statement (or profit and loss account) and the balance sheet. The discussion below considers each one in turn.

Income and expenditure statement

The income and expenditure statement in Figure 6.1 sets out that in the financial year 1 April 2007 to 31 March 2008 the ASA had a turnover of £10,065,000. Its day-to-day expenses were £10,103,000, which resulted in an operating loss of £38,000. However, the ASA also generated investment income of £57,000 (which is usually interest earned on surplus cash deposits) and this additional income was sufficient to turn the operating deficit of £38,000 into a surplus before tax of £19,000. After tax of £12,000 was charged, there was a final (or retained) surplus of £7,000. An alternative way of describing this financial performance would be to say that after the 2008 year's trading, the ASA's net worth increased by £7,000.

Having described what the financial performance has been, the next question to tackle is the extent to which this performance is good, bad or indifferent. There are two clues that give pointers in this regard. First, note how in Figure 6.1 the comparative information from the previous financial year (2007) is presented. In 2007 the 'bottom' line is that the ASA broke even, that is neither made a

simon shibli

	2008	2007
	£000s	£000s
Turnover	10,065	9,080
Operating expenses	−10,103	−9,104
Operating deficit	−38	−24
Investment income	57	29
Surplus on ordinary activities before taxation	19	5
Tax on surplus on ordinary activities	−12	−5
Surplus on ordinary activities after taxation	7	0

Figure 6.1 The ASA Income and expenditure account for the period ended 31 March 2008 (Source: The Amateur Swimming Association, 2008)

profit nor a loss. Thus in this context, moving from break even (£0 change in net worth) to a £7,000 surplus must be a step in the right direction. Second, in the Financial Review of the ASA's annual report it is stated that: 'the year ending on 31 March 2008 shows a surplus of £7,000 against a budgeted surplus of £4,000'. These two additional pieces of information lead to the conclusion that the ASA performed better than expectations (£7,000 v £4,000) and better than last year, which in turn can be taken to be evidence of successful performance. However, it should be noted that a £7,000 surplus on a £10m turnover is a very slim margin and leaves very little room for error. However, the basic point is that a sport organisation's financial statements show whether it made a surplus (or profit) for the year.

The balance sheet

The second financial statement is the balance sheet, and the ASA's for the years ended 31 March 2008 and 31 March 2007 is shown in Figure 6.2.

At first glance the balance sheet might look slightly daunting, but if the logic of what is presented is understood, it should be straightforward to interpret. The balance sheet is no more than a listing of:

- those things of value that are owned by the business (assets)
- those things that are owed to others by the business (creditors or liabilities), and as a logical consequence of subtracting creditors from assets

	2008	2007
	£000s	£000s
Fixed assets		
Tangible fixed assets	270	297
Unquoted investments	80	80
	350	377
Current assets		
Stocks	189	145
Debtors	2,437	2,457
Cash at bank and in hand	3,618	2,318
	6,244	4,920
Creditors:		
Amounts falling due within one year	−5,340	−4,050
Net current assets	904	870
Total assets less current liabilities	1,254	1,247
Capital and reserves		
Income and expenditure account	1,254	1,247

Figure 6.2 The ASA Balance sheet as at 31 March 2008 (Source: The Amateur Swimming Association, 2008)

■ a valuation of the net worth of the business.

This is easier to understand in the context of normal life. If a house is worth £350,000 and the owner has a mortgage with the bank of £150,000 then the net worth of the house to the owner would be £200,000. This can be expressed as a simple equation as follows:

Asset (house)	£350,000
less	
Creditors (mortgage)	£150,000
equals	
Capital (net worth)	£200,000

A balance sheet as shown in Figure 6.2 is no different in principle to the house and mortgage example. The only difference is that balance sheets for organisations like the ASA distinguish between different types of assets and creditors. A fixed asset is an item of long-term value to a business that is not normally converted into cash in the normal course of business. In the case of the ASA, its fixed assets are listed in its 2008 annual report and include land and buildings, motor vehicles and furniture, fittings and equipment. By contrast, any asset that is described as

simon shibli

'current' is either cash or expected to be converted into cash in the next year. It would be reasonable to expect that stocks of goods for resale and amounts that are owed by others be converted into cash within a year and hence they are called current assets.

The final structural note about the balance sheet is what it 'balances' with. In Figure 6.2 the figure for Total Assets less Current Liabilities is £1,254,000 and this 'balances' with the sum shown in Capital and Reserves under the income and expenditure statement of £1,254,000 (not shown in Figure 6.1). What this means is that the net worth of the ASA is £1,254,000 and this is represented by (or balances with) the accumulated surpluses (or profits) that the organisation has made throughout its history. This point can be reinforced by examining the link between the income and expenditure statement and the balance sheet. Note three things:

■ at 31 March 2007 the net worth of the ASA was £1,247,000
■ during the financial year to the end of March 2008 the income and expenditure account shows a surplus of £7,000
■ at 31 March 2008 the net worth of the ASA was £1,254,000.

The fact that the balance sheet has increased in value by £7,000 is no coincidence. The relationship between the two statements is this:

■ the opening balance sheet shows the net worth of an organisation at a given point in time (in this case £1,247,000 at 31 March 2007)
■ the income and expenditure statement shows how the organisation's net worth has changed over a period (in this case £7,000 over a year)
■ the closing balance sheet shows the revised net worth of the organisation at a given point in time (in this case £1,254,000 at 31 March 2008).

Using the preliminary analysis conducted on the financial statements thus far, the following features can be established for the ASA's financial performance for the year ended 31 March 2008:

■ the organisation made an operating loss of £38,000
■ money from investment income, i.e. cash on deposit, of £57,000 converted the operating loss into a surplus of £19,000
■ the investment income was largely derived by collecting money in advance from members and funders and placing it on deposit to earn interest
■ after tax, the organisation made a surplus of £7,000, which exceeded its target of £4,000
■ the net worth of the ASA is £1,254,000, that is to say: if all assets were converted into cash at the value stated in the accounts and all creditors were paid off, there would be £1,254,000 left.

The absolute minimum that should be understood is that:

- the income and expenditure statement shows how much the net worth of an organisation has changed over a period (usually a year)
- the balance sheet shows the overall net worth of the business at the start of the period and at the end of the period.

Having grasped the essentials of what financial statements are and what the information contained in them reveals about an organisation, it is now time consider how financial statements can be analysed and interpreted using a suite of widely used techniques.

FINANCIAL ANALYSIS AND INTERPRETATION

For all voluntary sport organisations it is important that the governance of the organisation is underpinned by proper financial management. Those people in charge of an organisation are said to have 'stewardship' responsibilities, which are particularly important when an organisation is in receipt of public funding. Without the need to have specialist training in finance, there are two common questions to which senior managers of a sport organisation should be able to respond positively.

First, 'Is the selling price higher than the cost?' For sport organisations this question can be modified to: 'Is the organisation operating within the resources allocated to it?' Thus in the case of the ASA, given that it made a £7,000 surplus in 2008, the answer to the question: 'Has the organisation operated within its resources?' is positive. If organisations do not operate within their resources, then it is highly likely that financial problems will follow. This chapter was written during a 'global credit crunch', which has demonstrated somewhat painfully what happens when people run out of cash. The same principle applies to voluntary sport organisations that do not operate within their resources. By contrast, why do certain organisations such as the IOC survive and thrive? The simple answer is that they make a financial surplus, or in other words the selling price is higher than the cost. When surpluses are made they can be reinvested in an organisation to improve it, to develop new services and to keep ahead of the competition.

The second question to answer is: 'Is the business well set to continue trading?' In practice the second question is a reference to an organisation's ability to pay its debts as they fall due and having the freedom to pursue strategies of its own without external influence. Many organisational failures occur as a result of running out of cash rather than lack of demand for products or services. In this regard the ASA is an example of a well managed business as it has plenty of cash and uses its surplus to generate interest, which in turn helps to make the difference between making a surplus rather than a loss. In voluntary sport organisations financial success depends on three factors:

- the ability to operate within the resources available
- the ability to pay bills as they fall due
- the ability to service debts.

In the next section the manner in which the two key questions underpin an understanding of finance will be demonstrated.

Analysing financial statements

There are two common uses for financial accounting data that managers of sport organisations are likely to encounter. First, financial statements can be used to explain an organisation's financial performance internally, for example the chief executive of the ASA explaining to the board how the organisation has performed over the last year. Second, financial statements are often the only publicly available information from which to diagnose the financial health of external organisations, for example other businesses that an organisation might consider trading with. There is little point in extending credit to a potential partner that has cash flow problems and therefore might have problems paying invoices. The skill of analysing financial statements is important because, if done correctly, it is possible to make an informed diagnosis about an organisation's financial health. Typical questions include:

- Can it afford to pay its bills?
- Does it have enough money to invest in new buildings or equipment?
- Would you be prepared to trade with it?

How a manager might set about answering these questions is best illustrated by developing our understanding of the ASA's financial statements using what is known as vertical and horizontal analysis.

Vertical analysis of accounts

Vertical analysis is where a key variable (usually turnover on the income and expenditure statement) is given a value of 100 per cent and all other lines on the income and expenditure statement are expressed as a percentage of this key variable. A fully worked example for the ASA can be seen in Figure 6.3, which simply develops the data shown in Figure 6.1.

Figure 6.3 shows that in 2008, for every £100 of the ASA's turnover there was expenditure of £100.40p, which when aggregated up over more than £10m of turnover led to an operating deficit of £38,000 or –0.4 per cent of turnover.

Investment income was equivalent to 0.6 per cent of turnover, turning the operating loss into a 0.2 per cent surplus before tax. Tax was –0.1 per cent of turnover leaving 0.1 per cent of turnover as a surplus. An alternative way of describing this situation is to say that for every £100 of turnover, around 10p was left over as a surplus. This is a paper thin margin within which to operate, but nonetheless the organisation did make a surplus of £7,000, which exceeded its budgeted target of £4,000 as discussed above. This type of financial performance is typical of voluntary sport organisations because they do not set out to make a profit.

Voluntary sector organisations do not exist to make a profit, but they do need to operate within the resources available to them. In this instance the ASA has operated within its resources and almost incidentally managed to make a small surplus. However, it is a rather sobering thought that for a £10m business, the difference between making a surplus and making a loss is about the same as three months' sick pay for one member of staff out of a total of 151 employees.

The ASA has clearly demonstrated a positive answer to the first key question: 'Is the organisation operating within the resources allocated to it?' It is conventional for financial statements to contain the data for two years' worth of trading activity, that is, the year in question and the comparative figures for the previous year. Therefore a follow-up question might be: 'How does this year's performance compare with last year?' Using the comparative data for 2007, it is possible to analyse how the 2008 data compares with the previous year. In the case of the ASA, in Figure 6.3 it is apparent that costs formed a marginally higher percentage of turnover in 2008 than in 2007 but the factor that has made the biggest

	2008 £000s	2008 %	2007 £000s	2007 %
Turnover	10,065	100.0	9,080	100.0%
Operating expenses	–10,103	–100.4	–9,104	–100.3%
Operating deficit	–38	–0.4	–24	–0.3
Investment income	57	0.6	29	0.3
Surplus on ordinary activities before taxation	19	0.2	5	0.1
Tax on surplus on ordinary activities	–12	-0.1	–5	-0.1
Surplus on ordinary activities after taxation	7	0.1	0	0.0

Figure 6.3 Income and expenditure account: vertical analysis for the ASA

simon shibli

difference is the doubling of investment income, which led to a surplus in 2008, which in turn compared favourably with a break-even position in 2007. In simple terms it can be concluded that the 2008 performance was an improvement on 2007.

Horizontal analysis of accounts

Generally, organisations need to increase their income streams as it is a harsh reality that costs tend to escalate every year. For example, in the current financial climate the costs of energy and utilities are rising at a disproportionately greater rate than the cost of living, which reinforces the need for income growth. It may be the case that sport organisations that receive funding to support their activities are insulated from the need to grow by having funding agreements that increase with inflation; however, this is unusual. Thus in the short to medium term, if an organisation wishes to operate within its resources, it must grow to keep pace with its increased costs (or alternatively reduce its cost base). Organisations also need to grow in order to invest in developing better levels of service and ensuring that key personnel have skill levels that are fit for purpose.

To illustrate the point, consider the case of how sport club administration could change as a result of investing in technology. In sport clubs it was traditional to have team selection meetings in midweek and for team captains to telephone players individually informing them of which team they were playing in, where the match was, and when and where to meet. Nowadays this type of administration can be done online subject to some investment in a computer, a website and some training. Thus clubs that wish to evolve and offer their members improved services also need to grow financially to fund the investments necessary to deliver better service.

Measuring growth is achieved by using what is known as horizontal analysis. Figure 6.4 shows the data from the ASA's income and expenditure statement subjected to horizontal analysis.

The growth calculation involve two parts: first, calculating the change in each component of the income and expenditure statement (this year minus last year); and, second, expressing the change as a percentage of last year. Thus in Figure 6.4, the absolute increase in turnover is £985,000, which is a 10.8 per cent increase on the previous year. It can also be seen that expenses increased at an even greater rate (11.0 per cent) than turnover, which could be a worrying sign. However, the 96.6 per cent increase in investment income made the difference between breaking even in 2007 and making a surplus in 2008. Signs of successful growth are an increase in turnover and an increase in surplus. In the case of Figure 6.4, the ASA's turnover increased by 10.8 per cent and the surplus increased by £7,000, which is a sign of successful growth. Note how it is not possible to compute a percentage increase in growth between 2007 and 2008 because the base figure

	2008 £000s	2007 £000s	Absolute change	% change
Turnover	10,065	9,080	985	10.8
Operating expenses	−10,103	−9,104	−999	11.0
Operating deficit	−38	−24	−14	58.3
Investment income	57	29	28	96.6
Surplus on ordinary activities before taxation	19	5	14	280.0
Tax on surplus on ordinary activities	−12	−5	−7	140.0
Surplus on ordinary activities after taxation	7	0	7	n/a

Figure 6.4 Income and expenditure account: horizontal analysis for the ASA

for 200[1]7 is zero. In summary, by applying some basic maths it has been possible to develop an understanding of the ASA's financial performance using vertical and horizontal analysis. It is of course possible to apply these techniques to the balance sheet as well as the income and expenditure statement, but space does not permit such a demonstration in a single chapter.

The answer to the second question: 'Is the business well set to continue trading?' can in part be obtained from examining the balance sheet. Understanding the relationship between certain items on the balance sheet enables vital information to be obtained about the financial health of an organisation. Two of the determinants of whether an organisation is well set to continue trading are the ability to pay its bills and the degree of control it has over its assets. The ability to pay debts as they fall due is called 'liquidity' and is measured by liquidity ratios. Liquidity ratios compare the amount of current assets available to pay current creditors. The first of these is called the current ratio and simply compares total current assets with total current creditors. Using the relevant figures from the ASA's balance sheet in Figure 6.2, it is straightforward to compute the relationship between assets that are cash or intended to be converted into cash in the next year, with bills that have to be paid within the next year as shown below.

Current ratio calculation:

	2008	2007
Current assets	6,244,000	4,920,000
Current creditors	5,340,000	4,050,000
Current ratio	1.16:1[1]	1.21:1

---

[1] (6,244,000 / 5,340,000):1

110

simon shibli

The current ratio calculation shows that in 2008, for every £1 of current creditors, the ASA had £1.16 in current assets. This finding suggests that the organisation can meet its bills as they fall due for payment. Comparison with 2007 indicates that there has been a small decline in liquidity from 1.21:1 to 1.16:1. However, the essential point is that generally liquidity ratios should be equal to or better than 1:1.

It is sometimes the case that organisations are unable to sell their stock as quickly as they would like. As an acknowledgement of this point, a second liquidity ratio, the 'quick ratio', also known as the 'acid test', can be calculated. The quick ratio is very similar to the current ratio and simply excludes stock from the calculation.

Quick ratio (or acid test) calculation:

	2008	2007
Current assets	6,244,000	4,920,000
minus stock	189,000	145,000
equals	6,055,000	4,775,000
Current creditors	5,340,000	4,050,000
Quick ratio	1.13:11	1.18:1

The acid test ratio reveals that in both years money tied up in stocks has a minimal impact on the ASA's ability to pay its bills. In 2008 the quick ratio was 1.13:1 which is only marginally lower than the 1.16:1 current ratio and a similar reduction occurs in the 2007 data. In some respects this should not come as a surprise as the ASA is essentially a service organisation and would not be expected to carry significant volumes of stock. The stock that it does carry tends to be confined to swimming certificates and badges, which young people buy when they have achieved a swimming award. Once a liquidity ratio falls below 1:1, further clarification might be necessary from an organisation's managers concerning their strategy for being able to settle debts as they fall due.

Liquidity ratios are one of the ways in which managers can assess the credit worthiness of potential business contacts. For example, the ASA might decide to enter into a sponsorship agreement with a commercial company. Whether agreeing to accept the sponsorship deal is a good idea or not depends on whether or not payment is received for the services provided to the sponsor. Checking the creditworthiness of a potential sponsor would be an important part of evaluating whether or not to accept a deal. Credit terms might be offered to a sponsor with a strong balance sheet and acceptable liquidity levels, whereas a sponsor without such credentials might be required to pay up in advance or indeed be declined. The importance of financial statements in this regard is that they are in the public domain and can be accessed quite readily by interested parties and potential suppliers can be vetted discreetly.

The extent to which an organisation is in control of its assets can be measured by the 'debt ratio', which is a measure of the extent to which an organisation's assets are funded by creditors. This point can be illustrated using an everyday example of two homeowners who both have houses worth £300,000. Owner A has a mortgage for £100,000 and Owner B has a mortgage for £240,000. Common sense tells us that Owner A is in a better position than Owner B, but how can the relationship be quantified to demonstrate the point?

	Owner A	Owner B
House (asset)	300,000	300,000
Mortgage (creditor)	100,000	240,000
Net worth (equity)	200,000	60,000

The debt ratio measures the extent to which assets are funded by debts, so the debt ratio for each house owner would be:

	Owner A	Owner B
House (asset)	300,000	300,000
Mortgage (creditor)	100,000	240,000
Debt ratio[1]	33%	80%

Owner A is in a better position than Owner B as a result of owning the majority of the equity in his house; whereas in the case of Owner B the mortgage provider has the majority stake in the house. Owner A would therefore be said to have greater control over his asset (house) than Owner B.

Applying the same logic to the ASA balance sheet using the data in Figure 6.2, the debt ratios for years 2008 and 2007 would be:

	2008	2007
Total fixed assets	350,000	377,000
Current assets	6,244,000	4,920,000
Total assets	6,594,000	5,297,000
Current creditors	5,340,000	4,050,000
Debt ratio	81%	76%

The debt ratio analysis for the ASA reveals that in 2008 81 per cent of the organisation's assets were in effect controlled by creditors, which is an increase on the position in 2007 when the corresponding statistic was 76 per cent. Whilst debt ratios of 80 per cent or more might be a concern in the commercial business world, they are common amongst voluntary sport organisations. As not-for-profit organisations it is reasonable to expect assets and creditors to be the same and therefore for the debt ratio to be 100 per cent. However, in the case of the ASA, the balance sheet tells us that the organisation has reserves of £1,254,000 which is largely represented by cash. So in this instance a debt ratio of 81 per cent is no cause for concern. Where the debt ratio might identify a problem for a voluntary sport organisation is if the debt ratio was higher than 100 per cent, that is to say more was owed to creditors than was available to pay them.

---

[1] Debt ratio = (creditors / assets) × 100

simon shibli

Any organisation that struggles to pay its bills because of a low liquidity position or which is not necessarily in control of its assets can be described as being not well set to continue trading. By contrast, if these indicators are positive, as they are for the ASA, it enables those with a business relationship with the organisation to be confident that they are dealing with a financially sound organisation.

There are many more ratios and analysis techniques that can be used to assess the financial statements of organisations. However, this section of the chapter has focused on the basic areas that managers of voluntary sport organisations should investigate. It is worth summarising what has been covered thus far.

- Sport organisations report their financial performance and financial position using financial statements.
- The two main financial statements are the income and expenditure statement and the balance sheet.
- The income and expenditure provides an analysis of how an organisation's capital (or net worth) has changed over a period.
- The balance sheet illustrates the capital, or reserves, of an organisation.
- The key relationship to understand is that the income and expenditure statement is an 'explanation' of how the balance sheet has changed between two accounting periods.
- Beyond the basics outlined above, it is possible to acquire an even better feel for a set of financial statements by conducting vertical and horizontal analysis on them.
- Selected use of ratio analysis to perform calculations such as liquidity ratios and the debt ratio can provide further insights into an organisation's financial health.

AN INTRODUCTION TO BUDGETING

Organisations do not drift from year to year and hope that their financial statements show a favourable outcome. Well managed organisations plan their activities in advance and monitor their financial performance on a regular basis. The process of budgeting is essentially about the plan for the organisation's programme expressed in financial terms. It is an estimate of income and expenditure, usually for a one-year period.

Creating a budget is a relatively straightforward process. It is necessary to know how much money will come in, how much money is being spent and how much money should be spent. This requires the following to be considered:

- sources of revenue, or how much money will come in, including in-kind contributions

- the costs of the services the organisation delivers
- overhead costs, including salaries, rent and electricity
- any other costs, such as investment in equipment, maintenance, fringe benefits, volunteer benefits and payroll taxes.

If the case of an amateur rugby club that owns its own clubhouse and pitches is considered, typical questions that need to be answered in order to create the budget might include:

- How many members are wanted and what price shall be charged for belonging to the club (subscriptions)?
- How much shall members be charged for match fees?
- What will be the cost of running and maintaining the clubhouse for the benefit of the members?
- What will be the cost of paying for match officials?
- How much revenue can be generated from bar and catering sales?
- How much money can be realised from fund-raising activities?
- What investments are necessary to improve the infrastructure and services of the club?

The budget should ensure that the organisation survives. Organisational survival can be achieved in a variety of ways such as:

- making sure that income is at least equal to or greater than expenditure
- generating sufficient surpluses to be able to maintain and develop an organisation
- delivering sufficiently well on social objectives so as to secure continued funding from external sources.

Thus whilst the simple act of having a budget does not guarantee that an organisation will survive, it can help improve the likelihood of an organisation surviving. The actual mechanics of compiling a budget will be illustrated briefly in the remainder of the chapter using an amateur rugby club as an example. As contextual background, assume that the club has 100 members and fields four teams per week. It owns its own clubhouse, which is equipped with a bar and basic catering facilities for providing meals after matches. In the voluntary sector it is conventional to identify expenditure first and then to match this with income. In the case of the rugby club example, the costs of running the club for a year are shown in Figure 6.5.

Numbers in isolation are not particularly helpful unless they are put into context and so it helps to have notes to explain what the numbers are and the underlying assumptions that have been used to derive them. Illustrative notes, which might be written by the club treasurer to justify the budget, and

114

Expenditure	£s
Gas / electricity / water	9,000
Playing costs	7,500
Club house rates	7,000
Maintenance of grounds	5,000
Insurance / security	4,500
1st XV coach / trainer	4,000
Bar costs	10,000
Administration costs	3,000
Total Expenditure	50,000

Figure 6.5 Rugby club expenditure

to explain the assumptions upon which the numbers in Figure 6.5 are based, are given below.

Gas / electricity / water, rates, maintenance, insurance, 1st XV coach

These costs are essentially fixed costs and do not vary in line with the number of rugby matches played. The costs have been derived by taking last year's known figures and adjusting them to reflect expected increases or decreases for next year.

Playing costs

Playing costs are based on the assumption that the club will field four teams of 15 players for 25 matches per season at an average cost of £5 per player per game (4 teams x 15 players x 25 matches x £5 = £7,500).

Figure 6.5 shows that the costs of running the club are £50,000 per year and from the contextual information it is known that the club has 100 members. In simplistic terms this is equivalent to £500 per year per member. It is highly unlikely that rugby players will pay £500 per head to be a member of a club (£100 is closer to the going rate) and therefore the club's committee will need to think carefully about how much it does charge for membership and how the shortfall in income will be recouped.

Now that the costs of running the club are known, the club treasurer and the rest of the committee need to put in place a plan to balance the books by finding the resources necessary to create a position whereby income is at least equal to expenditure. Essentially this is done in a similar way to expenditure as shown below.

- *Club subscriptions*: The purposes of club subscriptions is to put a cost on belonging to a club that in turn helps to pay towards the club's fixed costs (in this case the cost of owning and operating a clubhouse and grounds for the benefit of the members). For the purposes of this exercise, assume that all 100 members are happy to pay £100 as a club subscription. This will generate £10,000 in income and will cover 25 per cent of the club's total costs.

- *Match fees*: For those members who play in matches there are costs attached to staging each game. The notes to the expenditure above state that the cost of playing is £5 per player per match and this is equivalent to £7,500 per year. It is logical and fair that those players who play the most should contribute the most to the club. However, a key issue to address is should the club make a profit from match fees by charging players more than the actual costs incurred by the club (£5 per head)? Given that subscriptions do not cover the full cost of running the club then it makes sense that the club recovers some of its costs from match fees. If it is assumed that the match fees are charged to players at £8 per player per match, then the revenue generated by this plan will be £12,000 (4 teams x 15 players x 25 matches x £8 = £12,000).

- *Bar and catering sales*: Many sport clubs that have their own bar and catering facilities subsidise the cost of membership with the profits they make from selling food and drink. This rugby club runs four teams and plays 25 matches per year. Typically two teams per week will be at home and two will be away. This means that after every match there will be 60 players plus unspecified numbers of match officials, club officials from both teams and supporters at the club. It would be reasonable to assume that the number of people present would be around 100 and that on average they spend £10 per head on food and drink. Thus on each of the club's 25 match days it would be possible to generate £1,000 in income and over 25 matches this is equivalent to £25,000. However, it should be noted that this income is not all profit as the bar and catering supplies have to be paid for. A well run operation should be able to achieve a gross profit (the difference between sales and the cost of those sales) of 60 per cent. Thus the contribution of the bar and catering would be as shown below.

Bar and catering sales	25,000	100 per cent
Cost of sales	10,000	40 per cent
Gross profit	15,000	60 per cent

Note how the use of common size analysis helps to illustrate the relationship between sales, cost of sales and gross profit.

- *Gaming (or fruit) machines*: Another valuable income earner for sport clubs is gaming or fruit machines, particularly when they are located in bars. Assume that on match days the club can generate £200 in fruit machine income, then over 25 match days this is equivalent to £5,000 per year.

116

Income	£S
Bar and catering sales	25,000
Subscriptions	10,000
Match fees	12,000
Fruit machines	5,000
Sponsorship / fundraising	3,000
Total Income	55,000

Figure 6.6 Rugby club income

■ *Sponsorship and other fund-raising activities*: Sport clubs enjoy some success in attracting sponsorship, often from the businesses of members. In addition, they also engage in other fund-raising activities such as dinners, social events, raffles and lotteries. For the purposes of this exercise, assume that the rugby club makes £3,000 per year from sponsorship and other fund-raising activities.

The outcome of the assumptions concerning income can be summarised as shown in Figure 6.6.

Having modelled expenditure and income separately, a budget can now be constructed. This is shown in Figure 6.7.

Figure 6.7 shows that total income is £55,000, total expenditure is £50,000 and therefore the surplus for the year is £5,000. This is a promising outcome for the rugby club as it demonstrates that the club is capable of operating comfortably within its resources and could even have a surplus at the year end. However, what is planned out on paper using reasonable assumptions and what happens in reality are often two entirely different things. Nonetheless, it does provide the club's treasurer and committee with important information that can help them with the management of the club. Some of the key points are discussed below:

■ It is important that subscriptions of £100 are collected from all 100 members; any member that does not pay will adversely affect the projected surplus by £100. The club might even consider introducing a rule that no player is allowed to play for the club until their subscriptions have been paid.
■ Match fees must be collected from all players after each game. Anybody not paying is depriving the club of £8.
■ The bar and catering revenue (£15,000 net) is one third of the club's total income. The bar must be properly stocked and staffed when it is open so that potential sales are not missed. There are targets attached to sales such that on each match day the bar and catering facilities need to achieve sales of

managing finances

	£s
Income	
Bar and catering sales	25,000
Subscriptions	10,000
Match fees	12,000
Fruit machines	5,000
Sponsorship / fundraising	3,000
Total Income	55,000
Expenditure	
Category	
Utilities	9,000
Playing costs	7,500
Club house rates	7,000
Maintenance of grounds	5,000
Insurance / security	4,500
Staff	4,000
Bar	10,000
Administration	3,000
Total Expenditure	50,000
Surplus / (Deficit)	5,000

Figure 6.7 Operating budget for the rugby club

£1,000. Losses such as spillages should be minimised and this in turn means that people working behind the bar should be trained appropriately.
- The fruit machine must be kept in good working order and must never be out of order when the club is open. Appropriate levels of change need to be maintained and bar staff should be asked to give out change in coins so that drinkers are encouraged to spend their change on the fruit machines.
- Sponsorship and fund-raising is the financial 'icing on the cake' for the club and will make the difference between just breaking even or having sufficient funds left over to invest in improving services for members.

This type of information provides a framework around which managers can plan, make decisions and control their organisations. For example, if bar sales were not at the required level, what sort of action could the club take? A common strategy used by clubs with their own clubhouses and bars is to rent their facilities out to others. For example, the club could charge £100 so that a family could host a 21st birthday party on the premises and would also benefit from the bar sales generated that night. The profit on this night and others like them could then be used to make up the shortfall on the budget or to invest in improving services for members. Understanding an organisation's financial drivers and having rehearsed in advance potential responses to given situations, such as generating less income than expected, provides managers with the tools to manage effectively. This is equally applicable to voluntary sport organisations as it is to profit-making businesses. The key points covered under budgeting are listed below.

- The financial performance of sport organisations should be planned and managed in order to meet targets, even if the target is no more ambitious than to survive.
- Budgeting is a straightforward mechanical exercise, the more difficult task lies in making sure that the assumptions upon which the budget is based are accurate.
- An important benefit of budgeting is that it provides managers with vital information about what the key drivers of an organisation's financial performance are.
- It is good practice to rehearse responses to changes in the key drivers of financial performance so that managers can pre-empt how they might react accordingly.

SUMMARY

The key point arising from this chapter is that well developed financial skills are needed for mangers working in voluntary sport organisations. Financial accounting is the language of business as it uses standardised approaches for reporting financial performance (income and expenditure statement) and financial position (balance sheet). As all voluntary organisations are either required to, or should report a summary of their financial transactions using financial accounting techniques, it follows that understanding what these techniques are, is an essential skill. As the voluntary, public and commercial sectors now interact more than they have done previously, VSO managers need to be able to make assessments about potential partners as well as analysing and reporting on a partner's financial performance.

Second, the voluntary sector operates in a climate of increased accountability. Managers need the skills to plan, make decisions and control their spheres of responsibility. Use of management accounting techniques will not replace decision making by humans, but when used properly they can provide the basis from which the most effective decisions can be made.

ADDITIONAL ACTIVITIES

■ Obtain a set of accounts from a voluntary sector organisation in which you are interested. Diagnose the financial performance and position of the organisation using the techniques illustrated in this chapter.

■ What are the financial imperatives of managing a voluntary sport organisation? Can you give some examples from your own experience?

■ It is sometimes said that because sport club treasurers are volunteers and give their time and expertise at no cost, it is not realistic to expect them to work to the same standard as professional staff. To what extent do you agree with this view? What are the potential pitfalls of using under-skilled staff to manage an organisation's finances?

■ In practice, how feasible is it to compile a budget that accurately reflects both costs and income? Do you have any good or bad experiences from being involved in the budget setting process?

■ To what extent do voluntary sport organisations in your experience monitor their financial performance and take corrective action where appropriate?

FURTHER READING

Beech, J. and Chadwick, S. (eds) (2004) *The Business of Sport Management*. Essex: Prentice Hall Financial Times.

Robinson, L. (2004) *Managing Public Sport and Leisure Services*. London: Routledge.

Shibli, S. (1994) *Leisure Manager's Guide to Budgeting and Budgetary Control*. London: ILAM/Longman.

Trendberth, L. (2003) *Managing the Business of Sport*. Auckland: Dunmore Press Ltd.

Wilson, R. and Joyce, J. (2008) *Finance for Sport and Leisure Managers*. London: Routledge.

simon shibli

CHAPTER 7

PERFORMANCE MANAGEMENT

Leigh Robinson

Performance management can be quite simply defined as 'actively monitoring the organisation's performance levels to continuously improve' (Andersen et al, 2006: 63). It is a process that makes use of the systems and procedures that an organisation has, in order to meet the requirements of stakeholders. From this it is clear that performance management is an integral part of the organisational strategy and planning process that was set out in Chapter 4. Strategy and planning activities set the objectives and establish the plans that the performance management process must deliver. In short, performance management operationalises the strategic planning process.

This chapter addresses the need for performance management in the voluntary sport sector and its role in the delivery of services. It will consider issues relating to performance management and will focus, in detail, on performance evaluation and measurement. It concludes with a case study of the performance framework within which UK national governing bodies work.

THE PERFORMANCE MANAGEMENT PROCESS

The performance management (PM) process is a simplistic process and, as set out in Figure 7.1, is made up of four stages. The process starts with the *objectives*, which will have been set by the strategic planning process. This may need to be refined to a more applied level, for example, for the service, athlete or team. Performance objectives are a statement of what is to be achieved and as such should be directly linked to the objectives that the organisation is going to achieve (see Chapter 4). They need to be expressed clearly using SMART in that they need to be significant, measurable, action-oriented, realistic and time-bound.

Once the objectives are established, detailed plans to achieve these objectives need to be developed. Plans set out the activities that are to be delivered, how they are to be delivered and the resources required, such as time, equipment, athletes and coaches. These plans are then put into operation, which is the *process or service* offered to members, customers and other stakeholders. The operation phase needs careful management and will need resources that are

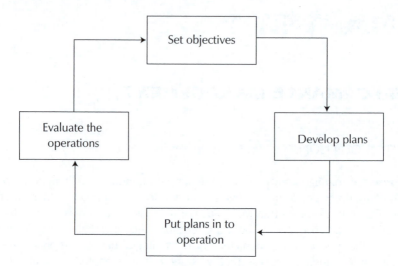

Figure 7.1 The performance management process

appropriate, well planned, in the right place and delivered in the right manner. Finally, the outcomes of plans and their subsequent operations need evaluation against the objectives they were intended to achieve and this is the role of performance indicators, which will be discussed later. This evaluation may lead to changes in the plan or operations or, as a last resort, a review of the objectives. This evaluation phase needs to be carried out at regular intervals in order to make sure that the final goal is achieved. For example, in Figure 7.2, which shows a performance management process for qualifying for the Olympic Games, the evaluation of plans would need to be done after each competition in which the athlete competes in order to assess whether qualification for the Olympics is on track.

This process is ongoing in that it will continue until the objective has been achieved. It is also possible that each performance management process may contribute to a number of objectives. For example, the plans made for sport science support of one athlete may contribute to the performance of another.

RATIONALE FOR PERFORMANCE MANAGEMENT

Performance management assists in five main ways. First, and somewhat obviously, performance management assists with planning as it provides a structure for controlling the implementation of plans to meet objectives, provides information on how the organisation is performing against targets and generates information that can be fed into future planning. Indeed, without performance management, planning is a pointless process. Second, organisations that manage

leigh robinson

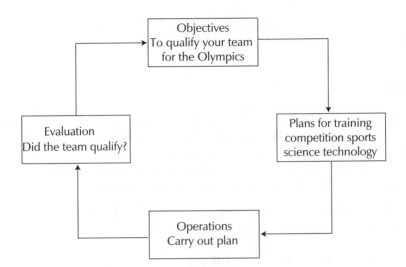

Figure 7.2 The performance management process for qualifying for the Olympics

performance are less likely to rely simply on subjective management judgement as managers are being continuously provided with up-to-date information on how well their operation is doing. Third, performance management allows managers to evaluate and communicate the success of the service in achieving strategies and in implementing policy. As a consequence, performance management makes sport organisations operate in a more transparent and accountable way. This is because the process allows managers to show members and funders how the organisation is performing and stakeholders can see this even if it isn't communicated to them. Fourth, performance management assists with meeting stakeholder expectations. If the performance objectives and indicators that are set are agreed by stakeholders, the service can be managed to meet these targets. The final benefit of performance management is that it allows managers to focus on key aspects of the service, such as participation or elite performance. The information produced from performance management allows managers to evaluate how they are doing against objectives set in targeted areas.

STRUCTURES FOR MANAGING PERFORMANCE

Performance management frameworks are sets of processes and procedures that lead managers to focus on the performance of all aspects of their organisation, in a detailed manner. They have been developed in response to a historical tendency to overemphasise financial performance to the detriment of other aspects of operations. There are many frameworks available to VSO managers, some of which, such as those described below, have been developed by external agencies, whilst others are created by the organisation to suit its specific needs.

Quest

Quest is a performance management framework that aims to set industry standards for customer-focused management, by encouraging managers to consider their operations from the point of view of their stakeholders. There is a Quest scheme for facility management and for sport development. It is the sport development scheme that is most relevant to voluntary sport organisations.

The Quest scheme for sport development identifies 11 critical management issues that are grouped into the following three areas:

- Strategy, which includes research, policy and strategy, sport development plans, continuous improvement and results.
- People, which includes management style and people management: training and development.
- Delivery, which includes process planning and improvement, health and safety management, customer relations and marketing.

A key strength of this programme is that it requires managers to address all aspects of their operations including customer satisfaction.

The assessment process for Quest includes three main stages:

1   Managers are required to carry out a self-assessment phase when they compare the operations of their organisation against the assessment criteria for the award. This indicates areas of strength and areas for improvement. For many managers, this process itself is enough to improve the performance of the service.
2   The next stage is an objective external assessment, undertaken by trained assessors from the industry. The assessment reviews progress against industry standards and provides a percentage score. Quest scores are classified into the following categories:
    - Approved – above 60 per cent
    - Commended – 68 to 74 per cent
    - Highly Commended – 75 to 83 per cent
    - Excellent – 84 per cent and above.
3   Finally, as Quest Approval status lasts for two years it is supplemented by an additional maintenance visit. This ensures that quality of service delivery is maintained and/or continuously improved in line with the Quest standards. After every two years the process needs to be repeated.

leigh robinson

The main benefit of Quest is its potential for reviewing procedures and getting feedback on these (Robinson and Crowhurst, 2001). As a result, the self-assessment aspect of this performance framework is considered to be vitally important. In addition, Quest is felt to be a useful tool for benchmarking the industry as it is the only industry-specific quality framework.

Towards an Excellent Service

The Towards an Excellent Service (TAES) performance framework, which has recently been piloted in NGBs, seeks to measure the performance of the governing body in terms of 'how' it is functioning and provides the NGB with an assessment that defines its strengths and areas for improvement. The intention is that the areas for improvement can then be incorporated into the overall business planning process. TAES focuses on eight themes, which are:

- ■ *Leadership*: The key decision makers in the NGB demonstrate leadership, a sense of ambition, direction and support for delivering and improving their sport.
- ■ *Policy and strategy*: A clear sense of direction and priorities based on effective consultation translated into measurable objectives, targets and outcomes.
- ■ *Community engagement*: The active involvement of communities in the process of planning, delivering and improving sport through communication, consultation and engagement.
- ■ *Partnership working*: Working effectively with other organisations to deliver and improve the delivery of sport.
- ■ *Use of resources*: The efficient and effective use of resources to achieve the delivery of sport.
- ■ *People management*: The effective management and development of people (paid staff and volunteers) throughout the NGB to support the delivery of their sport.
- ■ *Standards of service*: The development and maintenance of high standards of service in consultation with athletes, club members and participants to improve delivery.
- ■ *Performance measurement and learning*: The monitoring, review and evaluation of performance to facilitate learning and continuous improvement.

Within each theme, criteria have been developed that define the key aspects of a quality service, with 'equality' and 'service access' being effectively integrated into every theme. The NGB then has to provide evidence of performance against each criterion. The end result is that the governing body can plot the organisation at one of four levels:

125

- *Poor*: A poor organisation is one where there is little, or no, evidence of the specific criteria, or no awareness or commitment to create or develop the criteria.
- *Fair*: A fair organisation is one where there is evidence that the processes of planning and developing the criteria has commenced and is progressing.
- *Good*: A good organisation is one where there is evidence that demonstrates the key criteria are in place.
- *Excellent*: An excellent organisation can evidence all the aspects of a good organisation but will also be able to demonstrate that the key criteria have been in place long enough for it to evidence the impact of what it has achieved in terms of real outcomes.

The validation process involves three stages:

1   Independent review and challenge of the NGB's understanding of the process, the proposed scoping and the recording of evidence. This is done before the assessment commences and takes up to one day depending on the size of the organisation.
2   Independent review of the self-assessment documentation including random checking of selected criteria scoring against identified evidence. This seeks to validate the judgements made about the NGB. Again depending on the size of organisation it is anticipated that up to two days would be required for this stage. Return visits are required if validation could not be confirmed.
3   Independent review of the improvement plan and critical friend role to ensure the plan adequately addresses the agreed weaknesses. It is anticipated that up to a day would be adequate for this stage, again depending on the size of the organisation.

The validation is carried out by two people, one of which should be a senior peer from another governing body.

The Balanced Scorecard

One other popular framework is the *Balanced Scorecard* developed by Kaplan and Norton (1996). Underpinning the Balanced Scorecard is the establishment of a number of performance measures associated with targets in order to assess whether performance meets expectations. The original scorecard has been through many revisions and now has four main components:

- A destination statement, which sets out what the organisation will look like at a defined point in the future assuming that the current strategy has been successful.
- The strategic plan segmented into activities and outcomes.

126

leigh robinson

- A set of definitions for each of the strategic objectives.
- A set of definitions for each of the measures selected to monitor each of the strategic objectives, including targets. (Targets can be thought of as a standard or level associated with the performance indicator. For example, performance in a league is the performance indicator and second position is the target to be achieved.)

The Balanced Scorecard encourages managers to focus on four areas of their organisation's operations.

- *The customer*: Managers need to ask what existing and new members value from the service. In addition, they need to identify potential members and find out why they are not using the service. This area encourages the identification of measures that answer the question: 'How do customers see us?' For example, an assessment of member satisfaction would allow a club to answer this question. This allows targets that matter to stakeholders to be developed and incorporated into the performance management system.
- *Internal*: This considers the operations of the organisation in order to identify what has to be achieved to meet objectives. The purpose of this is to improve internal processes and decision making and encourages the identification of measures that answer the question: 'What must we excel at?'
- *Innovation and learning*: This requires managers to identify areas of improvement and to learn from past performance and encourages the identification of measures that answer the question, 'Can we continue to improve and create value?' This enables the organisation to identify its competitive position and to identify strengths and weaknesses that need incorporating into the planning process.
- *Financial*: Managers are required to consider the financing of the organisation in the context of creating value for stakeholders. Although finance has traditionally had a set of well established performance measures and targets, the choice of which to use needs to be determined in consultation with key stakeholders.

The scorecard is balanced as managers are required to think in terms of all four areas of performance and to measure their performance in these areas. A key feature of this approach is that it considers both the internal and external aspects of the organisation, in particular customers. In addition, it should be related to the organisation's strategy as it considers operations in the light of organisational objectives. Finally, it focuses on both the operational and social objectives of the organisation, which is important to stakeholders of VSOs.

This approach to performance management is flexible in that the process of deciding what should be the focus of the scorecard should allow managers to clarify the strategy of the service. However, like all management techniques, problems can arise in the implementation of the Balanced Scorecard. First, there may be a problem with conflicting measures. Some measures such as increases in gold medals and cost reduction naturally conflict. The balance that will achieve the best results must be determined after consideration of the service's objectives. Second, performance measurement is only useful if it initiates appropriate management action. There is little point in developing a set of measures for the four aspects of the scorecard if managers are not going to react to the information that these generate or cannot control the outcome. Finally, managers need to have the skills to be able to interpret the information that the Balanced Scorecard generates.

There are many other performance management frameworks that can be adopted, many of which have been developed outside sport. In order to support these, there are two factors that are integral to successful performance management. First, it is important for the organisation to have a culture that supports performance management. An effective performance management framework is more than just a system of controlling the operations of an organisation; it must also encourage staff to consider performance management as a fundamental way of doing things. As outlined above, staff are the key to making sure that procedures and operations actually meet targets and, thus, the organisation's culture has to support this process.

Second, in order to be effective, performance management systems must involve effective performance measurement and target setting. This is perhaps the key to making performance management effective, because if measures of performance are not established, then managers are not in a position to assess how they are doing, or to be able to take corrective action if required. In addition, it is important to set levels of performance, or targets that are to be achieved, as this aids comparison with other organisations and with previous performance.

PERFORMANCE EVALUATION AND MEASUREMENT

Evaluation usually involves a comparison between what 'is' and what 'ought to be'. Evaluation looks at how well plans have been followed through and it measures whether the work done will have the impact it is intended to have. In order to evaluate performance it needs to be measured and all possible aspects of operations should be evaluated in order to inform management practice. As set out earlier, performance measurement is usually carried out through the use of performance indicators (PIs), which can be defined as 'a piece of empirical data representing performance that can be compared over time or with similar organisations' (Taylor et al, 2000: 4). For example, number of members, athletes that qualify for championships or percentage of cost recovery. In order to make PIs more useful for management, they are usually associated with a target or level that managers need to obtain.

Several factors need to be considered to make performance indicators valuable for evaluation. First, it is important to be clear about the purpose of performance indicators. Managers must know who will be using the information and for what purpose. Members, funding agencies and other managers will all require performance management information and this needs to be provided in a manner that is accessible and appropriate to their needs. For example, members will want to know how their membership fee is being spent, while managers will want to monitor efficiency and effectiveness. These differing purposes are likely to require different PIs and will certainly require different presentations of the data. Second, performance indicators are meaningless unless they are evaluated in comparison with objectives. For example, you may be successful in increasing member numbers but may have done this by offering free membership. In this case, you have been effective from a membership perspective, but ineffective financially. Actual evaluation of performance has to be done in the context of what you are trying to achieve.

Third, sets of performance indicators used should give a balanced picture of the organisation's performance. The PIs chosen should reflect the main aspects of the organisation, including outcomes and the perspectives of users. In voluntary sport organisations, financial indicators should under no circumstances be the only performance measures used. Chappelet and Bayle (2005) have proposed six dimensions for measuring the performance of a voluntary sport organisation, notably at the national level. These are set out in Table 7.1

From this it is clear that performance should be evaluated across a range of dimensions, including an internal dimension and contributions to society. Chappelet and Bayle (2005) have also set out a range of PIs that can be measured both qualitatively and quantitatively. This emphasis on qualitative measurement is important as most managers will focus on what produces 'numbers', rather than seeking the richer detail available from qualitative measures.

Fourth, however, is that no matter how the data is collected, when it is used to form PIs it must be collected from the same sources and in the same manner. This will ensure that the performance is being evaluated accurately and allows comparisons. For example, if you are reporting on the success of four events encouraging children to join your sport, you need to decide whether the numbers attending the event or the numbers joining clubs is the measure of success. Fifth, PIs must measure what they are considered to measure, otherwise they may lead to mistakes in decision making. For example, counting the number of members of a national governing body is not a true indication of the number of participants in the sport. Membership numbers do not include non-members who participate outside the club system and often include people who are no longer active.

Finally, and of greatest importance, is that PIs should only be used as a guide for management, as they do not provide an explanation for performance. PIs will indicate areas of strengths and weakness, but will not say why these are

Table 7.1 Performance dimensions of voluntary sport organisations

Dimensions	Aims	Measurement
Sport	Obtaining the best sport results, increasing the number of members	Results and membership Quantitative and qualitative
Internal/social	Improving the social climate and the involvement of internal stakeholders	Satisfaction of stakeholders Qualitative and quantitative
Societal	Contributing to society and increasing social capital	Legitimacy and impact Qualitative
Financial	Obtaining the resources necessary to achieve the objectives Managing financial independence from main funders	Financial resources or value in kind Quantitative
Promotional	Improving the awareness of the sport among all stakeholders and the public	Reputation and image Quantitative and qualitative
Organisational	Well organised, clearly defined policies and procedures	Internal processes and assurance mechanisms Qualitative

Source: Adapted from Chappelet and Bayle (2005)

strengths and weaknesses. For example, a PI will show that athletes qualified for the finals, but not explain why they didn't win a medal. The management of the organisation will need to interpret the indicator and explain performance.

BARRIERS TO PERFORMANCE MANAGEMENT AND MEASUREMENT

Although there are clearly benefits to the performance management process, there are also barriers to its effectiveness. First, managers must accept the need for performance management and use it as a key management tool. If a manager's attitude to the process is negative, it will not be used effectively within the management of the service. Second, there needs to be a performance management structure in place in the organisation, which incorporates the setting of objectives, the procedures for the collection and analysis of information and for comparison with targets. The lack of such a process will be a barrier.

Third, using these techniques requires certain skills and, without these, performance management will not be effective. Indeed, without a clear understanding of the process involved and what the components mean, there is a danger that

130

mistakes may occur in decision making, resulting in the organisation performing poorly. Significant misuse of data or utilisation of incorrect performance measures can cause organisations of all sizes to experience difficulty in implementing performance management.

KPMG (2001) established that one of the most common weaknesses in performance management is a lack of data integrity and the inability of the processes to provide meaningful information to support decision making. The study also concluded that some performance measurement processes, integral to performance management, are not aligned with strategic business indicators, depend on indicators of past performance as opposed to future orientated indicators and are based primarily on financial indicators.

More fundamentally, however, although this chapter has highlighted how performance management can benefit voluntary organisations, there is some debate about whether it is actually possible in not-for-profit sport organisations. Sanderson (1998) presented several concerns regarding the use of performance indicators in public services and those concerns are also applicable to voluntary sport organisations. First, he is unconvinced that performance indicators can deal with environmental complexity, which is a characteristic of the operating context within which sport organisations work. For example, not only does a badminton club deliver services directly to its members, it may also be working in partnership with other agencies, such as BADMINTON England – the sport's governing body – and schools to increase participation in the sport. To try to identify the contribution the club makes to the partnership and to measure how effective it is, has been challenged by Sanderson (1998) as being too complex.

Second, performance management is based on the assumption of *controllability* – that all aspects of the organisation are under the control of managers. Sanderson (1998) argues that this assumption is also flawed, as managers have no control over changes in political priorities for sport, changes in legislation that affects volunteers or even the performance of their athletes.

Third, and perhaps most importantly, Sanderson (1998) argues that performance management and measurement is based upon a fundamental assumption of *measurability*. The underlying premise of performance management is that all aspects of management can be measured. This assumption is clearly flawed, in that although it is possible to measure many aspects of a voluntary sport organisation, there are some factors that cannot be evaluated. Performance indicators have existed for some time in areas such as athlete performance, member numbers and finance. However, they are yet to be fully developed to measure the contribution of sport in combating social exclusion or in contributing to 'human capital'. Sanderson (1998) feels that this will lead managers to focus on those aspects of the organisation that can be easily measured. For example, measuring the number of children in a swimming class, but not how well they swim.

This is a valid point as the creation of numeric key performance indicators (KPIs) has been at the forefront of the performance management agenda affecting VSOs, and this creates an overemphasis on aspects of performance that can be 'counted'. For example, his concern is evidenced by considering the KPIs for NGBs that are outlined in Figure 7.3, which focus on easily measurable aspects of the activity of an NGB. This means that activities of VSOs, such as their contribution to education, are often ignored, or measured in an inappropriate way.

It is difficult to present a direct argument against these concerns; however, these can be addressed in the way that PIs are interpreted and presented to stakeholders for their review. As long as a balanced set of PIs are collected and are interpreted in a sensible manner, then performance management is an appropriate tool for the management of voluntary sport organisations.

SUMMARY

This chapter has considered the role of performance management in the management of voluntary sport organisations. There are a number of benefits to the systematic management of performance utilising a holistic performance management framework. However, there have also been concerns expressed about the viability of performance management due to the complexity of the operating environment and issues to do with measurability and control. The main solution to these concerns is in the interpretation of the performance indicators collected, and managers must use their indicators to explain performance, which highlights the need for a holistic programme of evaluation.

CASE STUDY: THE PERFORMANCE FRAMEWORK FOR UK NATIONAL GOVERNING BODIES

The following case study sets out the performance framework within which the national governing bodies of the UK must operate. This framework, developed as a result of perceived inefficiencies in the management of NGBs, focuses on key aspects of the organisation in an attempt to drive up the effectiveness of these organisations.

The advent of lottery funding in 1996 provided a huge boost for sport across the UK, both at elite and grass-roots level. It may, however, be perceived as a 'mixed blessing' by the managers and governors of voluntary sport organisations. Although the extra funds have provided opportunities to thousands of people to enjoy their sport at every level, as a consequence of the extra funding the government shifted its funding policy from an input-based policy to an outcome-based policy. This meant a change from receiving funding for a well prepared budget to being accountable for the outcomes achieved by that funding. As

132

a consequence, NGBs have had to deliver quantifiable outcomes to justify continued funding, emphasising the need for good planning and even better performance management.

This shift to outcomes led to greater prioritisation within and between sports and it became clear that the administrative infrastructure of sport had not been performing as effectively as it could. In order to address this, the government-commissioned *Investing in Change* report was released by Deloitte & Touche in 2003. This report acknowledged that governing bodies are key to the delivery of sport in the UK. However, it also stated that if NGBs were to continue to play a full role in the delivery of sport, many required change in order to meet the challenges that they would face in the future. The report set out how some NGBs lacked basic administrative and professional support essential for any organisation, while others were too reliant on government funding. It was felt that this, along with other external factors, had led to some governing bodies not having the capacity to effectively manage growth and to deliver the outcomes necessary for the well-being of their sport. The key message from *Investing in Change* (2003: 1) was that 'for too long, many governing bodies have survived despite their weaknesses, rather than succeeded because of their strengths'.

As a consequence, a performance framework setting out success factors has been implemented into UK NGBs. In this framework, NGBs are categorised on the basis of size, using a series of criteria including turnover, membership numbers and participation levels. Five different categories of NGB were identified from the very smallest with a turnover of less than £35,000 per annum, no paid staff and fewer than 50 members or clubs, through to the largest mass participation sports. This categorisation was perceived to be necessary in order to reflect the resources and capacity of the NGB. For example, it is unrealistic to expect a small NGB with few members and limited resources to achieve the same level as a large NGB with professional athletes and significant commercial income. This model also acknowledges that small NGBs can be just as efficient and effective as a very large NGB when judged against criteria that are appropriate for that individual NGB.

This framework sets out specifically, and in detail, what an NGB in each category should aim to achieve across a range of 12 criteria, which are:

■ *Effective corporate governance*: The system by which organisations are directed and controlled.
■ *Sport and business administration*: The system by which organisations are managed based on a management audit.
■ *Financial management*: Requiring effective financial procedures and competencies.
■ *Exploitation of commercial opportunities*: This requires NGBs to identify ways to generate more income from 'commercial opportunities'.

- *Performance management*: NGBs need to develop a range of performance measures that are linked to more than just elite performance (see below).
- *Talent identification/development and elite performance*: Each sport should aim to develop a cohesive system to guide the long-term development and support of its talented athletes/players.
- *Coach education and development system*: It is essential that NGBs have an effective coaching structure in place.
- *Services to members*: It is vital that the services provided should be sufficiently compelling to ensure those who actively participate in the sport want to take up NGB membership.
- *Volunteer management*: It is essential that NGBs take an active role in securing, motivating and retaining volunteers.
- *Event management*: NGBs must organise competition and seek to host major events.
- *Partnerships with local authorities, education and the commercial sector*: It is essential that NGBs have a strong relationship with the other main delivery agents of the sport.
- *Structure of sport*: There needs to be adequate coordination between home country and UK/GB NGBs.

The content of the performance management success criteria is set out in Figure 7.3.

From this it is clear that NGBs have a structured performance environment that is intended to improve the management of their organisations. The framework certainly encourages NGBs to consider all aspects of the organisation and is valuable in that it takes into account factors that impact on performance such as size and income. However, this does not seem to be a feature of the KPIs set out in Figure 7.3 as all NGBs have the same KPIs. In addition, these KPIs are all numeric, which means that although they are relatively easy to collect if data collections procedures are in place, they do not provide any detail to explain performance. Thus, NGBs will need to supplement these KPIs with more qualitative indictors.

ADDITIONAL ACTIVITIES

- Develop a balanced set of objectives and PIs for a voluntary sport organisation of your choice.
- Develop PIs that measure the contribution that a tennis club makes to its local community. Make a note of the issues involved.
- Investigate the requirements of Investors in People.
- Read the full *Investing in Change* report.

leigh robinson

Performance Management

It is essential that NGBs develop a range of performance measures which are linked to more than just elite performance. The performance measures need to reflect the range of activities carried out by the NGB and need to demonstrate the added value that NGBs bring to sport.

Measurement Systems

Category 1	Category 2	Category 3	Category 4	Category 5
Conduct market research type satisfaction surveys with partners, clubs and members	Conduct market research type satisfaction surveys with partners, clubs and members	Obtain some feedback from partners, clubs and members to determine satisfaction with services	Obtain some feedback from clubs and members to determine satisfaction with services	Obtain some feedback from clubs and members to determine satisfaction with services
Obtain QUEST accreditation status	Obtain QUEST accreditation status	Obtain QUEST accreditation status	Obtain QUEST accreditation status	Undertake system of 'peer review' with other sports and with Sports Councils
Obtain Investors in People status	Obtain Investors in People status	Obtain Investors in People status	Undertake system of 'peer review' with other sports and with Sports Councils	Annual analysis of elite performance, attainment of medal targets and benchmarking of performance with other nations
Obtain EQFM status (or similar blue chip quality standard)	Undertake system of 'peer review' with other sports and with Sports Councils	Undertake system of 'peer review' with other sports and with Sports Councils	Annual analysis of elite performance, attainment of medal targets and benchmarking of performance with other nations	
Undertake system of 'peer review' with other sports and with Sports Councils	Annual continuous improvement plan focused on organisational effectiveness	Annual continuous improvement plan focused on organisational effectiveness		
Annual continuous improvement plan focused on organisational effectiveness	Collection of data relating to participation levels, coaching and volunteer workforce, all broken down by demographic group	Collection of data relating to participation levels, coaching and volunteer workforce, all broken down by demographic group		
Collection of data relating to participation levels, coaching and volunteer workforce, all broken down by demographic group	Annual analysis of elite performance, attainment of medal targets and benchmarking of performance with other nations	Annual analysis of elite performance, attainment of medal targets and benchmarking of performance with other nations		
Annual analysis of elite performance, attainment of medal targets and benchmarking of performance with other nations				

Figure 7.3 Success criteria for performance management

Figure 7.3 continued …

Key Performance Indicators (KPIs)

Key performance indicators (KPIs) are a valuable management tool to measure your NGBs performance in achieving the success criteria in this model framework. The KPIs detailed are indicative and not exhaustive. NGBs should consider what KPIs are relevant for their NGB and then set out up to 30 KPIs which can be used by the NGB to monitor its performance. Each KPI should be examined to determine the following:

- Is the KPI valuable to the NGB?
- Is the KPI already used and are there any learning points from its current use?
- Is the information required for its calculation readily available, or at least are there means to obtain the information, including from third parties where necessary?

The overall objective is to obtain a suitably broad range of KPIs which can be used to help drive the NGB forward, enable benchmarking and appraise current and past performance.

Indicative KPIs

Indicator	Calculation	Use/Implementation	Circulation Board	Circulation Management	Frequency
Ratio of Exchequer funding to total turnover	Total amount of Exchequer funding expressed as a percentage of total turnover	Important in order to drive down dependence on Exchequer funding If the ratio is not declining or is rising this may make the NGB vulnerable should Sports Council/ Government funding policy change Will allow the NGB to set targets for revenue generated from other sources such as from members or from commercial opportunities			Annually
Revenue per member	The total revenue generated from activities directly associated with members divided by the number of members	This will provide a valuable benchmark to assess the trend of revenue per member and allow comparison with other sports			Quarterly
Reserves to costs ratio	Total level of reserves expressed as a percentage of the total annual outgoings of the NGB before tax	In this way it will indicate how much security there is available to the NGB should the various sources of income be reduced If the ratio is declining it may indicate that reserves are being depleted or that costs are not being adequately controlled			Quarterly

Indicator	Description	Rationale	Frequency
Number of members	Total number of registered members currently listed on NGB database who have paid some form of subscription	Important in order to assess the success of the strategy to increase membership If the number is static or declining this may indicate that the NGB has failed to make the membership offer sufficiently compelling It may create financial problems in the future and indicate that the sport is not sufficiently attractive to new entrants	Quarterly
Number of affiliated clubs	Total number of registered affiliated clubs currently listed on NGB database who have paid an affiliation fee	Important in order to assess the success of the strategy to increase the number of affiliated clubs If the number is declining this may indicate that the NGB has failed to add sufficient value to the benefits offered to clubs in return for affiliating. Alternatively it may indicate that the sport is not sufficiently attractive to generate the demand for new clubs	Annually
Volunteer recruitment	Total number of volunteers who contribute more than 12 hours per year	Essential to understand whether the strategy on volunteer recruitment is successful If the number is static or declining it will seriously impact on the NGB's ability to host events and provide services to participants	Annually
Volunteer training	Total number of volunteers who received more than 3 hours training per year	Essential to ensure that volunteers are being developed so that they can fulfil their role adequately and that the CPD programme is working	Annually
Number of qualified coaches	Absolute figure of the number of qualified coaches who have registered with or are accredited by the NGB	Indication of success or otherwise of the strategy to encourage teachers and parents to get involved as coaches If the number is static or declining this may indicate that the NGB will have problems meeting its future performance targets	Quarterly
Performance in UK/World Rankings	Total number of elite athletes in the top 100 UK/World Rankings (if applicable)	Indicate between major competitive events (Olympics/Commonwealth Games) the performance potential of the elite athlete squad	Monthly
Juniors' Development	Number of junior players completing accredited coaching programme	Important to ensure that adequate numbers of junior players are being recruited and developed to help with talent identification programme	Quarterly
Schools' Affiliation	Number of Schools affiliated to an accredited training scheme	Important to identify how effectively the Education partnerships programme is working to ensure that your sport is adequately represented in schools	Quarterly

Source: Deloitte & Touche, 2003: 18–21

FURTHER READING

Chappelet, J. and Bayle, E. (2005) *Strategic and Performance Management*. Champaign: Human Kinetics.

Slack, T. and Parent, M. (2006) *Understanding Sport Organizations*, 2nd edition. Champaign: Human Kinetics.

Wiscombe, C. (2009) 'Planning, monitoring, controlling and evaluating sports organisations', in Bill, K. (ed) *Sport Management*. Exeter: Learning Matters.

leigh robinson

CHAPTER 8

THE MANAGEMENT OF CHANGE

Leigh Robinson

A changing operating environment is one of the constant factors that affects the management of voluntary sport organisations. Changes will occur inside and outside the organisation that will require 'things to be different' and managers will need to seek out management practices, procedures and services that need to change in order for the organisation to continue to operate effectively. In doing so, they are managing change. To be effective as a manager, it is necessary to recognise when change is desirable or inevitable and respond accordingly. For example, in recent times, NGBs are likely to have responded to at least ten new directives from stakeholder organisations such as UK Sport or their international federation, continually updated procedures in response to WADA, and handled the fallout from an athlete scandal. Clubs will have dealt with the increasing demands of legislation, seen their sport move away from amateurism and have attempted to obtain sponsorship.

Some of these changes will have been introduced willingly, whilst others will have been forced on the organisation, and in many instances there was likely to have been no choice about whether to change the way the organisation operated. Managers *have* to deal with athlete scandals and changes of major funding provider. The main point is that the organisation cannot continue to operate as it always has without becoming much less effective in its work. If it can, there is no need to change.

Changes usually have to be introduced alongside the day-to-day running of the organisation. Managers usually have to manage the introduction of change in addition to carrying out their usual work. This chapter aims to discuss the management of effective change within sport organisations. It will begin by considering how change should be understood and then outline how to prepare for the possibility of change and the reasons why people resist change in organisations. It will also discuss the factors that ensure the successful introduction of change. Finally, the chapter ends with an illustration of key points by discussing the implementation of change within the Amateur Swimming Association.

UNDERSTANDING CHANGE

It is necessary to understand how the need for change emerges as this allows managers to take account of the factors required to successfully introduce change. In addition, the introduction of change is sometimes unsuccessful or does not achieve the desired consequences and if managers are aware of how change has occurred they will be able to identify why.

Pioneering work carried out by Pettigrew (1987) suggested that change in organisations occurs as a consequence of the interactions between people, the organisation's history, the operating environment and the organisation's politics. Known as the *contextualist* approach to change, knowledge of these factors is important as change within sport organisations rarely arises as a result of a single factor in the external environment. Rather it emerges as a result of the interactions between the operating context and the people within the organisation. Thus, analysis of organisational change must take account of the organisational environment (Chapter 2), the type of change under consideration and the process of agreeing and developing the change.

In an attempt to explain the interactions, Pettigrew (1987) developed the Model of Strategic Change, which is based on the premise that strategic change cannot be regarded solely as a rational process undertaken by analysing the environments, suggesting alternatives and planning. Rather it is a complex, iterative process that is

> shaped by the interests and commitments of individuals and groups, the forces of bureaucratic momentum, gross changes in the environment, and the manipulation of the structural context around decisions.
>
> (Pettigrew, 1987: 658)

The Model of Strategic Change sets out three dimensions to change: context, content and process. The *context* of change refers to those environmental factors that have influenced, restrained or provided the opportunity for change within the organisation. Referred to as the 'why' of change, consideration of the context within which the organisation is operating is important as it is the knowledge of these contextual factors and their interactions that provides the basis for understanding why change occurs. Although each environmental factor is important in its own right they do not act in isolation, but react and interact with each other and on occasion cancel each other out. Table 2.1 has previously highlighted issues affecting a NGB that may lead to change in these organisations.

The content of change refers to the particular change being considered. For example, this may be the introduction of performance management and key performance indicators. Being clear about 'what is to be different' clarifies how and why the change has come about. The third part of the Model for Strategic Change is the process by which change comes about, and change within organisations

leigh robinson

often originates with people who have become aware of a mismatch between the demands of a changing operating context and the current performance of the organisation.

Thus, the model developed by Pettigrew (1987) provides the opportunity to consider not only key environmental factors, but allows these to be placed in the context of the historical, political and individual influences on the organisation. This allows managers to understand why a particular change might be appropriate, and also highlights the relationships that have to be considered when change is being planned.

PREPARING FOR THE INTRODUCTION OF CHANGE

Change is continual, so those who work with voluntary sport organisations need to be able to work in a constantly changing environment. However, in order to help volunteers and staff to be effective in such an environment, a state of readiness for change is necessary within the organisation. There are two factors that help accomplish this. First, managers need to be aware of what is occurring inside and outside the organisation and then communicate this information to volunteers and paid staff. This will allow potential changes to be identified before they become unavoidable and will allow appropriate time for planning what change should be implemented and when. Second, an organisational culture that is willing to accept change needs to be encouraged as this will reduce resistance to change.

Environmental auditing

In order to identify potential changes, managers have to be aware of what is occurring in both the external and internal operating environments of the organisation. This can be done by the process of environmental auditing, or scanning of the operating environments that was set out in Chapter 2. This will generate information about the environments and identify trends that may suggest a need for change.

Once the relevant information has been collected, managers can identify factors that may require changes in operations or services. These areas then should be prioritised in order to meet service objectives. Finally, the effect of these changes on the operation of the organisation needs to be evaluated. Some changes may require an immediate response, whilst other changes may be required in the future and can be planned and implemented over time. For example, suppose that in auditing the environment, it became clear that government policy was about to change from funding elite sport to promoting grass-roots participation. If the organisation worked with elite athletes, it would be necessary to identify other sources of revenue or change operations so that the organisation worked with grass-roots participants as well as elite athletes.

The purpose of environmental auditing is to help managers to be proactive in delivering services. By being aware of the threats and opportunities in the external environment and the strengths and weaknesses of the internal environment, they will be in a better position to anticipate and plan changes required of the organisation. This means that managers need to identify reliable sources of information about both environments. Information about the internal environment can be gathered by talking to colleagues and staff and by being aware of what is occurring in the organisation. Information on the external environment is harder to obtain, but it is often provided by organisations such as UK Sport, Sport England and by networking with others who work in the industry.

Developing a culture that supports change

As stated earlier, the working environment changes constantly and therefore an organisational culture that supports change needs to be developed. This can be done in a number of ways. Those involved with the organisation must feel that they are fully involved in or fully informed of the decision-making process so that the introduction of change does not come as a surprise. Managers must also be clear about what can and cannot be changed without great resistance. For example, the colour and style of team uniforms may have historical or local significance and attempts to change these will meet with strong resistance. Conversely, if managers know what can be changed, these aspects can be used to begin to introduce change to other aspects of the service. For example, if objective selection criteria for national teams are valued by those within the organisation, this desire for objectivity can be used to introduce other objective-led systems of performance measurement.

The creation of a culture that supports change requires good leadership as it is leaders that create culture. Leaders are those individuals who can influence other people on matters that are considered to be important (Gilgeous, 1997). In addition, leaders are those people who are expected to be, and are seen to be, influential on important matters. As a result, the successful introduction of change relies on the support of those who are considered to be leaders within an organisation. Without their support, change, particularly large-scale change, will be difficult to introduce. It is important to note that leaders are not necessarily managers. Some people because of personality or charisma will be seen by others as influential and therefore managers need to be aware of who these individuals are. Often change fails to be introduced into sport organisations because the people involved in promoting the change are not seen as influential.

leigh robinson

Leaders have five roles to play in the introduction of change. First, they create a culture that supports change. Second, they need to generate a commitment to the change. This can be done by outlining why things need to be different and how the change will benefit the organisation. Third, they need to develop a shared vision of what the change will entail and how it will work in the future. It is much easier to generate support for change if everyone is clear about what and how things will be different. Fourth, leaders have a key role in implementing the change programme as they should lead the activities that bring about change, be responsible for monitoring the process and help to overcome any resistance to the change. Finally, they have a responsibility to work in the manner required by the change. Leaders should be the first in the organisation to use new procedures or work to new objectives. This will allow the changes to be incorporated into the organisation's culture and to become the accepted way of working.

RESISTANCE TO CHANGE

Most change will lead to resistance amongst some or all of those who work with the organisation. The need to change suggests that the current way of working is no longer good enough, and often those carrying out the work will take this personally. It is also possible to argue that resistance to change is a logical reaction because people and organisations function best in circumstances of stability. Nonetheless, resistance to change needs to be identified and overcome if change is to be fully integrated into the organisation.

People resist change because of the following:

- Differences: There are likely to be concerns about what will be different in the working environment. Volunteers and paid staff may be unclear about or dislike what the change means for their position, their workload or their working practices.
- Competence: Unsurprisingly, people may have concerns about being able to carry out the new tasks required of them or being able to use new equipment or technology. Therefore they will resist the introduction of change that makes them feel incompetent. They may also be concerned about looking foolish or stupid.
- Ripple effect: Resistance to change may not come solely from those directly affected by the change. The introduction of change in an organisation usually has a ripple effect in that if change is introduced into one department, changes are usually required in other areas. For example, if the finance department implements a new system for claiming back expenses, the change will not only affect those employed by the organisation, but also volunteers.
- Workload: Most changes require more work. New procedures or operations will have to be learned, and this inevitably requires more work. Volunteers

and paid staff often have to attend training courses if new technology or new objectives are introduced. At the same time, people are expected to complete their usual workload. This increase in workload will lead to resistance to the change.

■ Resentment: The introduction of change may provide the opportunity to express resentment about what has happened to volunteers or paid staff in the past. For example, if a certain member thinks that they have missed out on an elected position, they may take the opportunity to express their resentment by undermining the need for change amongst other members.

■ Real threats: In some instances change represents a real threat to those who work with the organisation. For example, a change in regional structure may mean that some volunteers will lose their positions on a committee or have their influence significantly reduced. In this instance, resistance to change is understandable and is likely to be significant.

In addition to individual reasons for resisting change, staff as a whole may exhibit a general desire not to change. This is because of:

■ *Distorted perceptions of the risk*: Staff and volunteers within the organisation either do not perceive that there is a threat in the external environment, or they perceive the threat, but do not think that it is relevant to them and their service.

■ *A lack of motivation*: In this case the threat is understood, but there isn't the motivation to change in order to respond to the threat.

■ *Previous failures*: A lack of motivation to change often comes about because change that has been implemented in the past has failed or has been unsuccessful. A failed response to change makes organisational resistance more likely.

■ *Political deadlocks*: The introduction of change must be acceptable to the different groups within the organisation and occasionally change will be resisted because these groups cannot agree on what is needed. This leads to a deadlock that prevents change from being effectively introduced.

Resistance to change is inevitable and therefore a strategy for dealing with it is needed. Kotter and Schlesinger (1979) have suggested a number of strategies for dealing with resistance, which depend on the reason and the amount of resistance. In many cases, more than one strategy will be needed, particularly if large-scale change is being introduced. However, it is vital to communicate the reasons for change in the organisation. This allows those affected to become convinced of the need for change before resistance is established. Information about why change is necessary, the process to be followed and the consequences of both changing and not changing allows volunteers and paid staff to see the logic of what is being proposed. This is a useful strategy for overcoming concerns about competence and differences in the working environment.

144

The most effective strategy in overcoming all types of resistance, however, is to encourage those affected to participate in designing the required change. Involving volunteers in designing and introducing a new regional structure will build commitment to restructuring because it is difficult for people to resist changes that they have helped develop (see the case study below). Involvement can occur at any stage, but the more people are involved at the initial stages, the more committed they will be. This involvement must, however, be meaningful; otherwise resistance will become even greater when those affected become aware that they have been given a token role in determining their future.

Other strategies include:

- *Support*: This requires managers to work with their team members to overcome any concerns about what will be different and their competence. This is usually done on a one-to-one basis as the reasons for resisting change will be specific to individuals. This strategy is resource intensive as it requires managerial time and specific skills in order to be successful. In addition, the change may still be resisted.
- *Negotiation*: This involves the use of incentives to overcome resistance and is often used to overcome political deadlocks or when individuals are resisting change due to past resentments or because of a real threat. It is an appropriate strategy when it is clear that some people are going to be disadvantaged by the change. For example, when making people redundant, it may be necessary to agree to a redundancy package that is better than what is legally required. This will appease unions and may encourage people to volunteer to be made redundant. This strategy is usually expensive and often is a short-term way of dealing with resistance as it does not deal with the underlying cause of the problem.
- *Manipulation*: This is a covert attempt to influence those who are resisting change. Manipulation can occur by distorting the information that is given to those involved in the change, or by the selective use of information and restructuring of events. This way of overcoming resistance to change is bad for trust and often leads to others resisting change.
- *Coercion*: This may be implicit or explicit and forces staff to change through threats of dismissal or loss of job status. It should only be used when it is imperative that the change is introduced and all other strategies for overcoming resistance have failed. Forcing individuals to change causes problems as it builds up resentment, decreases the chances of the change being fully integrated into the organisation and breaks down the relationships between those being forced to change and those who are forcing the change.

Not all resistance is bad. Opposition to change may bring forward issues that had not been considered and that would have eventually had a negative impact on the proposed change. For example, changing the cut-off date for entries into a competition may result in no event being held if the entry period becomes too short. In most cases, resistance should be viewed as a means of identifying problems, which then need to be resolved. If resistance can be dealt with effectively, commitment to change is likely to be stronger than if resistance did not occur.

IMPLEMENTING CHANGE SUCCESSFULLY

A number of features increase the likelihood of change being implemented successfully. Although many of these seem obvious, once a potential solution has been identified it is easy to become overly concerned with what is to change, rather than how to go about making the change. The following features do not guarantee the successful implementation of change, but they do make it more likely.

Change as a good idea

Change must be perceived as being a good idea otherwise it is unlikely that it will be accepted. Not all potential changes will be appropriate, even if they appear to be a suitable response to changes in the operating context. For example, although the licensing of volunteers may be a sensible way to address increases in litigation, it may be unacceptable to the volunteers, leading many to stop volunteering. Therefore managers must involve others, in this case the volunteers, in deciding what changes should be introduced, and must seek feedback on any proposed change. This will allow issues to be raised that had not been considered.

Knowledge of factors that will promote and prevent change

Managers must identify what will work for and against the proposed change, such as people, resources, time, external factors and culture. This will allow factors that can be used to promote the change to be identified, such as the support of the president, or factors that will prevent the change, such as lack of funding. It is important to generate a list of these factors through discussion with people who have a vested interest in the change. If a manager carries out this process on their own, they are likely to miss concerns that may not be of importance to them but are of key importance to others.

Lewin (1951) developed a technique known as Force Field Analysis, which allows the driving forces for change to be shown in relation to those resisting change. The theory underpinning Force Field Analysis is that in any change situation there are forces for and against change. If these forces balance, then the organisation

146

will not change. Therefore in order for change to be introduced, the forces for change have to be strengthened and/or the forces against change, weakened. This will allow change to be introduced. The technique is relatively straightforward, consisting of four steps:

- *Step One*: The problem needs to be defined in terms of the present situation. This means stating clearly what the problem is, its strengths and weaknesses and the outcome to be achieved. For example, the competitive calendar needs to change to take account of changes in international competitions.
- *Step two*: The forces that will work for and against the proposed change need to be clearly identified. These can be based on people, resources, time, external factors and culture. As set out above, it is important that these forces are generated through discussion with a number of people who will be affected by the change.
- *Step three*: The forces then need to be rated in terms of their strength, for example high, medium or low. Theses should then be drawn as a Force Field Diagram, using arrows of different lengths or widths to indicate the different strengths of the forces, as outlined in Figure 8.1. This allows their importance in the process to be decided and provides priorities for action.

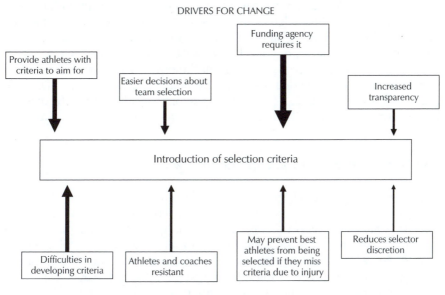

Figure 8.1 Force Field Diagram for introducing objective team selection criteria

- *Step four*: The most important forces need to be identified, which are usually those rated of high importance. For driving forces, a list of actions that will strengthen the force needs to be identified, followed by actions that will weaken the restraining forces. Those actions that will most help the introduction of change need to be part of the change strategy, alongside the resources to make them happen.

Force Field Analysis is a powerful technique that can be used to convince staff and volunteers of the need for change. It can provide a justification for actions that are part of introducing change and that allows resources to be prioritised.

Effective change team

Having a team of people responsible for implementing a change can be important. If a large change is being implemented, such as organisational restructuring, or a series of smaller changes that need coordination, such as the introduction of new technology, a team of people who are responsible for promoting the change will be needed.

An effective change team has a variety of members. It is necessary that the organisation's leaders either are part of the change team or support the team. The board or committee, aided by the financial director or the treasurer, must be part of the team since they control resources. Without the commitment of those who control money, facility or staff, changes will be hard to bring about. It may be necessary to include people who represent the organisation's main stakeholder groups, such as funding bodies, sponsors and members. The team should include a spokesperson from the parts of the organisation that will primarily be affected by the proposed change. This may include volunteers, paid staff or athletes.

Introducing change at the appropriate level

There are three levels at which change can be introduced. It can be introduced at the individual level, where a volunteer or member of staff may require new training. Change can also be introduced at the group level and may affect a particular team, region or department. For example, a change in drug-testing procedures will only affect those who are involved with drug testing. Finally, change can be introduced at the organisational level, which may occur with a change in organisational priorities, the introduction of new technologies or the introduction of operating procedures that affect the organisation as a whole.

It is necessary to identify exactly what and who needs to change so that the proposed change will bring about the desired outcome. For example, if certain staff members are performing poorly, they need to change their behaviour rather than asking colleagues to help with their work. If a particular part of a team is performing poorly, it is important to introduce changes into that part of the team, such as a change of coaching staff, rather than changing the team as a whole.

Communicate the need for change

As outlined earlier, organisations and people have a natural resistance to change as it challenges the existing way of working and often means additional work. It is therefore essential that the need to change is communicated clearly and convincingly in order to break down resistance. This should be done in a consistent manner, ensuring that there are no conflicting messages. It is also important that all staff who are perceived to be promoting the change are communicating the same message.

One method of convincing people of the need to change is to encourage dissatisfaction with the current ways of working. Highlighting weaknesses with existing practice is likely to encourage people to be more open to the idea of change. It is important, however, that if this tactic is used that there is a clear vision of how the proposed change can overcome the weaknesses of the current system. This is the role of the change team and/or leaders in the organisation.

Sufficient resources

The introduction of change requires money, training and time. Although money is important, allowing adequate time to develop and implement the change is even more so. A major factor that leads to the failure of change is competition from alternative activities. As suggested in the beginning of this chapter, managers usually have to continue with their day-to-day duties in addition to the activities that are required for the proposed change. In most situations, they will naturally continue to give their daily tasks priority because they know how to do these and the work has to be done so that the organisation can continue to function. This often leads to a low prioritisation of the activities associated with change.

In order to overcome this, managers should delegate some of their everyday work or ensure that other people are also involved in developing and implementing the change. They then need to make sure that these people have adequate time to devote to both their own work and the extra activities they have been asked to do. Deadlines may need to be extended or work reduced during the change process.

Implementation strategy

The final feature that leads to the successful introduction of change is a well-developed implementation strategy. This is particularly important when introducing large-scale change. All of the activities required to bring about the change need to be identified and put into an appropriate order. Tasks must be allocated to individuals and the whole process needs to be communicated to everyone who will be affected by the change. The implementation strategy should also include a period of evaluation in order to ensure that the change has been implemented successfully and is achieving its intended outcome.

Kotter and Schlesinger (1979) have outlined and discussed a number of approaches to introducing change into organisations. These are:

■ *A directive approach*: This is when change is imposed on the organisation by management. It has little or no staff involvement and requires power and authority to be successful. This type of approach should only be used when a very small change is required or when all other approaches would fail. In addition, as it is a fast method of introducing change, a directive approach is appropriate when the survival of the organisation is under threat. Directive strategies may also be used when legislation makes change mandatory.

■ *A negotiating approach*: This should be used when there are a number of groups that have to be involved in the change process. In this case, management initiate the change process and then enter into negotiations with key groups. This approach is useful when compromise is required, or if one group is going to be disadvantaged by the proposed change. Negotiating approaches tend to develop compliance with the change, rather than commitment to it. Although this may allow the change to be introduced, it does not guarantee that the change will be fully accepted into the organisation and may lead to further negotiations in the future. A negotiating approach would be appropriate when trying to change team selection criteria, where managers may need to negotiate with different groups in order for the change to be made.

■ *A normative approach*: This type of approach is required for large change or when staff and volunteers within the organisation must be committed to the change. This approach gets people committed to the change and makes it more likely the change will be fully implemented into the organisation. It requires involvement and participation, a good programme of communication and adequate resources. It is time-consuming, but will bring about effective change and help the change to become part of the organisation's culture. This type of approach is appropriate when trying to bring about cultural change. For example: developing an athlete focus amongst officials or when organisational objectives have changed.

150

- *An analytical approach*: This approach is useful when there is a clear problem and experts or consultants can develop a technically optimal solution. Although there may be some consultation with staff and volunteers, this is usually limited. This type of approach is useful when the manager lacks the expertise to develop a solution to a problem, or the organisation lacks the skills to be able to provide an answer. It is not appropriate for change that requires complete commitment, as the solutions proposed are unlikely to take account of the organisation's culture – the solution will be the most rational answer to the problem. An analytical approach is appropriate for the development and implementation of management information systems or specialised equipment.
- *An action-centred approach*: This is useful when there is a general idea of the problem, but no clear solution. It offers the opportunity to develop solutions and to try these out to see which is the most appropriate. This type of approach builds commitment to the change and may allow staff and volunteers to develop additional skills. It is time-consuming as the most appropriate change may not be the first tried. In addition, it may be costly as inappropriate change will lead to additional costs. An action-centred approach is most appropriate when the change required is small scale and does not directly impact on members. An example of this may be a new system for booking annual leave or an internal audit procedure.

The choice of approach will depend on several factors. First, the pace of the change will affect the choice of approach. The faster the change is required, the more directive the approach will need to be. If change is long term and can be introduced at a slower pace, then a normative approach may be more appropriate. Negotiating and action-centred approaches take time and therefore may not be appropriate if the need for change is immediate.

Second, the amount of resistance that is anticipated is important. If little resistance is anticipated, a directive or action-centred approach may be used. However, a directive approach may also be used when resistance is great, but change has to be introduced. Normative approaches are more effective at overcoming greater resistance and are useful when resistance arises because of a number of reasons.

Third, the power of the change leader will determine which approach is appropriate. If the person who is proposing the change is perceived to have a great amount of power and authority, then directive approaches are possible. Analytical approaches can be used when the initiator is perceived to be an expert or when consultants will be used. Finally, the stakes involved are important. When the consequences of not changing are great, a directive or analytical approach becomes more appropriate. Conversely, when the consequences are not great, an action-centred approach may be appropriate as this allows staff and volunteers to be fully involved in the change.

Most change situations will require a number of these approaches. For example, there may be instances where an immediate response to a breach of health and safety is required and a manager will tell staff and volunteers what has to be done. The development and introduction of the new operating procedures to prevent this breach from occurring again can be carried out via a normative, analytical or action-centred approach. What is important is to have a planned approach to the introduction of change. For example, if change is to be implemented via a normative approach, the required levels of involvement, communication and education must be part of an implementation strategy. If an analytical approach is to be used, appropriate consultants or experts must be employed, information must be provided and then their recommendations need to be acted upon.

SUMMARY

The keys to the successful management of change are preparation and knowledge of the people who will be affected. If managers are consistent and thorough when environmental auditing, they can be proactive in anticipating how and when practices will have to change. Managers also need to know their volunteers and paid staff well so resistance and how to deal with it can be anticipated. Most importantly, knowledge of the people involved in the change will highlight who has to be involved in the process, what can be changed in the organisation and the most successful way to go about it.

CASE STUDY: CHANGE IN THE AMATEUR SWIMMING ASSOCIATION

The Amateur Swimming Association is the English NGB for swimming, diving, water polo, open water, and synchronised swimming. It organises competition throughout England, establishes the laws of the sport and operates comprehensive certification and education programmes for teachers, coaches and officials as well as its renowned Learn to Swim Awards scheme. This case study shows how it is possible to implement large-scale change in the voluntary sport industry. Although managers may never be involved in change of this scale, this case study shows how the principles of effective change can be followed at an organisational level. The case study provides a brief description of the situation and then describes the process of change. It ends with an analysis of the process in terms of the principles outlined in this section.

At the Amateur Swimming Association (ASA) Annual Council in 2002, a paper was presented that dealt with the government's commitment to the regionalisation of government in England. This paper set out an intention to decentralise Sport England. The most significant impact of this to swimming was that most funding would subsequently be devolved to, and allocated by, the Sport England regions. The ASA Council recognised that the five existing ASA districts were not aligned to Sport England regions and in order to maximise direct and indirect benefits of funding, it was felt necessary to review the boundaries of the then five large districts.

Although the need to consider the structure of the ASA was felt to be primarily driven by external forces, there was an internal driver for restructuring in that one of the aims of regionalisation was to rationalise the size of the districts. It was felt that change was not only necessary to reflect the Sport England regions, but also that the size of the districts needed to be reduced to a more manageable level if a professional staffing structure was to be put in place and be able to make a difference. There was to be a fundamental change in the way the sport operated that was not perceived to be possible in the large districts.

At the Annual Council held in February 2002, five members of the ASA were nominated to form a Boundary Commission (BC) and were charged with boundary review. The five individuals who made up the commission had all worked for central or local government in one form or other. Their remit was to examine the structure of the ASA and they were given free rein in deciding the appropriate structure, although each of the new regions had to reflect one or more of the Sport England regions. In April 2002, the BC met to agree procedures and following this an invitation to comment was sent to all stakeholders. The BC received a number of submissions from the initial consultation and in June of the same year the commission agreed preliminary recommendations, which were then sent to all clubs and respondents.

The process followed to arrive at the preliminary recommendations was based on solid research. The BC had an open mind on the number of regions that might be appropriate and based their discussions on the size of the existing districts and the possible size of the new regions considering their general population, as well as size of the regions in terms of the number of swimming clubs and number of members.

In October 2002, the BC met to consider the submissions that had been received in response to the preliminary report and to prepare a final report, which was distributed to all stakeholders. The BC then presented their findings to the Annual Conference of 2003, which accepted the proposals. Communication underpinned the process and the BC produced a number of reports and booklets. The purpose of these was to ensure communication and involvement in determining the new regions. The review process led to a proposal of eight new regions. It was proposed that each of the new regions would be the same as a Sport England region with the exception of the new North East Region, which would reflect two.

The members of the BC were then charged with managing the process of introducing regionalisation and were renamed the Regionalisation Project Group

(RPG). Their remit was to oversee the process. The RPB recommended a shadowing process that allowed the new regions to put in place their management structures, while the old districts continued to operate. The process was considered to be vital because during that shadowing process the regions were able to set up their structures, to find out what volunteers they had and then find volunteers for the gaps. Regionalisation became operational on 1 October 2005.

In terms of implementing change, the process outlined above reflects many of the features required for successful change.

- *Change as a good idea*: The proposal to restructure the ASA was a good idea for several reasons. It responded to changes in the external environment and aligned the old districts with the new Sport England regions. This made it easier for the regions to identify and attract funding for their operations. In addition, it met an internal concern regarding the size of some of the districts. Although there were concerns about the size of the new regions, the new structure has resulted in regional bodies of a more manageable size. Finally, regionalisation has resulted in an increase in paid staff and an emerging culture of professionalism.
- *Knowledge of the factors that will promote and prevent change*: A desire for increased funding and more equitably sized regions were factors promoting the change. The establishment of the BC and RPB were major drivers for change, as was the shadowing process. Factors with the potential to prevent the change were concerns about loss of status and power, and simple resistance to change. These were overcome by the communication and consultation process that was part of the change strategy.
- *Effective change team*: Arguably this was the most successful feature of the change process. The change team was initially made up of five nominated members, who were later supported by a paid member of senior staff. Thus, the main stakeholders were part of the change team, actively promoting the need for change. The features that facilitated their effectiveness were:
  - nomination from the membership
  - experience of the group with regionalisation and/or government
  - autonomy from the ASA Committee
  - their approach to communication and consultation
  - the support received from the governing body.
- *The change team* can take much credit for the success of the process and without their involvement and the consultative approach they adopted, it is unlikely that the introduction of regionalisation would have proceeded at the pace it did, if indeed at all.
- *Sufficient resources*: The resources required to propose and introduce regionalisation were great. Of significance was the time that the BC gave to developing and communicating their proposals. Adequate time (two years) was given to develop the proposals, which was followed by a sensible

154

transition phase of 12 months. This increased the chances of regionalisation becoming fully integrated into the ASA.

- *Implementation strategy*: The change had a clear implementation strategy with allocated responsibilities and time frames. A taskforce was formed, charged with the development of proposals for change that were acceptable to the membership. The proposed restructuring required the approval of key stakeholders, which was given after consultation and discussion. This was followed by a period of transition that allowed the new structures to establish their ways of working. This was a well-planned process that occurred on a realistic time frame.

Overall, this research indicated that the process of change followed by the ASA when introducing regionalisation reflected best practice. The process of developing and implementing the change followed the steps characteristic of a well-planned and successful change programme, evidenced by the lack of significant resistance to the proposals. The membership were convinced of the need for change, involved in determining what it should be, and were prepared for the introduction of regionalisation in 2005. Although it will be many years before the full impact of regionalisation can be evaluated, the Amateur Swimming Association has, at this time, successfully implemented the process of regionalisation in an effective manner and brought about organisational change.

ADDITIONAL ACTIVITIES

- Identify two factors in the external environment that will require sport organisation managers to make changes to their services.
- Suggest possible changes that can be made in response to these factors.
- Consider the best solution and identify why people may be resistant to this change.
- What type of approach should be used to implement this change and why?

FURTHER READING

Abrams, J. (2001) 'The management of change in leisure and sport management', in Wolsey, C. and Abrams J. (eds) *Understanding the Leisure and Sport Industry*. Harlow: Addison, Wesley, Longman.

Senior, B. (1997) Organisational Change. Harlow: Prentice Hall.

Slack, T. and Parent, M. (2006) *Understanding Sport Organisations*, 2nd edition. Champaign: Human Kinetics.

CHAPTER 9

MANAGING MARKETING

Guillaume Bodet

Contemporary sport activities have been greatly affected by three major changes that have occurred in modern times (Enjolras, 2002). These are:

- Diversification: Which has been the increase in opportunities brought about by changes in traditional sport, such as snowboarding and kite surfing.
- Individualisation: Society has become more concerned about individual participation rather than group activities.
- Marketisation: Or commercialisation as the sport market has become increasingly focused on raising revenue and, for some organisations, profit.

As VSOs are not isolated from society these changes have directly impacted on the way they can operate and, as set out in Chapter 2, VSOs are facing increasing competition for resources, either in their sport specific market or in the wider recreational and leisure market.

For example, voluntary sport clubs offering sports such as tennis, badminton and squash face intense competition from public and commercial gyms, fitness and leisure centres. More generally, most VSOs target the same customers and stakeholders and are in competition with other organisations to increase grass-roots participation, to attract spectators to sporting events, to attract media coverage, to attract sponsors and to obtain public funding. This competition also occurs at a national and international level although the competition here is more intense, particularly for sport spectatorship, sponsorship and public funding. Consequently, VSOs have to progressively move from an inward looking operating perspective to become more market and 'customer' orientated to keep current members, attract new ones and increase self-generated revenue. In the long term this will help the organisation to fulfil its objectives and to be sustainable. This is the purpose of marketing.

Marketing can be defined as 'the activity, set of institutions, and processes for creating, communicating, delivering, and exchanging offerings that have value for customers, clients, partners, and society at large' (American Marketing Association, 2007). The essence of this definition relies on what the organisation has to offer, such as a service, product or brand, to the demand from members, funding agencies, partners and society at large. For VSOs, sport demand comes from participants, club members, spectators and communities, but also from other sport organisations, sponsors, public authorities, private facilities or TV and media companies (Ferrand and McCarthy, 2009). The matching of its offer with demand helps the VSO to meet its objectives in an increasingly competitive environment.

It is, however, important to note that organisational objectives do not 'belong' to marketing. Marketing provides a means of helping the organisation to fulfil its objectives, but it is not responsible for them. It is simply one mechanism by which a VSO can compete in its environment in order to achieve what it sets out to do. This difference is important as there is sometimes resistance to the concept of marketing as it can be associated with commercialisation and profit making, which may appear contradictory to the essence and status of VSOs. However, the role that marketing can play in raising awareness of a sport and increasing participation and attendance makes it a valuable management tool for voluntary sport organisations.

This chapter considers the two main dimensions of marketing, which are the strategic marketing process and the operational marketing mix. Marketing mix is a general phrase used to describe the different choices organisations have to make in the process of marketing a product or service. In the first part of the chapter, the concepts of identity, segmentation, targeting and positioning are defined and discussed as these underpin a VSO's marketing strategy. In the second part, the operationalisation of strategy is analysed and considered around the four traditional pillars of the marketing mix which are product, place, promotion and price (the 4Ps). These sections set out the managerial implications of the marketing strategy for a VSO. It is important to note that although Booms and Bitner (1981) extended the traditional 4Ps to 7Ps for the service industry, by adding people, physical evidence and process, these will be incorporated into the 4P framework. Finally, although sponsorship traditionally belongs to promotion, this issue is analysed separately as few VSOs use sponsorship as a promotion tool; they are more inclined to use it as a source of revenue.

THE STRATEGIC MARKETING PROCESS

The strategic level of marketing relies on four elements of which identity is the first. This is followed by segmentation, targeting and positioning. These four elements need to be considered carefully as they underpin the marketing process, providing direction for operational marketing.

Identity

Organisational identity can be defined by questions such as:

- What is the purpose of the organisation?
- Who are its members?
- How do the organisation and its members want to be seen by others such as other sport organisations, local community, potential sponsors?
- What are the core values of the organisation?

These questions need to be answered in consultation with stakeholders, in particular, members, as they will set out what is important to the organisation and highlight features that will assist with the marketing process.

Voluntary sport organisations tend to have a strong identity as identity is made from history and past members, traditions and culture. Indeed, at times the identity of the organisation is sometimes confused with the objectives of a VSO. However, identity goes beyond the purposes or the goals of the VSO as it defines the way the organisation wants to achieve these goals. Understanding the identity of the organisation is important to marketing as it determines the organisational objectives the marketing strategy will seek to help to achieve.

Segmentation

The next strategic marketing step is segmentation, which is the categorising of a market into several homogeneous groups. These groups need to be significant, in that they are worth targeting and that they fit with the organisation's objectives. They also need to be available for marketing actions (Kotler et al, 2004). The first step of segmentation is to split the market into two key relationships. The first is the relationship with stakeholders, known as the business to consumer relationship. The second is the relationship with other organisations, known as the business to business relationship.

Business to consumer relationships of VSOs fall into two main areas:

- Main consumers comprising current or potential members of the organisation and participants in general. They represent the primary segment for VSOs because an increase in participants is often a key objective for these organisations. It is worth noting that for young sport members and participants, parents also represent a type of 'consumer', even if they do not participate, as they play a significant role in their children's choice of sport organisation (Ferreira and Armstrong, 2002).
- Spectators, which can be both live and mediated. Increasing attendance at sporting events is important for VSOs as it helps to increase the level of

support for a team or athletes, but also it generates extra revenues both by ticketing and TV rights, and by merchandising and sales. The relationship with spectators is difficult as it can sometimes involve only few dozen live spectators, but thousands of mediated spectators.

Business to business relationships occur in three main areas:

- Those who belong to the same sport system (see Figure 1.1), such as other voluntary sport clubs, national and international federations.
- Public organisations, such as sport councils, city councils and governmental departments, which are often stakeholders and funders.
- Commercial organisations, which can be goods or material providers or sponsors.

Once this first segmentation step is completed, the second step is to identify if there are different homogeneous groups with specific expectations and needs within each of these relationships, and if the VSO is able to or wants to target all the segments. The most basic variable used to differentiate sport participants is an orientation towards performance, where high performance is at one end of the continuum and participation at the other. An alternative segmentation variable might be the difference between beginners and experienced or highly skilled participants.

Numerous others segments can be created according to gender, age, social and economic backgrounds, demographic variables, behavioural and psychographic variables such as the nature and the degree of participants' sport involvement. For instance Kyle et al (2007) identified several facets of leisure involvement such as the level of centrality in people's life the leisure activity represents, the level of self-expression or the level of social bonding, which may not have the same weight among all consumers and could be used for segmentation.

Targeting

When different segments or groups of consumers have been identified, the next step is targeting, which consists of choosing the appropriate segments to focus on. Many voluntary sport organisations, particularly clubs, have limited resources that do not allow them to attempt to satisfy too many segments with heterogeneous expectations. For instance, time and facilities are limited and all sport teams of the same local club cannot use the sport facilities at the same time, thus choices have to be made.

Therefore, decisions have to be made about which segment to target and this needs to be done in line with the objectives of the organisation and its capacities. For instance, should the organisation attract more beginners although the time

159

available for this segment is small? Or, should the organisation keep on targeting more experienced competitors although there is not enough high quality equipment?

Many VSOs do not have a specific targeting strategy because they do not focus on a particular type of participant since everybody is welcome. However, it is important to keep in mind that if everybody is welcome, everybody does not have the same motivations and expectations. Therefore, being aware of this is the starting point to understanding if the organisation's offer will meet the requirements of the organisation's targets in order for them to be satisfied. For instance, a frequent mistake in small clubs is that although they might welcome both participation and performance oriented membership they often favour one group over the other because of managers' interests, facility space or the reputation created by being involved with a particular group. This can often lead to conflict, dissatisfaction and switching behaviour. If VSOs target different kinds of participants, they have to be aware of their needs and of the type of offer they can provide. If the offer cannot match the expectations of some segments it is better not to target these groups. This is especially the case when organisational capacities are limited.

POSITIONING

Once the segments are clearly identified and can be targeted, the next strategic step is positioning, which uses the concept of the service and its image in order to give it a particular place in the targeted customers' mind (Kotler et al, 2004). An example of positioning can be provided by considering football, in the UK, where a five-a-side football team, a division two team and a premier league team occupy different conceptual positions in terms of the quality of the players, the club infrastructure and the merchandise associated with it.

The main goal of positioning is to distinguish the organisation's offer from the main competitors in the same market. As set out in Table 9.1 VSOs do not only compete in a specific sport. Indeed, from an economic point of view, they compete in a wider sport and leisure market. Therefore, two types of competitors can be identified. First, there are direct competitors, which are other sport organisations providing the same activity. For example, a basketball club is in competition with other basketball clubs to attract participants, even if they do not really compete in the same division. Second are the indirect competitors as the basketball club is in competition with unorganised activity and the offerings from other sports.

Why would members come to this club? For clubs, differentiation is primarily on the basis of sport results. Some clubs or teams are more successful than others and success is an appealing factor, even for those who are not performance oriented. However, there are other ways of differentiating sport clubs. Sport clubs

160

Table 9.1 The competitive market of a basketball club

Target consumers, prospects and stakeholders	Competitors (from direct to indirect)
Local, regional or national basketball players	The local basketball clubs
Casual players	The local indoor team sport clubs (volleyball, handball, netball)
Basketball fans	The local outdoor team-sports (rugby, football, field hockey)
Potential players	Other voluntary sport clubs
Volunteers and paid staff	Casually organised basketball participation (playgrounds)
Former players	Local gyms, fitness clubs and leisure centres
National sport organisations	School clubs
Local companies as potential sponsors and providers	Other local sport and recreation activities, organised or not, such as music schools, video games, cinemas and skate parks
Local and regional sport and non sport-related public authorities	Local professional clubs (spectatorship)
The local community	Entertainment industry
Players' parents and relatives (potential members and volunteers)	
Local media	
Local schools, teachers and educators (potential partners)	
Local and regional training centres	
Local sport hall managers or owners	
Local professional clubs (potential partners)	

offer a service based on different elements and each of these elements can lead to satisfaction or dissatisfaction with the club. For instance, Bodet and Meurgey (2005) identified 42 elements that make up the service offer of French not-for-profit fitness clubs, such as the sport results of the club, the manager's availability and friendliness, the number of coaches and instructors, the membership fee, the relationships between the members and the welcome of new members. These elements offer the potential to distinguish the organisation from its main competitors by increasing the satisfaction of members. Alternatively, a local club might wish to position itself on the basis of the social and community dimensions of the club, the ambiance or the fun to be had through participation. Having said this, on a more general level, because clubs are responsible for the delivery of a particular sport, the positioning of a club in the mind of participants and possible participants is often based on the results, the image and the representation of the sport created by the national team.

In many cases, the local club may be the only club of its particular sport in an area and therefore could consider itself to have no direct competitors, which therefore means it does not require the use of positioning and marketing in general. However, the current generation of young participants is prone to switch or 'zap' easily from one sport to another. In this case, the basketball club is also in competition with the volleyball or football club and therefore has to position and distinguish not only its own organisation but also its sport. A local club may also have to position its sport in comparison with video games, music or other leisure activities.

This strategic marketing chain (identity, segmentation, targeting, positioning) is not only relevant for participants, current and potential members, it is also relevant for current and potential spectators. For instance, it is particularly relevant for team sports because competitions are regular and often occur on the weekend and at fixed times. Thus, the games of other clubs represent competitors for local sport spectatorship. Furthermore, they are also in competition with other leisure activities such as watching TV and going to the theatre. At a regional or national level, even if sporting events do not occur at the same time, they are still in competition because the cost of attendance does not always allow spectators to attend as many events as they want.

In many cases, particularly at a local level, voluntary sport organisations are not fully aware that they are in competition with other sport organisations and that a strategy is needed to keep or increase their 'market share', in order to achieve the organisation's objectives over the long term. Moreover, the role of the strategic marketing process is often underestimated when compared with the marketing mix, although the strategic process underpins the operation process. In order to develop the strategic marketing process to provide support for the subsequent marketing mix, managers need to ask the following questions:

■ What is the identity of the VSO? What is its purpose? What are its values?
■ What are the short-term and long-term objectives of the VSO? What does the organisation want to achieve? What does it stand for?
■ What are the segments that make up the demand for the VSO? Who are the individuals and organisations that the organisation has relationships with? Among them, how many homogeneous groups are there?
■ Who are the targets of the VSO? Which individuals and organisations does the organisation want to attract, have a relationship with, satisfy and keep loyal to the VSO?
■ What is the positioning of the VSO in the different target markets and target segments? How should the organisation be seen by individuals and organisations it has a relationship with? Why would they choose this VSO and not the main rivals or competitors?

Once these questions have been answered, managers need to move on to developing the marketing mix, which intends to operationalise the answers to the above questions.

guillaume bodet

THE MARKETING MIX FOR VOLUNTARY SPORT ORGANISATIONS

This section discusses the marketing mix that allows practical and concrete strategies to be developed from the strategic marketing process. As stated earlier, this marketing mix for voluntary sport organisations is based on the extended 4Ps of:

■ product and process.
■ place and physical evidence.
■ promotion.
■ price.

These constitute the main operational variables for implementing a VSO's marketing strategy.

Product and process

In the sport context, the concept of a product constitutes a service offer that is based on one or more activities in a business to consumer relationship. This offer has to be appropriate for the targeted segment and has to meet expectations in order to bring about satisfaction so that people continue to want the offer. Therefore, the crucial point is to determine what the segment's expectations are and what they look for in this type of service.

A service is composed of a core or central service and several peripheral services (Langeard et al, 1981). In the case of VSOs, the core service is the opportunity to participate in a particular sport. From an organisational perspective, this central service represents the reason for the organisation's existence and, on the consumer side, often represents the main reason why members join the VSO. Historically, the core service provided by VSOs has relied on participation that has been concerned with training and competition. Consequently, the service has been based on regular training sessions designed to improve performance, and competitions in order to determine the best athletes or teams and an overall ranking.

However, this may no longer match the expectations and desires of many sport participants. Loret (1995) has analysed what he called a redefinition of the meaning of sport, which he considered to have emerged because of several counterculture movements that led to the development of new or individual activities such as roller-skating, surfing and windsurfing. These sport activities were driven by fun rather than performance, by challenge rather than competition (Loret, 1995; Heino, 2000). More recently, Seippel (2006) identified seven new meanings of sport: fun and joy, expressive action, keep fit, mental recreation, body appearance, competition and achievement, and social integration. In addition, James et al (2006) identified five major needs and benefits provided by sport characterised by the acronym SPEED, which stands for Socialisation, Performance, Excitement, Esteem and Diversion.

These studies suggest that some participants' relationship with sport has changed. Sport participants have become even more heterogeneous, looking for plural and diverse experiences. This means that voluntary sport organisations must change too, and they may need to re-evaluate the type of services they offer. It would appear that for some sports, services cannot just be based on the type of sport activities provided and more consideration has to be given to the way they are practised and experienced. This does not mean that all VSOs have to give up a focus on sport performance and competition as this particular segment is always likely to exist. However, it is clear that for some sports this change in participant expectations is going to require a reconsideration of the identity and segmentation aspects of the strategic marketing process.

The following two case studies show how two organisations have created a service offering to meet the differing needs of non-traditional market segments.

Case study 9.1: the Médoc marathon

The Médoc marathon was created in 1984 by several friends passionate about marathon and takes place in the Médoc region in the south-west of France. The main goal of the organisers is to get as many runners as possible to discover the benefits and the pleasure of long-distance running. It is limited on purpose to 8,500 participants, in order to keep its original spirit, which is based on four pillars: health, sport, conviviality and fun. In terms of the health pillar, two medical congresses are organised around the marathon in order to educate and prevent sport-related injuries, and the marathon serves as support for numerous medical studies. The sport aspect is obvious and even if the marathon is labelled as fun, it is a proper marathon distance. The most interesting are the conviviality and the fun pillars. The organisers are proud to say that the race was elected the most convivial race in France three years in a row. Conviviality is expressed through an individualised welcome, in the fact that participants receive a lot of presents, such as medals, bags and Médoc wine and in the attitudes of the local population and the volunteers. Finally, the fun aspect is based on several entertainment aspects. These include:

- a costumed party organised in a local castle the night before the race
- events that are organised before, during and after the race
- food and wine tasting stands provided alongside the race
- a party ending with fireworks is organised on the night of the marathon
- runners and volunteers can participate in a recovery walk or ride in the local area the day after the race.

164

The targeting of the event is explicitly mentioned on the website of the marathon and those for whom sport means health, fun and conviviality are welcomed. 'Spoilsports, thugs and record seekers are not invited!' The target market is not only French, and 20 per cent of the 2006 participants were foreigners, which has been driven by an English version of the marathon website. The demand for this event is strong (15,000 applicants in 2006) and does not seem to be decreasing.

Case study 9.2: the Daunat Beach rugby tour

The Daunat Beach rugby tour is a series of beach rugby summer tournaments organised by the French Rugby Federation in partnership with Daunat, a sandwich brand. About ten tournaments are organised in different places on the French coast and one event is organised in the Parisian region. Each event lasts between two and four days. During the events, tournaments are organised for children, adolescents, and mixed teams made up of women, men, beginners and experienced players, even family teams. In addition, a national championship is organised for club teams, the winner of which is considered to be the best beach rugby team in France.

This particular beach rugby format is a new discipline with specific rules. The ball is smaller than a normal rugby ball, the size of the pitch is less than half the size of a normal pitch, the game does not last more than ten minutes, tackles are replaced by a two-handed touch, and there is no line-out, scrum or kicking. This greatly amended version of rugby aims to be accessible and of interest to individuals who may not be familiar with this sport. Moreover, the rules are adapted to fit with the spirit of this sport, which is fun and generosity. As mentioned on the website, this form of the game relies on speed, technique and play. This complements the traditional values of rugby, which are considered by Bernard Lapasset, the former president of the French Rugby Federation, to be respect, sharing and conviviality. Aside from the sporting activities, numerous activities, stands and concerts contribute to the tournament. This tour targets a large audience made up of competitors, recreation seekers, families, anyone from 7 to 77 years old, and aims to increase the awareness and popularity of rugby in general.

As can be seen from these two case studies, the evaluation of the service should not only be about what is delivered but how it is delivered – the process of the service – as they are closely related. If participants are not focused on sport performance, they may be looking for a less regular commitment to training and participation. Therefore, one issue related to the process of delivery is regularity of consumption. Participants may increasingly look for more 'pay-as-you-go' participation opportunities, which is a challenge for VSO clubs in particular. Club structures are based on a commitment to the organisation through membership and a less formal commitment may undermine the collective nature of a club. However, it is possible to provide casual events, tournaments or friendly games for participants who do not want to commit to regular fixtures but are still willing to participate in a competition three or four times a year. In addition, in order to cope with the consumer demand for heterogeneity, voluntary sport organisations may create links with other sport organisations to provide a wider offer. For example, access to several sport activities could be available within one membership.

Place and physical evidence

The second variable of the marketing mix relates to how the offer is made available to customers, how the encounter between the offer and its demand is managed and organised. In the context of VSOs, Place is where the sporting activity occurs and can be as diverse as rivers, indoor arenas or rock faces. The concept of place also incorporates the location of sporting opportunities and this is impacted by a number of features such as the availability of facilities, the presence of a local club or the availability of experienced coaches and instructors. Therefore, for many sporting activities the place that the activity can occur is not uniform and will range from an absence of clubs in a rural location to the presence of several clubs in a city.

One key element attached to the place dimension is physical evidence and Booms and Bitner (1981) distinguished the servicescape (or place) from the other tangibles that can be associated with the service. For local clubs, the servicescape is mainly made up of the facilities enabling the sport to take place and the facilities that allow participation, such as the changing rooms, the entrance, the car park, the facility's direct surroundings, storage areas and perhaps a fitness room. These elements are not always required for a sport, but most are considered to be a normal part of the place of participation and their absence would be a sign of low service quality.

These servicescape elements should be as clean, attractive, functional and efficient as possible to meet participant expectations, as Zeithaml et al (2009: 319) have noted that the servicescape can be critical in forming initial impressions, customer expectations and organisational image in that it is a visual metaphor for the intangible service. This means that the servicescape has a key role to play in the positioning of the sport and thus must meet the expectations of targeted segments.

In addition, Zeithaml et al (2009) have identified the socialiser servicescape, which is particularly important for small VSOs, such as clubs. As noted by Seippel (2006), the socialising aspect of participation is important in clubs and can be the main reason for joining. This is acknowledged by some sports by the presence of a clubhouse, or a coaches' or a volunteers' room. This type of servicescape is becoming increasingly important as the general trend in sport participation is a bigger emphasis on the social and community dimensions of sport participation. It also represents a crucial aspect for enhancing the VSO's identity.

166

In terms of tangibles, they can be as important as the servicescape if they are necessary for participation. These are things such as sport equipment and accessories, such as shirts, balls, boats, ropes, hurdles and cones. They make tangible the service experience, which may help sport participants in their evaluation of the service offer. In this regard, some VSOs also provide badges, certificates or rewards to participants for their achievements or simply for participation. For instance, the British Canoe Union has set up the Paddlesport Performance Award scheme, which comprises five star levels designed to provide encouragement and an incentive for first-time paddlers.

At a national level, because sport participation services are often delivered by local clubs, the main issue to do with place is to do with the sporting servicescapes. Many national federations or major clubs possess their own servicescapes such as headquarters, and sport stadiums and arenas; for example, Twickenham and the Rugby Football Union (RFU). They can play a role in both providing a great sporting experience and in providing revenue. Moreover sport stadiums and arenas play a flagship role in building both internal and external image.

Promotion

The third marketing mix tool for VSOs is promotion, which can be considered as the function of informing, persuading, reminding and comforting the consumer's purchase decision (Kotler et al, 2004). This marketing variable comprises several dimensions that are more or less relevant to VSOs depending on their size and resources. The role of promotion is either to increase the awareness of non-participants or to increase the organisation's image in relation to strategic marketing. Promotion may be basic, such as informing people of the VSO as a potential place to practise a specific sport, or informing them about which activities are provided, where it is possible to participate, the time of the sessions, the date of a particular event or a person to contact within the voluntary sport organisation.

Promotion relies mainly on publicity and advertising, which is aimed at individuals or organisations known as targets. At a club level, this occurs mainly through local newspapers and radio, posters and leaflets and the Internet. Most of the time, the only presence of a club in local newspapers and on radio is the descriptive results and fixtures of local athletes or teams, which mainly attract the attention of the local sport community, essentially to increase awareness. Thus, it is often sport information for the already sport-interested community and, as most of these organisations do not consider themselves to be in competition with other local sport organisations for the recruitment of new members and the retention of the current ones, little is done to promote the identity and the image of the club.

This issue is strongly related to the product of the organisation. VSOs need to communicate to the type of participants they wish to attract, the type of sport and non-sport activities they provide, as well as the benefits of belonging to the club. Moreover, it is important to be in the media often in order to increase both the awareness and image of the organisation. This issue is unfortunately often neglected in local clubs due to lack of resources, but should be an area for investment. Whenever possible, promotion of the organisation is a role that should be allocated to a specific member of the organisation in order to be as visible as possible.

As for posters, they are mainly used by clubs to fulfil informational purposes and tend to be relatively poorly produced and thus low in terms of promotional impact. Managers need to be aware that posters can create an image that is not perceived as attractive. Many sport organisations underestimate the importance of this type of media although creative and innovative posters and leaflets are not difficult to do. Cost may obviously present a barrier but should be viewed as an investment because the impression created will go beyond the particular information given or the specific game promoted, especially for those who are not familiar with the VSO.

For example, Figure 9.1 shows a leaflet used to promote the Loughborough University rugby team. Although this leaflet does not provide a lot of information, it clearly gives an impression that something exciting is about to happen, something 'noisy', a real crunch match. It has the appearance of a movie poster rather than an ordinary sport game. This demonstrates how innovative and attractive this type of media can be in the promotion of a VSO.

Finally, Internet media is highly important and has to be considered by voluntary sport organisations as a necessity, although clubs are not likely to use this type of media to promote the organisation or a specific event because it is relatively expensive. They will, however, need to have their own website or blog. Obviously, highly technical, attractive websites are better in terms of promotion, but budget and skills often bound the enthusiasm of many managers. Nonetheless, the priority is to be Internet accessible because this media is intensively used to search for information, particularly by young participants. A basic website will match the awareness goal of promotion by providing information, such as the location of the organisation, who can join the club, contact details and times of training. A more sophisticated website will promote an attractive image of the organisation. It is important to note, however, that a website needs to be updated as often as possible as a wrong contact address or information that is out of date will not achieve the goals intended. Alternatively, social networks such as Facebook can also be used as they fulfil both informative and social interaction purposes.

For VSOs at a national level, the potential offered by media promotion is very important but again closely related to the size of the budget allocated. The main shortcomings that can be identified in promotion at a national level are similar to those at the local level and are a lack of originality, unclear objectives and non-targeted messages. However, with the wide and increasing use of the Internet,

guillaume bodet

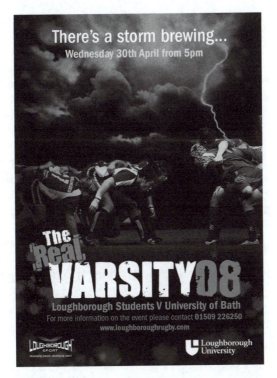

Figure 9.1 Promotional poster

a creative and successful advert can be extensively viewed with a minimum of cost. Thus, the Internet represents an important medium of communication that should be developed beyond simply a website. For larger voluntary sport organisations, the objectives of promotion are similar to local clubs but the role played by promotion in image creation is emphasised. The following two case studies show how two national federations have used promotion in a different manner to appeal to their target audience by creating an image of their sports.

Case study 9.3: 'Try rugby, you will be converted'

In 1999, the French Rugby Federation launched an advert that was broadcast on free-view French channels during and around rugby union games. The advert portrayed five French couples who described their son. After each parental comment, their son was pictured in a rugby game situation, such as a maul or tackling, in order to highlight the contrast between the parents' perception of their son and the way he behaves when he is playing rugby:

■ Couple 1: 'He is slim, not very sturdy, actually, he is small for his age.' The child is pictured driving into the defence, avoiding tackles.

- Couple 2: 'He does not speak, he is shy, even at school he does not speak a lot.' The child is pictured jumping and yelling in a line-out.
- Couple 3: 'This child is lazy.' The child is pictured energetically tackling a player.
- Couple 4: 'He is alone, always on his own, this is an introverted child.' The child is pictured scoring a try and publicly manifesting his satisfaction.
- Couple 5: 'Anyway, he will always be a loner.' The child is pictured being cheered by others and people clapping hands.

The advertisement finishes with the final slogan 'Try rugby, you will be converted'. This advertising is particularly interesting because it aimed to increase participation by playing on the sport image and by breaking stereotypes. It aimed to both attract parents, who are often the final decision makers in the family, and children. However, because of the design using parents' speeches, the main message targets parents to show that rugby practice represents a great source of achievement. It can be noted that the focus is on the values and individual characteristics this sport can develop and nothing is said about performance and competition.

Case study 9.4: 'Football's for girls, try rugby'

The advertisement was created by the Czech Rugby Association in order to attract new participants by developing the positioning of rugby in the sport environment. The advert starts with a football game, with a football player theatrically falling down after having jumped over a tackle. The football player keeps on rolling as if he was badly hit. A physiotherapist then quickly arrives and takes a comb and a spray to fix the player's haircut. After checking in a mirror that his hairstyle is fixed, the player gets up and starts running while the slogan appears: 'Football's for girls'. Following this, a football is squashed by a rugby ball and a new slogan appears: 'Try rugby'. The Internet address of the Czech Rugby Association is also displayed in the bottom right of the screen.

Beyond the fact that this advert might be offensive for women, the message is particularly interesting because it highlights that the Czech Rugby Association has understood the fact that they are in competition with other sports when attempting to attract new participants. In this case, the positioning of rugby is made in opposition to football and relies on the physicality, virility, toughness and authenticity of rugby. The segment targeted by the advert is men, potential participants interested in those features for a team sport. However, a negative outcome of this advert may be that it indirectly excludes men not interested in these features, who do not perceive they fit within this context, and women. Contrary to case study 9.3, this advert reinforces stereotypes regarding rugby and rugby players.

VSOs can also promote themselves via direct marketing, which can be considered as an interactive marketing process using one or several media in order to get an answer and/or a transaction (Kotler et al, 2004). Different techniques can be used, such as face-to-face communication or door sales, mass mailing, telesales, the use of traditional media with a contact phone number or address, or by promotional stands. Most voluntary sport organisations rely on mass mailing as a direct marketing technique, particularly emailing due to its limited cost. This does, however, require accurate and up-to-date databases with contact details, which are easy to obtain for current members but difficult for potential participants or spectators. It also requires an awareness of data protection issues and it is necessary to ask permission before sending messages as direct mail.

The last promotional tool available to voluntary sport organisations is public relations (PR). PR are the activities set up by an organisation to create, establish, maintain and enhance trust, understanding and sympathy towards the organisation through the development of the relationships necessary to ensure the organisation's survival. The main objectives of PR are to influence participants to join a club, to develop awareness of the VSO and to create a positive image, for both the organisation and the sport. In this case, the promotional targets are all potential participants, members, potential spectators, the community, the public authorities and potential partners, such as sponsors.

According to Cutlip et al (1997), PR encompasses several types of activity. Among them, the most useful for VSOs are probably media relationships, corporate communication and lobbying. Maintaining good relationships with the media is crucial due to their ability to create increasing interest in sport and generate financial resources. Thus, maintaining good relationships with the media, either local or national, is a key objective. Corporate communication represents all communication, internal and external, that focuses on the organisation and often relies on the creation of events. Birthday celebrations, conferences, expositions, lotteries, contests, dinners, treasure hunts and sponsor receptions are examples of PR events. The last activity, lobbying, can occur at both national and local level and consists of seeking to influence public authorities in the interests of the organisation. Because of the important level of public funding for VSOs in numerous countries, lobbying activity relies primarily on maintaining and increasing the level of public funding or provision of sport facilities.

Price

The final mix marketing variable is the price and is often not considered enough as a marketing variable by voluntary sport organisations, particularly small ones. Indeed, most VSOs consider attracting new participants as a major organisational objective and see economic cost, in general, and the price or membership fee, in particular, as obstacles to this. Moreover, at a local level, freedom over pricing is sometimes limited due to the fact that the membership/registration to the national federation has to be included in any club membership charged. Nevertheless, some consideration to price must be given.

First, membership and ticket fees are often disconnected from the internal costs and resources of a club or an event. Although a profit orientation may not be appropriate for a VSO, a no debt orientation is strongly recommended and fees should reflect this as much as possible. Moreover, from an ethical point of view, a debt situation means that the current members are paying for the previous ones, which could be considered as unfair.

Second, a VSO should adopt a market orientated approach, consider its main competitors and adjust its fees in line with them. However, there is a danger in being too focused on the market because not all organisations have the same capacities and resources. Moreover, adjusting fees in relation to market demand can be detrimental because it can give the impression to stakeholders that previous fees were either not justified, or they act as a barrier when fees increase and demand is volatile.

Finally, thought needs to be given to more innovative pricing structures. In this case pricing is closely related to the product variables. For instance, if annual membership fees are expensive, VSOs could introduce other types of membership that could vary, for example, by the length of the membership. This kind of modification would not concern regular competitors, but would be particularly suitable for recreational members. Some national federations already provide this kind of membership or affiliation, which lasts for the length of a specific event and which seems to fit well with contemporary participant expectations, as annual membership, in addition to regular training commitments, seems to be an increasing constraint to sport participants.

Another example of pricing adaptation can be linked to the offer of ancillary products and/or different packages. For instance, a membership fee for a participant could be merged with a spectator fee guaranteeing a discounted ticket price for parents of children who are members. Another package could comprise the membership fee plus equipment, ranging from a basic shirt of the VSO to more expensive and technical items, such as a helmet, paddle or bat. Finally, more could be learnt from commercial organisations in terms of innovation and pricing. For instance, although turnover in VSOs is becoming increasingly important (see Chapter 6), very little is done in terms of pricing to keep members, children in particular. Voluntary sport organisations should develop a long-term perspective and could therefore offer significant fee reductions for participants who are loyal, or reductions when several members of the same family join the club. This can simultaneously influence the loyalty of existing members and attract new ones.

The discussion above has presented the pillars that need to be considered when setting out to market a voluntary sport organisation. The process needs to start

guillaume bodet

with an understanding of the strategic marketing process and organisations need to be very clear about the identity they have, the segments they are going to target and where they intend on positioning themselves in the market. These factors can then be operationlised by considering the 4Ps discussed above. This will lead to the effective marketing of the services of voluntary sport organisations.

SPONSORSHIP IN VOLUNTARY SPORT ORGANISATIONS

Although, sponsorship is traditionally considered as a promotional tool, for VSOs it is more about revenue generation or the provision of services. Funding from sponsorship is vital for the operation of many VSOs, which produces an intensely competitive market for sponsors as well as focusing the attention of sponsors on what they get for their investment. For these reasons, Doherty and Murray (2007) have set out the necessity for VSOs to engage themselves in a strategic sponsorship process in order to fit with potential sponsor expectations and to differentiate themselves from competitors, other VSOs seeking a sponsor.

Sponsorship preparation

This is the first step of the process and requires the sport organisation to identify its objectives for corporate sponsorship, such as finance, material or expertise and then what they have to offer to a potential sponsor. This is closely related to the strategic marketing process discussed at the beginning of the chapter. The objectives of sponsors are numerous but most are associated with increasing sales, awareness, image and internal cohesion and motivation (Ferrand et al, 2007). Then VSOs need to identify which of these objectives they can help to achieve in relation to the organisation's assets and qualities.

The assets and qualities of a voluntary sport organisation can be evaluated according to Aaker's (1991) framework. For this author, brand equity comprises the four dimensions of perceived quality, brand loyalty, brand awareness and brand image. A strong brand equity means that customers have high brand name awareness, maintain a favourable brand image, perceive that the brand is of high quality and are loyal to the brand. An adaptation of this framework can provide a useful analysis tool for VSOs that are looking to identify what they can offer to prospective sponsors. Voluntary sport organisations with high brand awareness will be the most attractive to sponsors, such as the IOC, or Manchester United Football Club.

VSO managers should ask the following questions about their organisation:

■ Is the VSO well known? Among which population? Among which groups of individuals?

- What is the size of the non-sport community? Of the sport community?
- What is the image of the VSO? Is it positive? What are the characteristics of this image? Are these characteristics positive, strong and unique?
- Is the organisation perceived as providing good service quality? Are members satisfied? Are they considered to be satisfied? Does the VSO usually meet the expectations of its members? Of its spectators? Of its stakeholders?
- Are the stakeholders of the VSO loyal? Do they create positive word of mouth? Do they advocate the VSO?

It is important that managers try not only to answer these questions on their own – they must seek feedback to confirm understanding of the issues. For example, in order to identify different elements and attributes of the organisation's image, basic questions can be asked of members, such as: 'What are the first words that come to your mind when you hear or when you think about the VSO?' However, one of the main difficulties, especially for small clubs, is to identify the exact image of the organisation. When the level of awareness is low, it is likely that the image of the organisation will be that of the sport in general or will be the image of the national federation. In this situation all local clubs may have the same image and it will then be difficult for potential consumers to establish a difference and decide which one to join. This will make these clubs much less attractive to sponsors.

Finally, Doherty and Murray (2007) have highlighted how sponsorship preparation should also consider the potential risks for both the sport organisation and the sponsoring company. For VSOs, the major risk is a loss of control due to financial dependence and the potential to pay less attention to other stakeholders such as public authorities (Berrett, 1993). For the sponsor, the risks comprise:

- a lack of control over media coverage and thus of exposure
- the uncertainty of the sporting outcome
- a lack of fit between the image of the sport organisation and the sponsor
- a lack of return on investment
- a congestion of sponsors caused by too many sponsors, leading to confusion about who is a sponsor and who is not
- potential scandals and troubles, such as doping and disruptive fans
- ambush marketing.

(Desbordes and Tribou, 2007)

Identification of potential sponsors

The next step in the process consists of identifying potential sponsors. It appears sensible to look for companies that fit with the sport's image and its target market, but which can also allocate a specific and attractive budget to the sponsorship activities. Furthermore, companies with a direct interest within the sport or who are sport-related, such as equipment, drinks, transport, magazines and sport retail stores, should be targeted. Even if they are not able to support financially, the potential sponsor may be able to provide another type of resource, known as 'in-kind' sponsorship.

At a local level, small clubs often attract sponsors through personal relationships and community networks. For example, sponsorship often comes from a former member of the sport, a supporter of the club or from having a child who is a member of the club. However, this should not prevent small VSOs implementing a strategic sponsorship process with sponsors because it could, first, increase the level of sponsorship if they are shown how their company can achieve its objectives through sponsorship and, second, will enhance their loyalty and commitment as a sponsor. In this case, having loyal and committed sponsors will ensure a steady revenue for a VSO. In addition, the sponsor could act as an advocate for the VSO and may open their own networks of stakeholders, representing potential new sponsors.

When identifying potential sponsors it is important to be aware of any legal limitations on sponsors. For example, in several countries the public consumption of alcohol is strictly regulated, which may prevent some beverage companies from certain types of sponsorship. Similarly, ethical issues need to be considered and should be discussed in regards to the identity of the VSO. For example, it might not be appropriate to be sponsored by a 'sugary' cereal company when most of the organisation's members are children.

Sponsorship proposal

When the preparation is done and the prospective sponsors are identified, the next step is writing the sponsorship proposal, which, according to Moler (2000), should emphasise the benefits to a company of being a sponsor. According to Doherty and Murray (2007), the sponsorship proposal should:

- highlight the reasons why the company should become a sponsor
- describe and present the voluntary sport organisation
- present the potential targets, such as participants and spectators, which can be reached through the sponsorship
- set out the particular types and opportunities offered to the sponsor
- set out the length of the sponsorship deal
- define the nature and the amount of funding to be provided by the company
- anticipate the potential risks that could limit the benefits the sponsor would get from the deal.

Doherty and Murray's strategic sponsorship process leads to a strategic plan that should set out how the objectives of both the VSO and sponsor can be achieved.

This should be followed by an evaluation of the sponsorship, which in most cases will be carried out by the sponsoring organisation.

The growing costs of running a voluntary sport organisation mean that the need for sponsorship will become increasingly important. This is perhaps the most competitive aspect of the operating environment within which a VSO works. Much time can be wasted approaching the wrong sponsor with a poorly developed sponsorship bid and therefore it is important that the approach to sponsorship is planned, systematic and strategic.

SUMMARY

The fundamental purpose of sport marketing is to make available the right offer to meet the demand there is for the sport and other services offered by a voluntary sport organisation. It is essential that marketing is based on a thorough understanding of what the organisation has to offer and how it is perceived by its intended target segments. If this is the case the organisation can use the marketing mix to match up its service offerings with the expectations of participants.

ADDITIONAL ACTIVITIES

- Go through the strategic marketing process using a club that you are familiar with.
- Using the same club, use Aaker's (1991) framework to assess the club's brand equity.
- Identify what this club has to offer sponsors.

FURTHER READING

Ferrand, A. and Torrigiani, L. (2005) Marketing of Olympic Sport Organisations. Champaign: Human Kinetics.

Sullivan, M. (2004) 'Sport marketing', in Beech, J. and Chadwick, S. (eds) The Business of Sport Management. Harlow: Pearson Education Ltd.

CHAPTER 10

EVENT MANAGEMENT

Eleni Theodoraki

This chapter discusses the activities associated with event management as this is a major activity of many voluntary sport organisations. The chapter starts with an exploration of what constitutes an event, the principles that determine success and contemporary best practice. The chapter then goes on to a discussion of the challenges that are emerging because of mega events. A case study of a fund-raising event organised by a rowing club is included as an illustrative example of the structures, processes, environment and finances involved in event management.

DEFINITIONS AND TYPES OF EVENTS

An event is a happening of some significance that involves people attending a function or performance that is being hosted and staged to meet a particular set of aims. Events vary in their scope, size, significance, complexity and visibility from the small to the gigantic. They can be aiming to meet social, business, political or financial targets and they may involve organisations from the public, private and voluntary sector working together for the event related processes to take place (Getz, 2007: Roche, 2000). Organising a sport event is:

■ an essential objective for a large number of VSOs
■ the provision of a product or service that must satisfy a variety of stakeholders
■ a way of developing the organisation's image
■ a way of attracting and using human resources before, during and after the event
■ a process requiring risk management.

For an event to be successful, it must be part of the long-term development strategy of a VSO. Without adequate advance planning, the event will certainly become an activity that sits outside the overall strategic objectives of the organisation and therefore might not attract the importance it requires. To understand the risks and opportunities associated with an event, it is necessary to understand the characteristics of events. First, events are unique, non-repetitive and specific, even events that are held regularly, such as the Olympic Games. This means that

177

although an organisation can learn lessons from the staging of previous Games, it cannot stage the event in exactly the same manner.

Events must be completed by a fixed date, which requires careful planning. Organising events is challenging because success depends on the combination and interrelation of several elements and activities. Events are affected by numerous unknown contingencies, such as athlete participation, participation of the public, public contributions and sponsor involvement. They are also susceptible to conditions outside the control of the organisation, such as weather, environment, politics and society expectations.

Events are also staged under significant limitations, such as having to respect the rules of the sport, observing the regulations of the event owner (e.g. the IOC or an IF) and fulfilling the technical conditions required by the sport. Although often seen as constraints, these characteristics also provide many opportunities for establishing relationships and allow organisers to later exploit the success of the project and contacts and partnerships made during the event.

Sport events can be classified as:

- global, such as the Winter Olympics, or local, such as national championships
- popular, such as a fun run, or elite, such as the Commonwealth Games
- sport related, such as Grand Prix Athletics, or promotional, such as a taster event for new participants
- unidisciplinary, such as national swimming championships, or multidisciplinary, such as the Olympic Games
- single site, such as a club's championship, or multi-site, such as the Paralympics.

Examples of events hosted by voluntary sport organisations includes local and regional sport competition, fund-raising events, PR events, social events and award ceremonies, and reunions. As this list shows, not all events carry similar organisational challenges. A reunion for 150 past members will include less logistical challenges than holding of a training camp in another country that may include supervision of minors, transportation of sensitive equipment, safety and insurance measures as well as the financial tasks, such as day-to-day budgeting and handling of money transactions with outside contractors and service providers.

The dimensions that often distinguish small from mega sports events are the size of the event's budget, public participation and media coverage attained. Mega events, such as international competitions hosted by a national federation, may include thousands of people in the management and delivery of the event; they will be watched by numerous spectators or participants and the media coverage may include live transmission of the competition for television, radio and online audiences in all continents. Understandably, the budget of such events will be high and there may be investment in infrastructure needed for the event to take

eleni theodoraki

place, such as the development of appropriate competition or accommodation venues or transportation links. A local club competition will clearly be a much smaller task to organise and stage.

SUCCESSFUL EVENT MANAGEMENT

Before issues that are central to successful event management are explored further it is pertinent to consider what is meant by 'successful' in terms of event management. Successful event management involves the following:

- Achieving the aims set for the event: All events set out to achieve a certain 'something' – the aim of holding the event. Achieving this aim is an indicator of success. Having clearly defined goals is important for this process as unless the voluntary sport organisation knows what it aspires to achieve it will be difficult to chart a course of appropriate action. Goal setting will also be useful as a means to evaluate progress and measure the level of success.
- Having the least negative broader impact: All events make an impact on their stakeholders and the host community. A measure of success is to make the least negative impact possible when staging the event. Impacts can be physical, environmental, social, economic, technological or political. They may be felt in the host community or affect the broader region or country in which they are hosted. Importantly, events may have different impacts at various stages of their life cycle. For example, failed bids for major sporting events may have negative financial impacts but may also have positive ones as the momentum gathered in preparation of the bid may not be lost but be channelled towards partnerships for other developmental projects.
- Benefits to staff, host community and event participants: Events are projects that aim to achieve particular outcomes. Staff involved in the delivery of these can benefit from the exposure they have in the process. This could be through training and development and by gaining experience in event management. Host communities may benefit from the event in terms of tourism or redevelopment. Other benefits may accrue such as civic pride and respect for members of the community as well as financial gain for local businesses and staff who become temporarily involved with the event. Likewise, event participants may have such a positive experience that it benefits their future involvement with the sport specifically as well as their overall well-being more broadly.
- Being economical with the spending of resources: This critical success factor relates to the central notion of sustainability. If events are wasteful of resources, be it human (e.g. wasted manpower), physical (e.g. damage to natural reserves), financial (e.g. unnecessary costs) or intangible (e.g. goodwill of volunteers) then they are damaging the sustainability of the organisation hosting the event, of the broader community or both. The current focus on

the CO_2 emissions of events is an example of this and many events make commitments to reduction of emissions as part of their bid or as a KPI.

THE STAGES OF EVENT ORGANISATION

Events have a start and end date that is preceded by a date when the idea of the event was conceived and born. From that point steps and processes are put in motion for the event's life cycle to unfold.

Event organisers may become overwhelmed by the volume of work facing them but careful planning can ensure that critical targets are met at the right time. The pacing and exact nature of the steps in the event's execution need to be decided in line with the event's aim, objectives and scope. There are seven stages to the planning of events.

Stage one: final confirmation of the event's aims

Notwithstanding the importance of having an initial clear vision of the event's aims, once the decision has been made to proceed with the event, the process of planning and negotiation with various stakeholders may reveal the need to reconsider these aims and adapt them to the reality of the circumstances surrounding the event. On many occasions bid committees for sport events state overambitious aims in their attempts to win the hosting of the event. When awarded the event the organising committee is faced with delivering its promises and it is then appropriate to consider what can be realistically delivered. As prices fluctuate and budgets are affected by economic cycles, successful event organisers should strive for flexibility in the expected deliverables.

Stage two: a feasibility study

The conduct of a thorough feasibility study for the event is often the suitable second stage in process, although an initial study should have been carried out at the bidding phase. This will assist organisers in identifying whether the critical requirements for the event exist or can be available in time. This study will also identify all relevant stakeholders and their relative power in supporting, shaping or altering parts or aspects of the event. Financial and general resource considerations will also be included, in addition to a SWOT analysis (Chapter 4) and an analysis of the external environment, which will help organisers build a picture of the event's viability.

eleni theodoraki

Stage three: identifying the necessary functional areas

Once the feasibility study has confirmed the viability of the event, it is then necessary to identify the functional areas that will be involved in the planning and delivery of the event. Planning tasks is an essential aspect of organising a sport event. Even if the planning is based on precise event regulations and on the organisers' past experience, which gives them greater insight and responsiveness, planning is essential for ensuring that the unique characteristics of each sport event are taken into account and for adapting to the inevitable unexpected challenges.

The areas that are often required include human resources for the recruitment and training of the event management team, marketing, finance, security, facilities management, operations management, communication and accreditation of competitors or participants, and guests. As the functional areas take shape and activity commences within them, a better overview of the tasks required becomes clearer. At this stage, event managers also identify any infrastructure works that are required by the facility owners and commence discussions with sponsors, if applicable. Within each functional area sub-projects are then identified. Common functional areas for an event include:

- Function 1: management and coordination: This function affects the following areas: budget estimates and financial engineering; functional organisation, hierarchical structure and personnel management; task planning, follow-up and adjustment of tasks; and legal and regulatory issues.
- Function 2: managing sport operations: This function ensures that the event actually happens. It puts in place the plans of the management and coordination function, and its activities involve everything from evaluating the human and material resource requirements to appraising the work performed by personnel, including setting up competition spaces and warm-up areas.
- Function 3: secretarial, administrative and management work: This function includes administrative and secretarial tasks, but it also involves financial relations with service providers, accounting, ticketing management and additional services. This function plays an important supporting role for the other functions, occurring in all phases of the event. The secretarial tasks of communicating with the public and key stakeholders, managing mail and record keeping are vital to the success of the event.
- Function 4: logistics: This function has two main areas. The first involves setting up the facilities to be used for the event, with security being the number one priority for all audiences. This occurs when the infrastructure of the event is put into place. The second main area of work for this function involves managing and maintaining amenities during and after the event, with the dismantling or transferring of facilities being of key importance.

- Function 5: promotion and sales: The promotion and sales function deals with marketing, communication and media partnerships. This function includes the following tasks, which require substantial work at an early stage when planning the event:
  - setting up a marketing strategy for the event
  - defining a communication strategy and a media action plan
  - researching, managing, following up on and initiating partnerships.

Stage four: project management

This process will be discussed in greater detail below; however, the success of an event relies on careful project management. Critical dates for achievement of milestones should be identified and risks calculated for a number of choices and the implications of sub-projects running late or failing to deliver on time. With time, activity within each functional area becomes more established.

Stage five: event testing

It is important that event planning includes the opportunity for tests of preparedness of staff and facilities to ensure gaps are identified and remedial action can be taken before the event. Test events are often carried out at this stage that allow managers to gather valuable data on how the overall management and any systems on which the event relies perform. Facilities are inspected and details of operations can be made available to any stakeholders who may be awaiting reports on progress and delivery of commitments. As the event date approaches, participants and other stakeholders need to be contacted for information on the exact arrangements and what will be available and expected of them at the event.

Stage six: delegation of tasks

When the event starts, the delegation of tasks in the venues becomes essential as the event team play their respective roles. The event manager is often called upon for decisions to be made on issues that arise during the event and it is crucial that these are not issues that could have been anticipated, or should have been dealt with by another member of the team. In addition, they should not lead to the event manager being away from the centre stage of the event to resolve them, unless the manager's authority has been fully delegated to another team member. The welcoming services, performers, officials, hosts, the media and facility managers, as necessitated by each event, need to perform their roles until the event draws to a close.

Stage seven: finishing the event

At this seventh stage, the challenge is to maintain the interest of the event team and any stakeholders in order to complete remaining tasks. Bills need to be paid and accounts audited and closed, volunteers, patrons and sponsors officially thanked, staff that may now be looking for a new job need to be provided with letters of support and the press representatives may need to be chased for reviews and any post-event coverage. Until these tasks have been competed the event has not finished.

KEYS TO THE SUCCESSFUL DELIVERY OF EVENTS

It is widely accepted that prescribing how events should be planned can be disadvantageous as organisers may follow the letter but not the spirit of the guidance. Notwithstanding this proviso, a number of key issues emerge in event management that are central to the chances of an event's success.

Timely preparation

Events are invariably time bound. A date is set for their hosting and once set it is rarely able to be changed. Events typically have a very short time of intense activity (a morning, day, week, one or few months but not any longer). Such time constraints mean that there is seldom any room for delays. Preparations need to start in time for all activities to be completed before the event; and if parts of the event organisation are not completed in time, sub-projects may need to be cancelled so that the main event's integrity is not compromised. If, for example, there are delays in the planning permission for building necessary new sports facilities, it may be necessary either to pay a higher premium to the contractor who will have to work under pressure to deliver on time or to reconsider the event requirements or contractual obligations and host the event using alternative or existing facilities. In some circumstances it may be actually better to cancel the event altogether as this will minimise costs and risks even at the expense of the reputation of the failed hosts.

As the date of the event approaches and plans are progressing, the event team needs to better acquaint itself with the facilities where the event will be hosted. In some cases it may be necessary for the event team to move to temporary offices in the event's venue, a process called venuisation, whereby the final preparations and the event itself are managed by a team physically based in the venue. This is to ensure that the team fully understands the particular features of the venue and has a better overview of the event as it will unfold in that particular environment. As stated above, during event preparations it is also important to perform test events. If, for example, the regional sport competition event relies on the work by volunteers to perform crowd management in the venue, it is important to provide real life training to these volunteers in an event that is less challenging and publicly visible, such as a local competition.

Inclusion of key stakeholders and understanding their expectations

Whoever leads the event's preparation needs to understand the roles of others in the success of the event and event, stakeholders may be found inside or outside the immediate boundaries of the voluntary sport organisation. The line manager of the event manager hosting a friendly football match, his/her superiors, the event manager's peers, participants or spectators that are expected to attend, other staff in the organisation involved with the facilities and promotion have expectations of the event manager and their own means of assessing the effectiveness of the event's preparations and hosting.

Other stakeholders outside the organisation may include sponsors, regulators, funders, the local or regional government, media and the press. When the event is hosted by the voluntary sport organisation on behalf of another organisation, contractual obligations often predefine the success criteria that the host needs to consider. An example of this occurs in European competitions that are hosted by the national federation and a local organising committee. The 'owners' of the event have their own development agenda that is not necessarily identical to the agenda of the local hosts of the event. In this case, event requirements are predetermined and any planning by the hosts needs to work towards meeting these requirements. Legacy considerations need to also be in the forefront of the event manager's efforts as local communities will judge them by what remains in the host environment after the event is finished.

The various stakeholders that the event manager needs to works with and whose agendas will shape views on the event's ultimate success or relative failure include:

- the event owners who will expect the strength of the brand of their event to be maintained and enhanced through this particular staging
- the budget holders who will expect value for the investment of their resources
- any elected officials who were influential in the decision to host the event and will take the credit for its success or will be held accountable if it fails
- the colleagues of the event organiser in the sport organisation as they are likely to be involved in planning the event
- the guests, participants and spectators of the event as they are central to the operation

184

- the owners or managers of the facilities used for the event as their quality standards will affect the event's execution
- the sponsors of the event as they will expect to see a positive association of their brand name to the event
- the media and press representatives.

All the above stakeholders have the power to affect perceptions of the event's success and the event manager's performance. It is therefore of paramount importance to understand what the stakeholders expect from the event and what power they have over resources (financial, physical and human, as well as intangible, such as goodwill and brand name). Time and effort needs to be dedicated to meeting with stakeholders so that their interests are clear; and if competing interests exist between them, as is invariably the case, compromises must be reached before the event with agreements in place of what is considered acceptable. Juggling the expectations of the stakeholders becomes a fundamental task of the event manager who should also have a vision for the overall event and what its purposes are. The next step is to create synergies amongst stakeholders who will then collectively benefit from the event.

Project management

A project is a group of interrelated activities that are planned and then carried out in a certain sequence to create a unique service within a specified time frame. Therefore, an obvious example of a project is the staging of an event. Project management is necessary to deliver the event by a certain time, to a specified level of quality, with a given level of resources.

The characteristics of a project are:

- definable and measurable outcomes such as an event
- a start and end date
- a balance between time, cost and quality – the event should be the best it can be within these constraints
- a governance structure such as an organising committee
- a well defined multidisciplinary project team with the skills necessary to make the event a success
- involvement of stakeholders such as athletes and sponsors
- criteria to measure project performance such as satisfied athletes and officials, or money raised.

The management of a project such as an event involves the following elements:

- Planning and scoping: No matter how small the project, time must be spent on a clear definition and statement of the areas of the project. The scope of the project is more than the work involved and includes:

- outcomes: the project itself – the event
- stakeholders: individuals or groups with a vested interest in the project
- work required
- resources: money, time and volunteers.
- Governance: The management structure of the project is known as the governance of the project. In the case of the event, this is the organising committee. The structure identifies the specific players, their roles and responsibilities and the way in which they interact. In short, who does what.
- Stakeholder management: Stakeholders are the people or organisations who have an interest in the project process, outputs or outcomes and will be involved in ensuring the project's success. They need to be involved early, communicated with regularly and their involvement carefully planned and managed.
- Risk management: Risk management involves identifying, analysing and planning a response to potential threats to the project (see Chapter 12).
- Resource management: This is more than simply managing the money. It requires:
  - managing what people need to do
  - how and when they do their tasks through scheduling
  - providing suitable accommodation for the project team
  - managing information between stakeholders
  - working to an agreed budget
  - meeting deadlines.

This is perhaps the key to a successful project.

- Quality management: It is important to agree on the level of quality the project owner, such as an NOC, expects as this will have an effect on the budget. Quality can be managed by engaging staff and volunteers with appropriate skills, monitoring progress against an agreed schedule and delivering an event that meets requirements.
- Status reporting: Status reports should be given on a regular basis and include details about major activities and tasks that have been achieved, the budget, issues of concern and risks.
- Evaluation: Measurement against well defined criteria is necessary for all projects so that success can be demonstrated.
- Closure: The formality of the closure process will be determined by the project itself. It may involve:
  - formal handover to the project owner, such as the Olympic Delivery Agency handing the venues over to the Organising Committee
  - a review of the project outputs and outcomes against the plan
  - completion or reassignment of outstanding tasks
  - finalising records and documentation

- deciding what to do with staff and volunteers that have worked on the project
- 'loose ends', which is anything else that may be left to do!

Gantt charts

There are a number of project planning tools that can help to deliver the event on time at as high a level of quality as possible. The most helpful of these is a Gantt chart, which is a tool for helping plan and monitor projects. Gantt charts can be created by simply using 'post it' notes or a whiteboard. Basic word processing software within a table format can also be used.

The essential concept behind project planning is that some activities are dependent on other activities being completed first. For example, it is not a good idea to start building a sport stadium before it has been designed. These dependent activities need to be completed in a sequence, with each stage being nearly completed before the next activity can begin. Dependent activities are known as 'sequential' or 'linear'. Other activities are not dependent on completion of any other tasks. These may be done at any time before or after a particular stage is reached. These are non-dependent or 'parallel' tasks.

Drawing a Gantt chart

To draw up a Gantt chart follow these steps:

- Step 1: List all activities in the plan. For each task, show the earliest start date, estimated length of time it will take, and whether it is parallel or sequential. If tasks are sequential, show which stages they depend on. This will result in a task list like the one in Figure 10.1, which shows the task list for staging a simple event.
- Step 2: Head up graph paper with the days or weeks through to task completion.
- Step 3: Plot the tasks onto the graph paper and draw up a rough draft of the Gantt chart. Plot each task on the graph paper, showing it starting on the earliest possible date. Draw it as a bar, with the length of the bar being the length of the task. Above the task bars, mark the time taken to complete them. Schedule them in such a way that sequential actions are carried out in the required sequence. Ensure that dependent activities do not start until the activities they depend on have been completed. This will produce a diagram like Figure 10.2.
- Step 4. The last stage in this process is to prepare a final version of the Gantt chart. This shows how the sets of sequential activities link together, and identifies critical path activities. At this stage the resources of the various activities need to be confirmed and, while scheduling, it is important to make best use of the resources available, and to not overcommit resources.

187

Task	Earliest start	Length	Type	Dependent on
A. Deciding to stage the event	Week 0	1 week		
B. Forming an event committee	Week 1	1 week	Sequential	A
C. Allocating responsibilities	Week 1	1 day	Sequential	B
D. Choosing and booking venue	Week 2	1 week	Parallel	
E. Deciding sponsorship strategy	Week 2	1 week	Parallel	
F. Determining competition structure	Week 2	2 weeks	Parallel	
G. Attracting sponsorship	Week 3	5 weeks	Sequential	E
H. Attracting volunteers	Week 3	5 weeks	Parallel	
I. Sending out entry forms	Week 4	4 weeks	Sequential	F
J. Organising officials	Week 4	4 weeks	Sequential	F
K. Arranging programme	Week 8	1 week	Sequential	I
L. Setting up for event	Week 9	2 days	Parallel	
M. Training of volunteers and officials	Week 9	1 day	Parallel	
N. Stage event	Week 9	1 day	Sequential	D–M
O. Review and evaluate	Week 9	1 week	Sequential	N

Figure 10.1 Staging an event

Gantt charts are useful for planning and scheduling events as they allow an event manager to assess how long an event should take to organise, determine the resources needed, and lay out the order in which tasks need to be carried out. They are useful in managing the dependencies between tasks. When the organisation of the event is underway, Gantt charts are useful for monitoring progress. What should have been achieved at a point in time is immediately clear, and organisers can therefore take remedial action to bring the event back on course. This can be essential for the successful implementation of the event.

CHALLENGES FOR EVENT ORGANISERS

Although events often bring a number of benefits to the sport organisation staging the event and its host community, some authors (Flyvbjerg et al, 2003; Flyvbjerg, 2004) offer worrying views over the consequences of major sport events. The challenges associated with the staging of large, or mega events are:

■ The owner of the event and their relative monopoly power over the organisers: Under the strict confines of a host contract, event organisers are

188

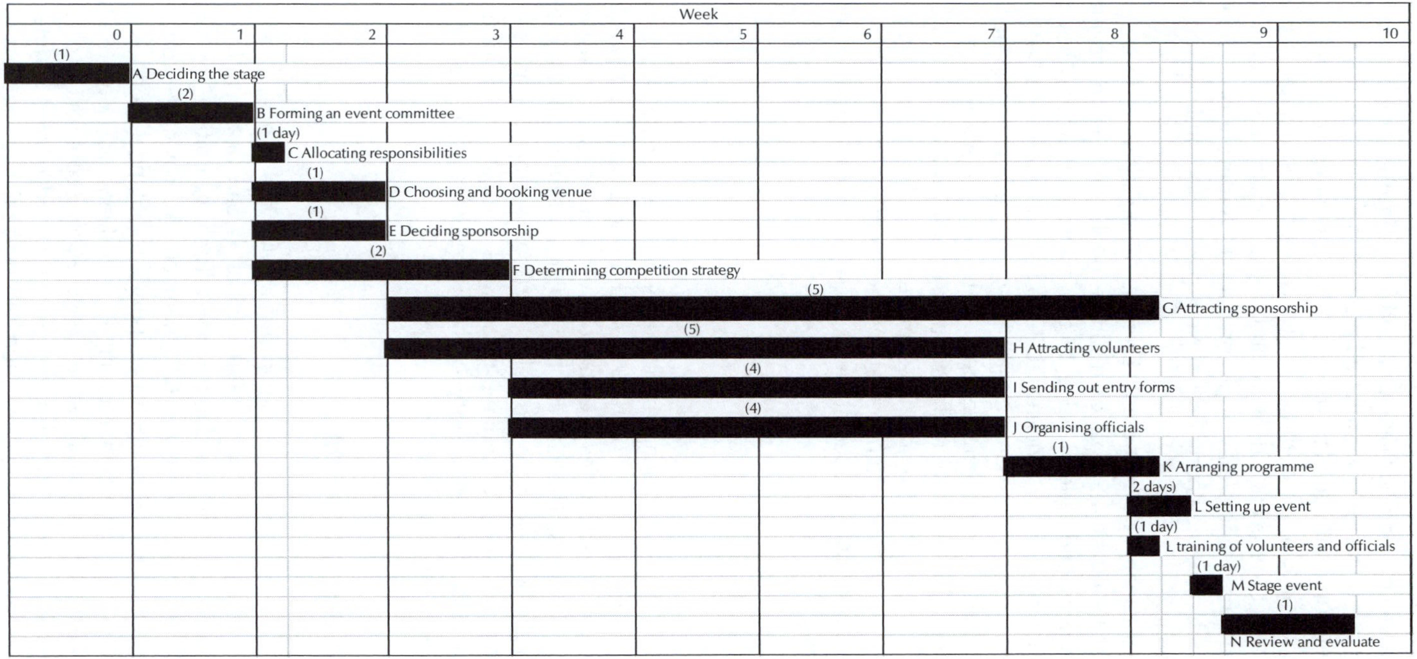

Figure 10.2 Gantt chart for organising an event

obliged to protect the brand of the event and follow instructions that may run counter to common sense or established practice in the host environment.

■ The local development agenda: There are often attempts to hijack event preparations to fit such an agenda. Budget overruns and delays may then accrue that affect the event's delivery and overall impact. Local politicians as well as business leaders may apply pressure to the event organisers for additional work or reorientation of the event preparations in line with their personal agenda.

■ The cost of sustainable development: Event sustainability refers to an event that is not achieved at the cost of resource depletion. On the contrary, sustainable events offer added value to the community where they take place and opportunities for synergies that would have otherwise been lost. For an event manager to ensure sustainability, the parties affected need to be considered and event organisers need to be alert to practices that may be wasteful, or against the law, and harmful to people and the environment. Unfortunately, many host communities are left with the results of a series of actions that were taken often in haste as the event's start was looming or when business interests prevailed at the expense of what would truly benefit the community.

SUMMARY

The need for skills in event management has grown worldwide as specialist knowledge has been required to cater for the increased demand from communities, companies and cities seeking to use events for social, marketing and development purposes. This chapter has defined and discussed the types of events that might be hosted by the voluntary sport sector and has set out the stages an event organising committee might work through. In addition, the chapter has highlighted what is necessary for the successful staging of events and some of the tools that might assist with this.

CASE STUDY: ROWING CLUB DINNER

This case study sets out the event management tasks and processes as they unfolded in a voluntary rowing organisation, which is part of a nautical club that also includes sailing and tennis club members. The organisation has been in operation since 1931 and currently has 600 members. Approximately one year ago the idea of establishing closer links with existing and potential sponsors of the club was aired during a club meeting among its president, two vice presidents and secretary general. The intention was to invite existing sponsors and senior members of the local community in business, education and local government to be associated with the club as corporate members with privileged access to the club's facilities. In return they would offer guidance on the club's future plans, access to possible sources of funding and add kudos to the organisation.

Following internal approval of the idea by its board, the club's secretary general was asked to undertake the task of sourcing suitable candidates from business, education and government and approaching them to establish whether they would be interested in joining the club. After careful consideration 50 nominees were sent formal invitation letters from the president that outlined the brief and future terms of engagement with the club if they were interested. Thirty accepted the new posts and after a couple of months the board decided that the club should host a formal gala dinner to officially welcome the new corporate members. This event was to have a celebratory tone and would be an important occasion to enhance the internal and external image of the club.

The board sought ideas on how best to host this event and who would be the most qualified person to do this. The secretary general recommended one of the full-time coaches of the club that had led preparations for similar events in the past. The coach (Maria) agreed to take responsibility for organising the event on a voluntary basis and she was promised the full support of the secretary general and other members of the board. This was three months prior to the event that was intended to be held in the adjacent premises that belonged to the club.

At that early stage Maria felt that it was important to understand what the senior management was trying to achieve and what the background was of the people for whom she was preparing this event (i.e. the new corporate members). Following a number of short discussions with the secretary general she realised that she had to find a date that would suit most persons and set out to find out the availability of the club's senior management. Once a date was established she checked the availability of the corporate members by e-mailing them a message that outlined the nature of the invitation and sought a response on availability. The vast majority of the members were available and enthusiastic about the event.

Having secured a date she checked for suitable venues to host the dinner in-house and booked the appropriate rooms in the club's premises. One reception room was going to be used for the guests before and after the dinner and the other would be laid out for the dinner. There was no charge for the two rooms as the venue was owned by the club. Maria then had meetings with the person on the board that was in charge of marketing, publicity and public relations and together they agreed a list of what needed doing before the event. Although Maria would not hold the budget herself (the secretary general did) she was given a relatively free rein on decisions that related to expenditure. After booking the venues approximately two months before the event, she had to decide on the menu. With suggestions from the catering manager Maria chose a menu that had proven appropriate in similar occasions and cleared the cost of £20 per person with the secretary general. Additional expenditure that had to be agreed included the decoration of the two rooms with flower arrangements. This was in the region of £150.

One month prior to the event Maria thought that the corporate members would welcome a reminder of what they agreed earlier and that this should come from the president of the nautical club. She drafted a letter that was given to the president and after some additions and alterations it was sent from his office to the 30 corporate members. It also contained questions about any dietary requirements and advice on parking arrangements was offered. The latter had been previously agreed by Maria with the security office of the club and there would be allocated parking available for 30 cars on the day.

Most corporate members responded overwhelmingly positively by replying to the president's invitation, but half a dozen did not reply at all. Some reported dietary requirements and these were noted by the president's secretary and passed on to Maria who then informed the catering manager. At approximately the same time, the board member in charge of marketing and publicity contacted Maria to agree how best to promote this event externally by securing newspaper or television coverage. He drafted a press release and Maria showed it to the secretary general and the president for suggestions and any comments.

The club used an outside public relations company with links to the media and Maria realised how important publicity would be for her event to be successful. As she knew from previous events and discussions with the secretary general, the sailing and tennis clubs within the nautical club were important stakeholders and their perceptions of the dynamism and success of the rowing club were highly significant and affected decision making related to funding and infrastructure development.

Although a small core of staff including the president, the secretary general, the board member in charge of publicity and the catering manager more or less knew what Maria was doing, she had the overall view and it became apparent that she needed to keep the secretary general better informed of preparations as these were progressing rapidly. Maria realised that other staff in the rowing club had heard of the preparations and were eager to find out what was happening. Following discussions with the secretary general on whom to invite, Maria informed the internal guests, and all were able to attend. Some were senior representatives from the sailing and tennis clubs and others included the respective head coaches and assistant coaches. Twenty people in total were invited and Maria updated the catering manager with the numbers and the respective catering requirements.

One week prior to the event, preparations were culminating and final numbers were needed by the caterers. Maria contacted all corporate members that had initially accepted the invitation but not replied to the president's official letter. It transpired that some were unable to attend because of other commitments but others had somehow not received the president's letter. Eventually five more positive replies were secured and the final number of 46 guests was given to the catering manager two days prior to the event. At the same time, the press release was sent by the communications company to the media on their contact list, and the president's office got in touch with Maria and the secretary general about the president's speech at the dinner. The group whose idea it was to invite the corporate members brainstormed again over a few email communications to rehearse the main ideas behind this initiative and a briefing note reached the president two days prior to the event. Table plans were also needed by the catering manager. She had to take into consideration the layout of the room and was assisted by the catering manager who was able to send her plans of the seating and also recommend the nature of the layout, i.e. round or rectangular tables and number of guests per table.

Maria tried to intersperse the external with the internal guests and also position the president appropriately. The table plan was cleared by the president's office and the secretary general and then sent to the catering manager. Name badges were produced by Maria to be taken to the event venue. One day prior to the event, the photographer that covered the club's competitions contacted Maria to ask the timing of the event and inform her that he would be taking photos, at the president's recommendation. At the same time, journalists from the local newspaper contacted the secretary general to find out what the club was trying to achieve and how this would enhance the sporting opportunities for the town's youth. The following morning the local radio representative also telephoned to find out more and promised to run a short story on the club's new initiative. The journalist was particularly interested to find out what the business, education and local government people had to offer to the club and what they were getting in return in terms of use of the seafront club facilities.

At the start of the event day Maria had last minute email communications with the president, the secretary general and the catering manager about the event and spent a few hours at her desk answering emails and phone calls from the guests. Some could no longer attend and were writing to send apologies, others wrote to say they would be slightly late and others contacted her to find out the time of the event as they had misplaced the invitation letter. The local photographer also got in touch, as well as the photographer from the main town newspaper. They both wanted a photo of all the guests as they gathered and Maria asked the two photographers to arrive at the start of the event for that to take place. As the day passed, Maria felt confident that things were overall under good control and looked forward to seeing the guests arrive.

Two hours prior to the start of the event she went to the adjacent venue to see the room decorated and laid out with the menus, the table plans and the name plates and she then took some time to herself to get ready for the start. Forty-five minutes prior to the start of the event Maria took the name badges to the venues and was joined by the secretary general and other internal guests. The secretary general informed Maria and the others that the event had just been mentioned in the local radio and that he thought the newspapers were also running a piece for the next day. Thirty minutes from the start of the event the photographers arrived.

The club's president arrived shortly after and then the rest of the guests. A few of the other rowing coaches helped Maria distribute all the name badges and chaperoned guests towards the reception room where drinks were offered and music played. The rooms appeared full of energy and it was clear that the guests were enjoying each other's company. Just after 7.30 p.m. the catering staff prompted guests to find their table by looking at the table plans that were posted on the entrance doors and the name plates on the tables. At around 7.45 p.m. the president gave his speech that welcomed all new corporate members and emphasised the importance of the relationship. He praised the club's paid and unpaid staff for the club's success and outlined his vision for the future, which included additional links to schools that would foster participation and links with the industry that would bring in sponsorship and management expertise. Soon afterwards a three-course dinner was served and the guests appeared to be having friendly and lively discussions. The table plan arrangements had worked although there were some last minute changes from cancellations that the catering manager had to take care of.

As the event drew to a close and people started leaving it was clear it had been a success. The event was celebratory and had run smoothly. Staff congratulated Maria and she thanked all for their hard work. The chef had asked for feedback on the menu, which the secretary general offered and passed on some of the guest comments. The next day the board member in charge of publicity reported that three newspapers had covered the event, one had also included a photo and that two radio programmes mentioned it. Maria was thanked again by the secretary general.

Looking back Maria realised that the success of the event was secured by a number of critical factors which were:

- the clarity over the event's aims and unanimous support of the overall idea
- the early allocation of tasks to her and the team of people surrounding her
- the role she played in pulling everyone's efforts together and respecting other's opinions
- the preparedness to adapt plans when new information came in
- her relative free rein over decisions without having to report everything to the secretary general
- the timely communication with stakeholders
- appropriate decisions over budget and who to invite
- special attention to the needs of the media
- respect for protocol regarding the president's and senior management's role
- last minute availability and checks

194

- the early marketing and public relations plan
- timely transfer of operations from office to venue
- the constant liaison with the facility managers.

Having these features in place meant that the development and implementation of the event went smoothly. Most importantly, Maria had planned the event in a systematic and comprehensive manner. She had started planning in plenty of time, consulted regularly with key stakeholders, clearly understood the aims of the event and was able to develop and implement an event to meets these aims. Her planning meant that the unique characteristics of the event were taken into account and she was able to adapt to the inevitable unexpected challenges. As a consequence, the event was successful.

ADDITIONAL ACTIVITIES

- Select a voluntary sport organisation you are familiar with that is involved with event hosting.
- Which of the types of events mentioned earlier does the organisation host? Consider the event held most often:
  - What is the rationale for holding this event?
  - Who are the stakeholders that will influence the event's success?
  - How are the impacts of the event assessed?
  - How is the performance of the event manager assessed?

FURTHER READING

Allen, J., O'Toole, W., McDonnell, I. and Harris, R. (2005) Festival and Special Event Management, 3rd edition. Sydney: John Wiley & Sons Australia Ltd.

Getz, D. (2007) Event Studies: Theory, Research and Policy for Planned Events. Oxford: Butterworth-Heinemann.

Masterman, G. (2009) Strategic Sports Event Management: Olympic Edition, 2nd edition. Oxford: Butterworth-Heinemann.

PART III

ISSUES IN THE MANAGEMENT OF VOLUNTARY SPORT ORGANISATIONS

CHAPTER 11

THE LEGAL DIMENSION

Andy Gray and Sarah James

Voluntary sport organisations, like any other organisations, have obligations under law. To fulfil these can at times be no small task as the range and quantity of laws affecting the sector can make it difficult for voluntary organisations to keep abreast of the relevant laws and the latest developments. Unfortunately this chapter is not able to offer legal advice to voluntary sport organisations, as the subject is simply too large to cover! However, it is recognised that there are certain areas of law that repeatedly cause voluntary sport organisations anxiety. They include the following:

- governance issues
- the employment of coaches and support staff
- management of volunteers
- data protection rules
- child protection
- sale of alcohol by sport organisations
- gambling
- playing of music at sporting events
- health and safety.

All of the above are intrinsic to the running of a voluntary sport organisation. It is therefore hoped to give a flavour of the principles underpinning these areas. Where there are any questions or concerns, there can, however, be no alternative to proper legal advice by a qualified legal professional.

GOVERNANCE ISSUES

As set out in Chapter 3, the good governance of a VSO is essential because it helps to map out how authority and responsibility is shared between the governing body (be it a committee, board of trustees or board of directors) and the wider organisation; it also serves to limit the liability of the governing body arising from its various responsibilities. The basis of operation for the governing body will be set out in the governing document of the voluntary sport organisation, sometimes called the 'constitution'. This is a critical document, as not only must it take into account any applicable legal requirements but it also sets out quite practical details regarding the running of the organisation.

There are a number of different forms that the governing document may take. The appropriate form for any one voluntary sport organisation depends upon how it has been set up. If it has been set up as a members club, the governing document is a relatively simple set of rules regarding the running of the voluntary sport organisation. If it has been set up as a charity and/or company it will need to comply with the regulatory requirements prescribed for each and/or both, and therefore the governing document will be quite a technical and complex document.

A large number of voluntary sport organisations in the UK are members clubs. The most likely reason for this is that they are very simple to set up and also to run. To assist affiliated members, many sport governing bodies have produced model documents for them to tailor to suit their individual circumstances. That said, there are often mandatory clauses that are required for affiliation and which must be preserved at all costs in order for membership to be bestowed by the governing body. For example, all members must pay membership fees.

Two of the different (and, at present, the more common ways) in which a voluntary sport organisation may be set up are expanded upon briefly below.

Members clubs

A members club is recognised in law as a creature of contract,[1] with the rules of the club forming a contract between members. For that reason, it is important that new members are provided with and sign a copy of the current rules and by-laws. Any failure to do so may present problems subsequently, if they seek to rely upon the conditions of the 'contract' – for example, in the event of a dispute. Along the same reasoning, any amended rules must be communicated to the membership and it is recommended that this be undertaken by individual notification, rather than simply placing the information on the club noticeboard, to make sure that all members receive notice of the amendments.

The above notwithstanding, there are legal limits placed on the ability of minors to enter into contracts that must be factored into the governing document. Whilst younger members may stll be given membership rights (e.g. voting), this is different from being able to enforce responsibilities. For this reason, it is usual to have an acknowledgement from the young person's parent or guardian.

On an operational note, the arrangements for the day-to-day management of its affairs are a matter for individual clubs to decide but this is usually delegated to a committee, who are elected by the members. Because a committee's powers are delegated from the membership, all committee members must agree unless the rules provide for a majority of members to determine issues. Provided the committee acts within the powers granted to it and does not act incompatibly with its governing document, it is otherwise up to the members of the committee to determine their own methods and procedures. However, the guiding principle should always be that the powers of a committee are only to be exercised in the interests of the club as a whole and not in the interests of any particular section of the committee.

It is also often more practicable if the detailed regulations for the operation of the voluntary sport organisation come in the form of by-laws, which are again usually delegated to the committee. The advantage of this is that they can be altered in a normal meeting rather than requiring a special majority of membership votes at a general meeting. Of course, such delegated power is not suitable for all rules; they are, instead, often reserved for matters such as membership categories and club championship conditions.

There is, however, a significant downside to creation as a members club. As a creature of contract, the organisation does not have a legal existence as an entity separate from its members. It can therefore not sue or be sued in its own name, only through its officers. 'Officers' here mean the members of the committee/management body. This usually includes posts such as chair, secretary and treasurer, all of which are considered critical to the good governance of a members club. As a result, in legal terms there is a risk to these people and potentially the club's members, for debts and damages if not adequately covered by insurance.

That said, it is quite possible to include in the governing document certain indemnity clauses that if adopted by the voluntary sport organisation will cover these liabilities provided that they are incurred whilst acting entirely within the voluntary sport organisation's rules and any other rules, regulations and/or policies. To do otherwise means that insurance cover may not apply. It is also important to note that insurance cover may not extend to fines and penalties imposed under criminal law.

Company limited by guarantee

Given the above risks of liability, some voluntary sport organisations choose to register themselves under company law, so as to benefit from the resulting limited liability that this provides. Voluntary sport organisations that take this approach are said to be 'incorporated' and they will then have their own distinct legal identity (unlike members clubs). Incorporation can take one of two forms, and it is for the voluntary sport organisation to elect which is most appropriate to it:

■ it could become a company limited by shares

■   it could become a company limited by guarantee.

The difference between the two is that a company limited by shares normally has a working capital created by the issue of the shares. Members invest their capital into the company by purchasing the shares in the expectation that a dividend will be paid in respect of those shares. Such companies are therefore formed with the intention of trade or profit. For that reason, many sport organisations seeking incorporation do so in the other form, and it is therefore that form that will be considered at more length.

A company limited by guarantee is not allowed to have any share capital. Instead of buying shares, the members of the company give a guarantee. The amount of the guarantee must be stated in its governing document, which must also state that the liability of members is limited. The usual guarantee used in the voluntary sport sector is small: usually in the region of £1.

The main benefit of incorporation from the members' point of view is that their liability is limited to that nominal sum that the members guarantee to pay on the winding up of the company. Other benefits are that it can also hold property and that it can sue and be sued in its own name. A disadvantage is the cost of incorporation. There are many formalities with which it is necessary to comply, such as setting up the company in the first place and subsequently in preparing and filing the annual return and audited accounts. Further, there is a great deal of regulation in this area. Company law can be complex and failure to comply with it can result in criminal action. It is therefore not by any means an easy option, or one that would suit most voluntary sport organisations. Further information is available from the website of the regulator in this area, Companies House: www. companieshouse.gov.uk.

In addition to the above distinct ways in which it is possible to set up a voluntary sport organisation, it is also possible to pursue certain special statuses in recognition of the special type of activity undertaken. In the sport sector, two are particularly relevant: charitable status and registration as a Community Amateur Sport Club.

Charitable status

Voluntary sport organisations may be eligible for charitable status if they are established for purposes that are exclusively charitable. Generally speaking charities are organisations set up for the benefit of the community. However, in the legal sense of the term, 'charitable' is quite a technical term.[2] Roughly speaking there are four elements to a charity:

■   It must be not for profit (i.e. any profits must be reinvested into the organisation).

- The formally stated objects of the charity must fall within 1 of 13 categories of charitable purposes listed by law:
  - The prevention/relief of poverty.
  - The advancement of education.
  - The advancement of religion.
  - The advancement of health or the saving of lives.
  - The advancement of citizenship or community development.
  - The advancement of the arts, culture, heritage or science.
  - The advancement of amateur sport.
  - The advancement of human rights, conflict resolution or reconciliation or the promotion of religious or racial harmony or equality and diversity.
  - The advancement of environmental protection or improvement.
  - The relief of those in need by reason of youth, age, ill health, disability, financial hardship or other disadvantage.
  - The advancement of animal welfare.
  - The promotion of the efficiency of the armed forces of the Crown, or the efficiency of the police, fire and rescue services of ambulance services.
  - Any other purpose accepted as charitable on the day that that part of the Act came into force and any purpose that is analogous to or within the spirit of the purposes listed in the Act or accepted as charitable after the new law comes into force.
- The object(s) must be exclusively charitable.
- The organisation must operate for the public benefit.

Several different types of organisation can qualify as a charity – for example, some charities are registered companies, some are trusts. However constituted, all charities must have a written formal governing document.

The main advantage of charitable status is the financial benefits derived from various taxation exemptions plus the public recognition that may accompany being a registered charity. On the other hand, charities are subject to various laws and if they have an income of more than £5,000 per annum, must register with the Charity Commission if they are based in England and Wales (Scotland has a separate charity law system). Thus if a charity was also, for example, set up as a company limited by guarantee, then it would also fall under the regulatory jurisdiction of Companies House.

It is therefore important that the voluntary sport organisation knows fully of the expectations upon it before registration as a charity. Moreover, once registered, the members of the management body will become known as 'trustees', and will in turn owe particular duties to the charity and have particular obligations under law. In broad terms they have the ultimate responsibility for managing the affairs of the charity and checking that it is well run, complies with its obligations and delivers its charitable objects. This may be summarised as owing duties of compliance, prudence and care. Further information is available from the website of the regulator of English and Welsh charities, the Charity Commission www. charity-commission.gov.uk.

Community Amateur Sport Club[3]

The Community Amateur Sport Club (CASC) scheme is designed to support grass-roots sport by acting as a financial recognition by the government that sport clubs pay a vitally important role in their communities. It does this by distinguishing between amateur sport clubs and businesses for business and tax purposes, thereby ensuring that money is kept in clubs.

The financial benefits include:

- 80 per cent mandatory business rate relief (it is possible for local authorities to offer up to 100 per cent relief to clubs at their discretion).
- Ability to raise funds from donations under Gift Aid. A registered CASC can reclaim £28 in tax for every £100 donated (although this does not presently apply to all types of donations).
- Tax free income from interest and capital gains (used for qualifying purposes).
- Exemptions from corporation tax on trading income (up to £30,000 per annum) and gross income from property (up to £20,000 per annum).
- CASCs whose income does not exceed those thresholds will no longer be required to complete an annual corporation tax return.

There are, however, certain eligibility requirements in order to have CASC status. The organisation must:

- be recognised by the sport council (e.g. Sport England) as a sport
- be organised on an amateur basis
- be community focused and open to all without discrimination
- have the promotion of amateur sport as its core purpose
- reinvest any income back into the club – the club must not operate for profit
- in the event of the club being wound up, all its remaining assets must be distributed to the sport governing body, another CASC or a registered charity.

The above requirements should normally be included in the governing document, and the regulator of CASCs, HM Revenue and Customs, must approve the document before CASC status can be granted. It should be noted that it is possible for CASCs to apply to the Charity Commission for charitable status too, providing it is also able to meet the required elements of a charity. Further information is available from the CASC website (run by the Central Council of Physical recreation, CCPR) at www.cascinfo.co.uk. Information is also available from HM Revenue and Customs website at www.hmrc.gov.uk/CASC/CASC_guidance.htm.

204

THE EMPLOYMENT OF COACHES AND SUPPORT STAFF

As the above section briefly highlighted, the employment of staff is one of the responsibilities that may open a voluntary sport organisation (and in particular the management body) up to liability. It is also a very technical area that can be difficult to fully comprehend. Across the sector, there are many active personnel delivering the services: some are engaged on a self-employed basis, others are employed under a contract of employment, and some donate their time free of charge as volunteers. Issues relating to volunteers will be considered later in this chapter as they do not need a contract in order to provide their services. The self-employed and employment routes on the other hand do necessitate certain formalities, and in the case of the latter, there are particular legal requirements that must be met by the employer when drawing this up.

The starting point is to decide whether it is a self-employed or employed position. There are certain advantages of each, which include:

Advantages to sport organisations of engaging a self-employed person:

■ The club will not have to take on the administrative difficulties of income tax, national insurance (including costs of employers' contributions) or statutory sick pay.
■ In law an employer is legally responsible for things done by his/her employee during the course of his/her employment. A club is unlikely to be similarly liable for the actions of a self-employed worker.
■ The club does not have to issue written statements of terms and conditions of employment (but is advised to use a standard form contract for services).
■ The club is not liable for unfair dismissal or redundancy on the termination of a relationship.

Advantages to coaches and support staff of being self-employed:

■ He/she will be free to undertake work from other sources without gaining permission from the club.
■ He/she can agree a pattern of work to fit in with personal commitments or other jobs.
■ He/she may engage other qualified persons to undertake the work when unable personally to provide it.
■ He/she may be able to negotiate better contractual terms than the equivalent employee.

Advantages to a voluntary sport organisation of engaging employees:

■ The contract of employment requires personal services, i.e. that a particular person must deliver the services.

- The club maintains a higher level of control over employees, particularly where the club wishes employees to perform tasks on the periphery of the job description.
- Disciplinary procedures and sanctions are available to the club as employer.
- The relationship is viewed as requiring a much greater degree of loyalty and good faith (and there are implied terms in the contract to this effect).

Advantages to coaches and support staff of being employees:

- There is less financial input and risk and less administration required by the individual – for example on tax matters. He/she may also be required to organise his/her own insurance if he/she is a volunteer.
- He/she is entitled to sick pay and other benefits, plus a pension scheme (where applicable).
- He/she is entitled to holiday pay (if applicable).
- There is greater job security by virtue of statutory rights, e.g. unfair dismissal, and also benefits of other statutory rights such as equal pay, and legally required terms and conditions.
- Indemnified by the club for expenses and liabilities occasioned in the course of employment.

However, it is not possible to simply elect which contract is most favourable – the law has established requirements as to when a person is fulfilling the role of employee and when they are an independent contractor. A voluntary sport organisation therefore needs to be careful that it does not find itself in a position where the relevant authorities do not accept the parties' classification of the working relationship, since the wrong classification can carry with it financial liabilities.

Generally the features of an employment context is that the person:

- has to do the work him/herself
- has a manager telling him/her at any time what to do, where to carry out the work or when and how to do it
- has to work a set amount of hours
- is paid by the hour, week or month
- is entitled to overtime pay and/or a bonus payment.

Generally the features of a self-employed arrangement are that the person:

- is able to hire someone to do the work for him/her or engage helpers at his/her own expense
- risks his/her own money on the venture
- provides the main items of equipment needed to do the job (not just the small tools many employees provide for themselves)

206

- agrees to do a job for a fixed price regardless of how long the job may take
- can decide what work to do, how and when to do the work and where to provide the services
- regularly works for a number of different people
- has to correct any unsatisfactory work in his/her own time and at his/her own expense.

Where the nature of the relationship is ambiguous (in the sense that it does not clearly fall within either of the above categories), it is possible to stipulate in an agreement what the legal relationship between them is to be. So, in borderline cases it may be that the inclusion of a specific clause in the contract to the effect of the status of the employee/contractor may be helpful. However, be warned: this is not a way to circumvent the above legal definitions; courts and tribunals will always be prepared to look behind the parties' express intentions and labels to ascertain the true nature of the relationship.

Where there is any doubt as to whether a person is rightly an employee or self-employed contractor, sport organisations may wish to seek professional advice in order to avoid potential problems with the HM Revenue and Customs (www. hmrc.gov.uk/index.htm) and also the Department for Work and Pensions (www. dwp.gov.uk/).

Recruitment and selection to an employed post

Once it has been decided that the post is correctly one of an employee, it is important to be aware of the considerable law in this area. The law applies as soon as a post is advertised and also extends through to the recruitment and selection process.

Potential employers should focus only on the requirements of the job when advertising, and should select objectively and consistently. Thus, there should not be any discrimination (for example, on the grounds of sex, race, disability, sexual orientation, religion or belief, or age) in the choice of the successful candidate, unless it falls within the exceptional circumstances allowed for by law.

Once a successful candidate has been chosen it is usual to send to them a letter containing a provisional offer of employment, which is conditional upon receipt of the usual pre-employment checks: satisfactory references, immigration checks, medical (if applicable) and Criminal Records Bureau (CRB) clearances (if applicable).

For the successful candidate, references from the previous employer should always be followed up in full in order to support or deny the information about the candidate. Equally, a CRB check (or 'CRB disclosure') should also be sought for the appointed person if applicable. The CRB produces considerable guidance

207

on this area, about which it is essential employers are aware (www.crb.gov.uk). In addition the voluntary sport organisation's governing body will have a policy with which it must comply. This area is considered in greater detail below under 'Child protection: safe recruitment strategies'.

In addition to checking the person is suitable for the post, it is also important to ascertain whether the person is eligible to work in this country. The Immigration, Asylum and Nationality Act 2006 (in force from February 2008) sets out the current law on the prevention of illegal migrants working in the UK. This puts the onus on the employer to check anyone it proposes to employ and to make sure that they have the right to work in the UK. Guidance is available from the UK Border and Immigration Agency at www.bia.homeoffice.gov.uk.

Obligations owed by an employer to an employee

Once the suitable candidate has been appointed, duties arise on each side. The ACAS website (www.acas.org.uk) is a good place to start to get a practical grounding in this area of law; ACAS is a governmental organisation that provides advice and support to employers and employees.

If it hasn't already done so, the voluntary sport organisation also needs to set itself up as an employer with HM Revenue and Customs. The following is a general overview of the obligations on employers:

- It is the duty of an employer to provide an employee, within two months of the employee commencing work, with a written statement of certain terms of employment (and further to keep the statement up to date as and when changes in those terms are agreed). This must be given to an employee even if his/her employment ends before this two-month period.
- The statement must include as a minimum the names of the employer and employee, and the date the employment began (including, if different, the date upon which the employee's period of continuous employment began).
- The statement must also contain the following (as at a specified date not more than seven days before the statement):
  - the scale of rate of remuneration or method of calculation of remuneration
  - the intervals at which remuneration is to be paid (e.g. weekly or monthly)
  - any terms and conditions in relation to:
    - hours at work
    - entitlement to holidays (including public holidays) and holiday pay (the particulars being sufficient to enable the employee to precisely calculate his/her entitlement including to accrued holiday pay on the termination of employment)
    - incapacity for work due to sickness or injury including any provision for sick pay

208

- pensions and pension schemes.
- the job title or brief description of duties
- the place of work (or if the employee is required or permitted to work at various locations an indication of that and the address of the employer)
- the length of notice that the employee is obliged to give and entitled to receive to terminate the employment
- where the employment is not intended to be permanent, the period for which it is expected to continue, or if the employment is for a fixed term, the date upon which it will end
- details of any collective agreement that directly affects the terms and conditions of employment
- where the employee is require to work outside the UK for a period of more than one month, certain information regarding the period manner of payment and other benefits and arrangements, and the conditions for his/her return to the UK.

- Where the employee is to commence work outside the UK before the expiry of the two-month period for furnishing of the statement, he/she must be given the statement no later than the date of his/her departure.
- If there are no terms and conditions relating to any of the matters covered above then this should be stated.
- With regard to any terms and conditions relating to incapacity, sick pay and pensions etc., the employee may be referred to some other document provided it is reasonably accessible them.
- The statement should note whether there is in force a contracting-out certificate issued in accordance with the Pension Schemes Act 1993.
- The written statement must also include details of the person to whom the employee should address any grievance relating to his/her employment and to whom he/she may apply if dissatisfied with any disciplinary decision relating to him/her. Any disciplinary or grievance rules should be specified or, alternatively, the employee may be referred to a separate document, again provided that it is reasonably accessible. All employers are required by law to have in place disciplinary and grievance procedures that comply with the statutory minimum requirements. For further details, visit the ACAS website. At present, there is no requirement to include any reference to any other matters such as, for instance, normal retirement age or maternity or other rights.

The above summary sets out the minimum legal obligations upon the employer. There may well be other matters that sport organisations and their legal advisers will need to consider when preparing a contract of employment or, indeed, a contract for services of a self-employed coach/support staff.

The provision of this statement does not automatically bestow upon the document the status of 'contract of employment'. However, at the very least the statement may be taken to constitute the employer's view of the terms of employment, and whether it can be taken to constitute the contract, or at least a part of it, may turn upon the basis by which the document is received by the employee. It would assist if an acknowledgement is taken from the employee, for example:

I acknowledge receipt of the particulars of terms of employment dated [ ] and further acknowledge and accept that some terms shall constitute terms of my contract of employment.

....

[Name of Employee]

In addition to the above contractual points, the employer needs to have in place disciplinary and grievance procedures, and other policies such as equality and diversity. Furthermore, it needs to ensure compliance with health and safety and undertake the necessary risk assessments; health and safety will be considered in further detail in Chapter 12.

Minimum wage

There is also a legal obligation on the employer to pay workers a prescribed minimum wage. Under the law, the onus is on the employer to prove that the minimum wage has been paid or is not due. The national minimum wage is applicable to most adult workers who:

■ are working legally in the UK
■ are genuinely not self-employed
■ have a written/or implied contract.

There are three levels of minimum wage. The rates from 1 October 2009 are:

■ 16–17 years old: £3.57
■ 18–21 years old: £4.83
■ 22 years and older: £5.80.

Clubs need to check to see what the current rate is for the national minimum wage as it is reviewed annually on 1 October. Since April 2009 employers who do not pay the correct minimum wage have been issued an automatic penalty of up to £5,000 even if it was simply a mistake. For the most serious of cases, they may be the subject of an unlimited fine.

Usually voluntary 'workers' do not qualify for the minimum wage. Thus there are clear advantages in having workers classed as voluntary workers as opposed to employees. That said, voluntary sport organisations need to be careful when they have in place arrangements for those who receive expenses for their volunteering or receive other benefits in certain circumstances, as these arrangements could inadvertently trigger minimum wage obligations.

MANAGEMENT OF VOLUNTEERS

In addition to employees and contractors, the sport sector relies heavily upon the generosity of volunteers. It is generally understood that a volunteer provides services free of charge. This of course means that there is a lack of any obligation on behalf of the sport voluntary organisation to provide work to the volunteer or, indeed, for the volunteer to accept any work offered.

The categorisation of a person as a volunteer is important. For example, whereas duties are owed to HM Revenue and Customs and the Department for Work and Pensions in relation to its employees, this is not the case for volunteers. However, care must be taken that these duties do not inadvertently arise in relation to volunteers, as a result of them receiving expenses or other forms of payment/ benefits in kind for the services they perform. For example:

■ Match day volunteers: Where a worker has access to a sporting event as part of their voluntary role (e.g. monitoring/assisting crowd safety, selling programmes, operating turnstiles), access to the event will not be treated as a non-cash benefit for minimum wage purposes.
■ Provision of uniform, jumpers etc.: Where a worker or someone acting in an official capacity at a sporting event is provided with clothing to enable them to be distinguished from competitors and members of the public, the provision of such clothing will not be treated as a non-cash benefit for minimum wage purposes. It should be noted that:
  ■ the item provided has to be reasonable, i.e. a jumper or a jacket for a worker may be acceptable, expensive sporting equipment may not
  ■ the item should be necessary to perform duties, i.e. for a worker to stand out from the crowd
  ■ if the item is allowed to be retained, it has to be a gift, i.e. they might expect to receive it but it must be the case that they're not entitled to receive it.
■ Free food or drink and honoraria: Where a free basic meal or drink is provided, such provision will be treated as reasonable subsistence. This could also cover cases where a reasonable honorarium is made, which may be expected, although there should not be any entitlement to the sum received. In such cases the provision of the food and drink or an honorarium would not on their own trigger eligibility for the minimum wage.

HM Revenue and Customs does reserve the right to take enforcement action where they believe workers are being exploited; for example, where benefits in kind are being offered on a scale as a replacement for monetary payments.

Workers also have the right to take their own case to an employment tribunal for recompense.

Expenses can be paid at a flat rate if they represent a fair and reasonable estimate of out of pocket expenses and it would be otherwise administratively cumbersome for the provider to calculate individual expenses. Therefore, a flat rate figure that represents genuine average expenses for a group of people would be acceptable. Records should be kept of all expenses paid and the organisation or club should be able to explain how they arrived at the level of expenses paid.

A coach (or similar) can provide additional time coaching on a voluntary basis and this time will not be considered as unpaid overtime. This will be the case as long as no payment is received for this period other than for actual or estimated legitimate expenses. However, it is critical that what happens in practice is not simply an extension of what the coach provides under his/her contract. For example:

- there is no obligation that the coach will be volunteering his/her time
- the original payment by the voluntary sport organisation is not provided on the basis of additional voluntary time being worked
- the coach is not under the direction of the voluntary sport organisation during the voluntary period, other than in connection with mandatory statutory obligations (e.g. in connection with child safety)
- the coach is free to go after the contracted time is completed and does not suffer any detriment if he/she does not volunteer.

Office holders are exempt from the minimum wage. Their defining characteristic is that the office, which exists independently of the person who fills it, defines rights and duties of the office holder. An office holder could be a club secretary or treasurer. However, if the office holder also holds a worker's contract with a named individual/employer, or he/she is working with both the expectation of and an entitlement to an honorarium, then he/she may be brought within the scope of the minimum wage.

Clubs should retain entries in cash and petty cash books, keep records of the identities of those receiving payments, when they 'work' and for how long. Clubs need to keep a record of how estimated expenses are calculated. This record keeping is for the club/s own benefit as the onus of proof lies with them should an individual claim that the minimum wage should have been paid.

Although volunteers are not subject to the same kind of obligations in law as employees, it can be useful to have a volunteer agreement in place. This sets out what the volunteer can expect from the organisation and vice versa. It should be stressed that this should not simply be the standard template employment contract otherwise used by the voluntary sporting organisation, with a few minor adjustments; rather, it should be a bespoke agreement specifically drafted to

212

cover the volunteering arrangement. The Volunteering England website is an excellent source of further information (www.volunteering.org.uk), including example volunteering agreements.

DATA PROTECTION

Within the structure of sport, there is usually a need for information relating to competitors, members and other participants to be passed between governing bodies, clubs, local and regional associations and event organisers. This use of information places the sector squarely within the data protection regime.

Data protection compliance in the UK is monitored by the Information Commissioner's Office (ICO). That is the independent authority set up to uphold information rights in the public interest, by promoting openness and requiring data privacy (www.ico.gov.uk). The law the Office works with, the Data Protection Act 1998, is not, however, the draconian regime it is often portrayed in the media: it seeks to strike an effective balance between the interests of individuals on the one hand and, on the other, those who wish to use the personal information. This is reflected in the stated main aims of the Act, which are to:

1   protect individuals' rights to privacy
2   ensure individuals' rights to access and correction of information held about them
3   prevent against any excessive and unreasonable retention of 'personal data'.

With the advent of the Act, all organisations holding personal data (referred to in the Act as 'Data Controllers') must comply with the principles of good management, as set out in the Act. The Act contains eight principles:

■   Personal information must be lawfully and fairly processed. In other words, there must be a legitimate reason for collecting and using personal data. Transparency is paramount, and it is important that a data protection notice (otherwise known as a 'privacy notice' or 'fair processing notice') be present when collecting data. It should contain details such as:
    ■   identity of organisations
    ■   purpose(s) for which the organisation intends to process the information
    ■   any extra information that might be required to process the information fairly.

The ICO has templates and a code on its website. This aims to ensure that organisations are open about their reasons for obtaining personal data and that what they do with the information is in line with the reasonable expectations of the individual.

- It should be processed for limited purposes.
- The personal information stored must be adequate, relevant and not excessive.
- It must be accurate and up to date.
- It must be kept for no longer than necessary, i.e. no more information to be stored than is required for the purpose for which it is being held. How long personal data (and indeed different categories of data) are retained depends upon the purpose for which it was obtained and its nature. Matters to take into consideration include:

  - The current and future value of the information
  - Costs, risks and liabilities associated with retaining the information
  - Ease/difficulty of making sure it remains accurate and up to date.

- It is processed in line with the subjects' rights. Data subjects have a number of rights:

  - a right of access to a copy of the information held about them
  - a right to object to processing that is likely to cause damage or distress
  - a right to prevent processing for direct marketing
  - a right to object to decisions made by automated means
  - a right to have inaccurate data rectified, blocked or erased in certain circumstances
  - a right to claim compensation for damages for breach.

- It must be held securely. This is to guard against unauthorised use, loss, destruction, disclosure or in any other way compromise the personal data held. Appropriate security measures very much depend upon the circumstances of the organisation and rather than a 'one size fits all' approach, it is best to adopt a risk-based approach that takes into account the nature of the information in question and the harm that might result from its improper use, loss, destruction or disclosure.
- It must not be transferred outside the European Economic Area (EEA) without adequate protection.

'Personal data' has a wide definition and includes both facts and opinions about a living individual from which it is possible to identify them. 'Identify' in this context does not just mean a person's name. Other identifying information will be sufficient to constitute personal data. The following is likely to be considered personal information:

- information on a computer (including emails) about an individual who can be identified from that information
- information in paper files
- information collected with a view to processing the information/storing it in the above ways.

Therefore name, address, national insurance number, photographs and email address are all examples of personal data that a voluntary sport organisation might regularly encounter.

Special rules apply where the data is of a 'sensitive' nature; for example information relating to race/ethnic origin, health and any criminal convictions/proceedings is all sensitive. In many cases (although not all), the individual's written permission to hold such information should be sought. That notwithstanding, there are special rules permitting the collection of information for equality of opportunity monitoring, providing there are adequate safeguards for the data subjects' rights. Given the nature of sensitive data, there are more stringent conditions for processing than with personal data.

In order to process personal data lawfully it must be processed in accordance with one of the conditions in Schedule 2 of the Data Protection Act 1998. Broadly speaking the consent of the individual is required unless one of the other conditions is relevant – for example when it is to comply with a legal obligation or under a contract. Consent for this type of data can be obtained by ensuring that members are given the appropriate clause to read (e.g. by publishing it on the website, membership form or noticeboard at the organisation's headquarters).

In relation to sensitive data, there are additional conditions, contained in Schedule 3, which must also be satisfied. This requires explicit consent to be obtained unless one of the other specified circumstances apply – for example it is necessary to comply with employment law or it has already been made deliberately available to the public.

Data protection law requires parental consent for the collection of data from children 12 years and under. Many sport governing bodies have, however, aligned their stance with their child protection policy and impose a higher threshold. Affiliated organisations are therefore required to adopt that higher threshold as part of their membership conditions.

All data controllers must comply with the Act. They must also register with the Information Commissioner unless they only have paper files (with the exception of computerised accounts and payroll activities, and the computerised membership records where members have consented to the records being kept and those records are only kept to send information to the members). Further information is available from the Information Commissioner through the notification hotline and the website, in particular, 'Notification Exemptions: A Self-Assessment'.

Voluntary sport organisations should be aware that in addition to requirements regarding the retrieval and the retention of data, there is also a right for members to see information about themselves, known as a 'subject access request'. Failure to cooperate with the process can result in enforcement actions being taken by the Information Commissioner. Equally if an individual or organisation considers that their personal information is not being processed in line with the eight principles above, they can also complain to the Information Commissioner, with enforcement action potentially being taken.

For most voluntary sport organisations, it will generally be the governing body who registers with the ICO and therefore there will not be any need to register independently. That said, there is still a requirement for them to comply with the conditions and principles of the Data Protection Act, as briefly outlined above. More information is available on the Information Commissioner's website. This includes guidance on how to store information securely (www.ico.gov.uk).

CHILD PROTECTION: SAFE RECRUITMENT STRATEGIES

Voluntary organisations in sport (typically private members clubs) are ultimately accountable to NGBs for sport through a process of affiliation. The jurisdiction of governing bodies is effectively consensual and based upon the contract formed or deemed to be formed (i.e. the 'contractual nexus') around the affiliation process. It is perhaps somewhat surprising that notwithstanding the significant public funding of sporting governing bodies (particularly in the UK) that there exists no statutory basis for their actions, which means the governing body has no powers over members of the public at large participating in their sport. The limitations of governing bodies to regulate their sport in a complete and harmonised manner is perhaps most starkly seen in the area of child safeguarding.

In many sports, with the advent of awareness of issues of child protection/child welfare, sport governing bodies have had to encounter the so-called 'parent from hell' syndrome. What action can the football authorities take against a parent attending a football match in which their child is participating and who is engaging in abusive actions possibly towards both their own child and the officials in question? To the extent that the individual is present on a public park where neither the participating teams nor the local county football association exercise powers to regulate under licence the admission of spectators (e.g. a ticketing regime), it is easy to see how such individuals can represent a painful challenge to governing bodies.

In such circumstances what is clearly required is common sense 'joined up thinking' involving all affected responsible bodies to ensure a just and appropriate outcome. In the situations described, the sport bodies may be well advised to liaise with the local authority, children's services and/or the police authorities in order to seek an effective resolution.

However, notwithstanding the strict legal position, there is clearly an expectation in the minds of the public that those asserting governing body authority in relation to a particular sport, be it the football association, the Amateur Swimming Association or a local club, should not seek to absolve themselves of responsibility for dealing with problems within their sport on such a dry legal

andy gray and sarah james

ground. Indeed governing bodies are expected by government to recognise their broader responsibilities partly by virtue of the recognition of their governing body status by the relevant governmental authorities such as Sport England, UK Sport and the sport lottery fund.

The Criminal Records Bureau – an analysis and evaluation of the current vetting process

The CRB was created in 1997. Prior to its establishment, access to criminal records information on individuals was regulated by a series of Home Office circulars or by determination of the Association of Chief Police Officers (ACPO) Sub-Committee on the Disclosure of Convictions. Information was made available for pre-employment checks and other purposes in a host of widely varying circumstances.

Accordingly, one immediate advantage of the establishment of the CRB was the intent to provide uniform and harmonised access to police records on a structured basis throughout England and Wales. However, as revealed in the Bichard Inquiry Report in connection with the Soham murders, practice has varied amongst the various police forces with regard to the retention and disclosure of criminal records information and other relevant police intelligence. This has resulted in the establishment of the Independent Safeguarding Authority, which is mentioned below, under the auspices of the Safeguarding Vulnerable Groups Act 2006.

Under the CRB checking regime the cooperation of the individual concerned is required in completing a standard application form, which is processed by an accredited registered person (or umbrella body) who is responsible for checking the identity of the individual applicant and forwarding the application form together with the fee payable (if applicable) to the CRB. Once the CRB checking process has been completed, a form of certificate is provided by the CRB to both the individual applicant and the registered person (or umbrella body) who submitted the application.

Where the registered person is the direct 'employer' this information can then be utilised as part of the employer's internal vetting process to ascertain the suitability of the candidate for the post applied for. If the application is submitted by an umbrella body (and many sport governing bodies have assumed this mantle), in most cases the information will be passed on by them to the 'employer', subject to the terms and conditions of the scheme as to confidentiality and other matters. Alternatively the umbrella body may make the recruitment decision on behalf of the prospective 'employer'.

The system allows access to information in relation to individuals who are prospectively to be involved in working with children and young persons, which clearly is of great significance to many sporting organisations whose membership predominantly comprises young people. The process is not limited to persons to be in paid employment and equally applies to those wishing to take up volunteer positions. Again, this is of crucial importance to many sporting governing bodies who are highly dependent upon volunteers providing support in club administration, coaching and teaching, and chaperoning/'helping' in various capacities in the grass-roots club environment. Dependent upon the structures within the sporting governing body acting as an umbrella organisation, either the information will be disclosed to the employing club to enable a recruitment decision to be made or alternatively the decision will be made centrally by the governing body subject to the relevant jurisdiction/constitutional framework.

Who can be required to complete an application?

A sporting organisation must ensure that it has the requisite lawful authority to compel an individual to participate in the CRB scheme. Two levels of checking are currently available, the Standard and the Enhanced Disclosure. The advantage to sporting organisations of the 'Enhanced' certificate is that it provides details not only of any criminal conviction, caution or warning and entries on the statutory Protection of Children Act (POCA) and Protection of Vulnerable Adults Act (POVA) lists but also 'other relevant information' made available at the discretion of the police force concerned, to assist in the recruitment process. However, as indicated above, concerns (and/or legal advice) received by police forces across the country would appear not to be consistent. Consequently, it would appear that differing views have been taken with regard to the possible application of the Data Protection Act and/or rights of confidence/privacy and with the disclosure of information.

With individuals seeking employment with an organisation, the necessary lawful authority can conveniently be contained within the organisation's recruitment policy. An applicant for employment will be required to submit to CRB checking as a condition of the application process. Fundamental to checking of both volunteers and paid employees is the establishment of clear criteria for the roles for which checking is required. This determination of relevancy should be based upon sound principles of risk assessment, at the heart of which is an analysis of the role to be performed by the individual and in particular whether the individual by virtue of the role to be performed will have an opportunity for direct access to children or young persons. For instance, an individual performing the role of referee or other official in the sport would arguably be outside the scope of CRB checking on the basis that the role to be performed would not involve the individual in unsupervised one-on-one contact with young persons. However, a coach/teacher whose role may involve not only unsupervised access but also an element of physical handling of children/young persons from a coaching/teaching

218

perspective would clearly be an individual who should be made the subject of CRB checking.

Child Protection in Sport Unit (CPSU) guidance recommends that Enhanced Disclosures be obtained for posts involving, for instance, the post holder in regularly caring for, training, supervising or being in sole charge of children or vulnerable adults.

At the present time CRB checks for volunteers undertaking relevant roles is provided by the CRB free of charge. This was originally, and remains, an area of major concern to many national sporting governing bodies for whom possibly tens of thousands of individuals perform voluntary roles involving direct access to children. Were payment to be required for such individuals, the standard fees for an Enhanced Disclosure would either prove a deterrent to recruitment/retention of volunteers or alternatively represent a significant drain upon the financial resources of the governing body concerned.

Determination as to suitability

The CRB have helpfully produced a Code of Practice and Explanatory Guide for registered persons and other recipients of disclosure information. Contained within the Explanatory Guide are a series of factors to be taken into account before reaching a recruitment decision. In particular, it states in paragraph 4.1.2:

Employers shall consider the following:

■ whether the conviction or other matter revealed is relevant to the position in question,
■ the seriousness of any offence or other matter revealed,
■ the length of time since the offence or other matter occurred,
■ whether the applicant has a pattern of offending behaviour or other relevant matters,
■ whether the applicant's circumstances have changed since the offending behaviour or the other relevant matters, and
■ the circumstances surrounding the offence and the explanation(s) offered by the convicted person.

These criteria, based upon established principles of objective risk assessment, will obviously need to be applied on a case-by-case basis dependent upon the particular facts and circumstances of the applicant, and the role applied for.

Independent Safeguarding Authority

The government had cause to review the vetting processes available to prospective 'employers' under the CRB system in light of the horrific Soham murders and the findings of the Bichard Inquiry Report, which noted (inter alia) failures of record keeping, vetting and information handling surrounding this case. This review resulted in the enactment of the Safeguarding Vulnerable Groups Act 2006, which introduced a new framework for checking prior to the engagement of employees or volunteers by sporting organisations.

At the heart of the new legislation is the definition of 'regulated activity', which includes sport training/teaching if either 'frequent' or 'intense'; for these purposes 'frequent' involves the activity being undertaken on more than one occasion per month and 'intense' would entail involvement on three or more days in a consecutive 30-day period. Whilst involvement as employee or volunteer member of a sport club would ordinarily involve an individual engaging in 'frequent' activities as defined in the new Act, shorter term involvement, e.g. an intensive summer school training programme that does not involve any ongoing membership/employment role, is similarly caught by the Act.

Under the Act, to undertake a regulated activity an individual must become registered with the Independent Safeguarding Authority (ISA). This clearly is primarily an individual responsibility akin to an individual making an application for a CRB disclosure. However, whereas the CRB system was ultimately optional it will now be a criminal offence for an individual to undertake a regulated activity without being so registered.

Legislation does not confine itself to the imposition of responsibilities on individuals, with ultimate criminal sanctions in the event of non-compliance. An employer must not 'engage' in a regulated activity a person who is barred or otherwise not registered. This organisational responsibility again has with it an ultimate criminal sanction for non-compliance. For these purposes 'engage' includes the engagement of an individual in a voluntary capacity.

The ISA registration process seeks to offer a 'one stop shop' facility integrating the information/intelligence presently maintained in a series of separate lists including the POCA and POVA lists, List 99 and Disqualification Orders.

At the heart of the new system is an ISA board empowered to make determinations as to an individual's suitability to work with children (and with power to delegate to individual case workers dependent on the seriousness of the case), which on the face of it removes this responsibility from individual sporting organisations and other employers of persons working with children. However, it may well be that many sporting organisations will wish to continue their own independent vetting processes; and whilst clearly an individual who is the subject of a barring order cannot be engaged by the organisation, it may be that certain individuals who are not the subject of a barring order may nonetheless be declined membership/ suspended by sporting organisations on the basis of the organisation's own risk assessment.

It is intended that the scheme will provide continuous updating with automatic notification of changes in the status of an individual to any employer who has registered their interest. However, based upon anecdotal experience relating to the establishment of the CRB systems, the logistical challenges of the operation of such a system should not be underestimated.

Other recruitment measures

Prior to the creation of the CRB many sporting organisations, under the guidance of the National Society for the Prevention of Cruelty to Children (NSPCC) in particular and more recently the CPSU, required prospective members who would be engaged in roles involving children to submit to a self-declaration process. Under the terms of self-declaration, individuals are typically required to disclose the following information:

- Have you been convicted of any criminal offences?
- Are you a person known to any social services department as being an actual or potential risk to children?
- Have you had a disciplinary sanction relating to child abuse?

The self-declaration process continues to perform a valuable function for a sporting organisation for a number of reasons:

- As a pre-engagement check and the first stage in the application/vetting process. Anecdotal evidence suggests that the very posing of these questions may serve as a deterrent to individuals who would otherwise seek to engage with the sport and who may have a history that would suggest unsuitability for such role.
- A self-declaration form can be used as a source of disclosure of relevant governing body/sporting sanctions that would not otherwise be revealed by a formal CRB disclosure search unless the information had previously been provided by the sporting body by way of formal POCA referral. Again this step is unlikely to have been undertaken in all but the more serious type of situations.

Additionally, and obviously, references as to an individual's suitability for a particular post should be taken up, as what is said (or perhaps what is not said) in a reference can be a valuable tool for a prospective 'employer' to ascertain a person's suitability for a particular post. Readers should, however, be aware of the evolving law pertaining to the duty of care surrounding the giving of references, which is outside the scope of this work.

LICENSING

For some activities, a licence is required from the appropriate enforcement agency. For most organisations, the most relevant is entertainment and food. The law recognises that volunteer and social clubs give rise to different issues for licensing compared to commercially run premises selling directly to the public.

Sale of alcohol

In England and Wales the law governing the sale of alcohol is primarily found in the Licensing Act 2003; in Scotland it is the Licensing (Scotland) Act 1976. The licensing of the sale of alcohol is the responsibility of the local authorities, who issue the necessary licence to sell alcohol. The type of licence depends upon the nature of the proposed activity.

The sale of alcohol to members of a club differs from the usual retail sale in that the members of the club jointly own the assets of the club, which include the alcohol, and therefore any payment is not strictly speaking a sales transaction, but monies to replenish the jointly owned stock. It is for the management body to ensure that members behave appropriately and in accordance with club rules.

In the context of sport organisations, the relevant form of authorisation is a 'club premises certificate'.[4] A club premises certificate enables club premises that fulfil specific membership criteria to supply alcohol and other club activities for their members and guests on a non-profit basis. It authorises a members club to carry out licensable activities, such as:

- the supply of alcohol
- provision of regulated entertainment.

Unless stated otherwise, a club premises certificate has no end date and will continue until withdrawn by the licensing authority. It perhaps goes without saying that a club premises certificate does not immunise the club from the broader obligations under law: alcohol must in no circumstances be sold or otherwise supplied to under-18s or to anyone buying it on behalf of a person under 18 years old. To do so is a punishable offence by law.

'Qualifying clubs' for the purpose of the club premises certificate are those organisations that meet the following legal criteria:

andy gray and sarah james

- under the rules of the club, persons may not be admitted to membership or as a candidate for membership without an interval of at least two days between their nomination for membership and their admission
- the club is established and conducted in good faith as a club
- the club has at least 25 members
- the alcohol is not supplied to members on the premises otherwise than by or on behalf of the club.

There are also additional general qualifications:

- The purchase and supply of alcohol by and for the club is managed by a committee of elected members of the club aged 18 years and over.
- No arrangement may be made for any person to receive any commission, percentage or other similar payment at the expense of the club in respect of the purchase of alcohol by the club.
- No arrangement may be made for any person to derive directly or indirectly any monetary benefit from the supply of alcohol to members or guests apart from to the benefit of the club as a whole or any indirect benefit to a person derived by reason of the supply contributing to a general gain for the club as a whole.

However, the benefits of a club premises certificate is that the club is granted the authority to supply alcohol to its members and sell it to guests without the need for any members/employees to hold a personal licence (as is the usual case for businesses). There are also more limited rights of entry for the police and other authorised persons as the premises are considered private and not generally open to the public.

Please note that qualifying clubs should not be confused with proprietary clubs, which are clubs that are run commercially by individuals or businesses for profit. Such clubs would require a normal premises licence.

Application forms can be obtained from the relevant local authority's licensing unit where the premises are situated. Once completed, a copy of the application must be served on a number of authorities (such as the fire service, police, environmental health, children and family service, and trading standards) and a fee is payable. A qualifying club may choose to obtain a normal premises licence if it would like to offer its premises commercially for use by the public. Alternatively, if the club wishes to provide licensable activities to the general public on a limited number of occasions it might be possible to serve a Temporary Event Notice on the local authority.

Music licences

Sport organisations that use audio-visual equipment and play music for performance need to gain formal permission to do so in advance of using the recording, by obtaining a licence from the copyright owner. The reason is that the copyright owner has many rights over recorded music and videos including:

■ the exclusive right to play them in public
■ the exclusive right to communicate them to the public
■ the exclusive right to copy them.

These rights are entrenched in copyright law,[5] and include common occurrence situations, for example playing music at social events such as discos, as well as for music sport purposes, such as performing dance sequences to music.

In the UK, there are two different bodies working in this area: the Performing Rights Society (PRS) and Phonographic Performance Ltd (PPL). They each represent different owners of the copyright in the creative works: the PRS represents music composers, songwriters and publishers; the PPL is very similar but works with the owners of the copyright sound recordings rather than the original musical works that may have been embodied in them. When a licence is issued by the PRS and/or the PPL, the monies it receives in return are paid as royalties to the copyright owner it represents.

At the moment sport organisations such as sport clubs are exempt from the requirement to purchase a licence from the PPL. This is, however, currently under review and may in due course change.

Failure to obtain a licence where applicable may result in civil action for breach of copyright infringement, which carries with it the potential sanction of damages and costs. Indeed, to ensure compliance, the PRS has representatives in and around the UK who visit public premises and regularly contact businesses. Further information is available from the PRS website, www.prsformusic.com, and the PPL website, www.ppluk.com.

Gambling

Gambling and betting is another highly regulated area. The applicable law is now found in the Gambling Act 2005, which came into force in September 2007. The aims of the new regime includes protecting children and the vulnerable from being exploited by gambling, and ensuring that it is conducted in a fair and open way. The body that oversees this is the Gambling Commission.

For sport organisations, the significance of the new law may be primarily in the distinction between prize competitions, free draws and lotteries. Although the

224

Gambling Commission has no statutory responsibility for the former, it does monitor the boundary between them and lotteries as holding a lottery is subject to considerable regulation, including licensing requirements in most circumstances. There are pitfalls for the unwary: if a competition relies upon chance, it may be a lottery and therefore unlawful in the absence of a licence. The licensing unit of the local authority should have more information.

Another pitfall comes in the form of sponsorship by overseas gambling providers. Under the Act it is an offence to advertise foreign gambling unless the provider is from the EEA or an approved country. This therefore means that a voluntary sport organisation that accepted sponsorship from a foreign gambling provider may in certain circumstances have broken the law and therefore be liable to prosecution. For this reason, care should also be exercised when receiving visiting teams from abroad. Further information is available from the regulator of gambling in Great Britain, the Gambling Commission: www.gamblingcommission.gov.uk/.

OTHER LEGAL OBLIGATIONS

Other legal obligations with which an employer must comply include:

- Organisations must hold employers' liability insurance and display the certificate in a prominent position to prove this. This type of insurance will cover employees in the event of an accident, disease or injury caused or made worse as a result of work. It should usually cover any associated legal costs but will not pay out for fines. In most sports, it is the governing body who arranges for appropriate insurance at the time of membership (and which usually includes employers' liability insurance).
- Every organisation with paid employees must register the fact. With whom depends upon the activity being undertaken – generally speaking this requires registration with the Environmental Health Services Department of the local council and the local fire service. The Health and Safety Executive (HSE) may be able to advise further via its website (www.hse.gov.uk) or InfoLine.
- Employers must appoint a competent person to help the organisation to meet its health and safety duties.
- Employers must display the Health and Safety Law poster 'What you should know'. This includes basic health and safety information and lets people know who is responsible for health and safety in the organisation. Alternatively, it is permissible to distribute HSE leaflets containing the same information (both of which are available from the HSE).
- They must maintain an accident logbook, which contains details of all accidents. This is a requirement of all workplaces with ten or more employees (and all factories), and should also record any sickness possibly caused or aggravated by work and any 'near misses'. All entries are highly confidential

and therefore must be stored in full compliance with the data protection laws. This means that after an entry into the logbook, the logbook should stored in a secure place.

■ Voluntary sport organisations that are employers or in control of work premises have to report to the authorities some work-related accidents, diseases or dangerous events. This includes death or minor injury; injury that results in the injured person being unable to work for more than three days; and work-related disease.

■ Organisations that do not have employees nor own their own premises, such as clubs, are not subject to reporting regulations but must of course inform their insurance company of any incident or accident.

■ All workplaces with employees must carry out a Control of Substances Hazardous to Health (COSHH) assessment. The HSE has produced a step-by-step guide to help organisations to fulfil this obligation. Further information is available on its website (www.hse.gov.uk).

■ All employers have a duty under law to provide first aid facilities that are adequate and appropriate for the organisation. This can only be properly ascertained by carrying out a first aid assessment. As a very minimum there must be one properly equipped first aid box that is readily accessible and a person appointed to take charge of first aid arrangements.

■ All organisations must make appropriate arrangements to minimise the risk of fire. Premises that are used by the public must obtain a fire certificate (or exemption) from the local fire brigade. Employers must undertake a fire risk assessment to identify hazards and put into place procedures to remove or limit the likelihood of those hazards causing a fire.

However, the above examples serve as just a flavour; there may very well be additional obligations imposed upon the voluntary sport organisation as part of its membership and under the conditions of its insurance – regardless of whether it is staffed by employees or volunteers. The HSE also provides sector specific guidance on its website (www.hse.gov.uk).

SUMMARY

This chapter has set out a brief overview of the key aspects of the legal environment that impacts on the operations of sport organisations. It is clear that this is a highly technical area that will need expert support, and managers must have access to a source of legal advice. For clubs, this advice can come from the NGB, which will have, in most cases, their own source of legal assistance.

Nonetheless, it is important that managers are aware of the implications of the law in terms of the way they run their organisations. This is particularly important for safeguarding the participation of people in their sport. Awareness of health and safety legislation and the regular review of safeguarding policies would seem to be the minimum that a voluntary sport organisation should undertake in this area.

NOTES

1 Conservative Central Officer v Burrell [1982] 1 WLR 533 CA at 527.

2 Charities Act 2006.

3 Details of the legislation in this area can be found in Schedule 18 of the Finance Act 2002.

4 The Licensing Act 2003 (Premises, Licences and Club Premises Certificates) Regulations 2005.

5 Copyright, Design and Patents Act 1988.

CHAPTER 12

RISK MANAGEMENT AND PROTECTION

Leigh Robinson and Dick Palmer

The management of risk is integral to managing voluntary sport organisations effectively. Everyone involved with the organisation has a responsibility to take well-judged, sensible risks to develop the organisation. However, to make sure that risks are well judged and sensible, risk management needs to be part of the management procedures that operate within the organisation. Risk management is a fairly straightforward process; however, unless it is also considered to be an essential function of the governance process, there is a danger that it may not be carried out properly.

Board members must take responsibility for risk management since they are ultimately responsible for what happens in the organisation. In some countries, this may make them legally liable for accidents to spectators, financial failures and bad publicity for sponsors. The responsibilities of the board, in terms of risk management, are:

- Approving the risk management policy statements, strategy and subsequent revisions of this.
- Monitoring the organisation's risk management and internal control arrangements.
- Considering the key risks associated with their decision making.
- Reviewing immediately any changes relating to primary risks.

This chapter sets out the risk management process that should be carried out in VSOs, highlighting areas of risk and how organisations can be protected against risk. It also sets out a key area of risk, which is health and safety.

ASSESSMENT OF THE RISKS FACING THE ORGANISATION

Although each organisation is unique, there are certain risks that are common to most sport organisations. When assessing risk, the following areas should be considered:

228

- Effectiveness of the board: Because the board provides strategic direction for the organisation and is ultimately responsible for what the organisation can do, it is important for the board to operate effectively. Questions to be asked include: Does the board have the right type and level of skill needed to ensure the organisation works effectively? Are members fully aware of their responsibilities and liabilities? Is there a process of succession planning that ensures that not all members come up for election at the same time?
- Financial climate: The importance of finances to VSOs is well understood and was discussed in detail in Chapter 6. In order to evaluate the risks associated with the financial environment, managers should consider the following: Does the organisation rely on one source of funding? How easy would it be to replace that source of funding? What would happen if the major funder withdrew its support?
- Policy and strategy: Risk arises in this area from both inside and outside the organisation. The organisation itself may have a policy that leads to risk, such as poor communication with stakeholders. Alternatively, government policy towards physical education in schools or the role of sport in society may bring about risks. When evaluating risk in this area, managers need to ask whether the organisation has an appropriate strategy for the resources it controls and the services it needs to provide.
- External factors: As outlined in Chapter 2, the external context can have a major impact on the way the organisation can operate. Managers should use the information obtained by completing the PESTLE process to evaluate the risks of the external environment.
- Operating effectiveness and efficacy: The way the organisation operates may lead to risks, such as a loss of sponsorship, loss of membership, poor use of resources, or recruitment of inappropriate staff and volunteers. The two main questions that should be answered in order to assess risk in this area are as follows: Does the organisation have a clear and appropriate strategy for achieving its objectives? Is this strategy backed up by appropriate operating principles?
- Financial prudence and probity: The use of finances in an efficient manner for the purpose they were intended is an ethical responsibility for a VSO. When assessing risk in this area, you might ask the following questions: Does the organisation have financial controls in place? Can these controls be circumvented by those in authority? Can the organisation account for all of its revenue and its expenditure? Does the organisation offer audited accounts to its stakeholders?
- Legal risks: The manner in which the organisation is constituted will greatly determine the extent of legal liability it can bear as an independent legal entity, as well as the corresponding extent to which individual members, or board members, may bear personal liability (see Chapter 11). In addition, it is necessary to confirm that all contracts the organisation enters in to be reviewed by a legal expert to ensure that legal risks are properly identified.

229

Contracts even of low value may carry a large potential legal risk exposure, so it is not sufficient to adopt crude thresholds for contract review; instead, a proper assessment of the risk should be made. The VSO must also, of course, ensure it complies with all applicable legislation, such as employment law, data protection law, and health and safety law. The following questions should be considered: Is the organisation an unincorporated association in which the individual members have personal liability, or is it a partnership or perhaps a corporation with liability limited by guarantee? Are board members aware of the extent of their personal legal liability? Are contracts reviewed for legal risk? Are the assets properly protected by law? (This is especially important in relation to intellectual property protection for your brand and merchandising or sponsorship rights.)

■ Any other identifiable risks: These may be risks to do with the sport itself; for example, judo is likely to have more inherent risks than badminton. There may be risks to do with the activities of the organisation, such as attending major events. There may be risks associated with the skills and tacit knowledge of key staff or volunteers that might be lost if they leave. Finally, there may be systems, such as computer systems, that the organisation is dependent upon and whose failure could cause major difficulties.

BENEFITS OF RISK MANAGEMENT

Risk management is a time-consuming process; however, there are many benefits of this to the VSO. A good risk management process enables:

■ an understanding of the level of risk exposure that can be tolerated by the organisation
■ the type of risk to be understood and the level of risk to be measured
■ the ongoing effectiveness of mitigation and protection to be assessed
■ action to be undertaken by management to design and establish suitable levels of mitigation and protection
■ an awareness of risk at all levels of the organisation, but in particular that there are appropriate mechanisms to ensure that risks can be responded to.

A risk management process will not get rid of risk: its intention is to reduce or protect against it. This process needs to be robust and transparent and subject to regular review and reporting.

THE RISK PROCESS

Piekarz (2009) has identified the five key stages of the risk process. The first is context and he suggests that it is vital to understand how the organisation and its

230

services affect the risk exposure of the organisation. For example, a tennis club is likely to offer less risky activities than a rugby club. This allows the organisation to determine how much risk it has to carry and how much protection it may need. The second stage is the carrying out of a risk analysis. This requires the identification of areas of risk (see above) and how features in these areas may lead risks to occur. For example, how might a poor accounting procedure lead to fraud? The third phase is a risk assessment and this is carried out through the identification of risk to the organisation, an assessment of their impact and the likelihood of the risk occurring. The fourth phase is the implementation of control measures. This is fundamental to the risk management process as there is little point in identifying risk, if nothing is then done about it. At this point it will become clear whether risks can be controlled, or whether the VSO needs to invest in protection against the risk. Finally, the process needs to be subject to constant monitoring and evaluation in order to make sure that the risk assessment is up to date.

Defining organisational risk appetite

Sport is risky and therefore all voluntary sport organisations will deliver services with some element of risk. Part of the risk management process is to identify the amount of risk that the organisation is prepared to accept, tolerate or be exposed to at any one time. This is called the appetite for risk and this needs to be communicated throughout the organisation and used in decision making regarding the priorities placed on policies, procedures, services and the funding that goes with them.

Key to risk appetite is risk ranking, which is the identification of where risk sits within an organisation and how that risk should be managed. Risk ranking serves two purposes: first, it describes the probability of the risk occurring and, second, it describes the impact of the risk on services. From this it is possible to identify the risks that pose the highest threat to the organisation, taking into account the organisation's risk appetite. This can then be incorporated into the risk register; an example of which is set out in Table 12.1.

Quantifying risk

Quantifying risk involves multiplying the likelihood of the risk event occurring by the extent of the impact it will have if it does indeed occur:

Risk = likelihood × impact

Once a review of risk has been carried out, each risk needs to be ranked and quantified. Managing the risk then involves identifying tools, processes and

Table 12.1 An example of a risk register for a club

Risk	Likelihood of risk	Potential impact	Control procedure	Monitoring process	Ownership	Further action	Date of review
Members not paying fees	Low	High	Regular reminders to members	Regular reviews of membership payments	Membership secretary	Report on progress each month	3 months from start of procedure
Player getting injured during training	High	High	Meetings with athletes regarding health and safety Well qualified coaches Appropriate training regimes	Club committee to monitor number of injuries	Coach	Evaluate cause of injuries as they occur	12 months from start of procedure
Loss of head coach	High	Low	Regular communication with coach to reinforce commitment Succession planning to ensure skills are not lost	Club committee to monitor process	Club Chair	Review plans for succession in 6 months	12 months from start of procedure

procedures to prevent or minimise the risk by reducing the likelihood or the impact. Insurance is one tool to reduce the impact of a risk. Another option is to accept the risk, but this will depend on the organisation's risk appetite and should always be taken after careful assessment of the risk and possible consequences of accepting it.

Although risk management is the responsibility of the board, a risk officer should be appointed to take the lead in risk management. The risk officer should be responsible for preparing and updating a risk register, as outlined in Table 12.1. This will form the basis of the risk management strategy.

There are a number of ways of reducing the risks that affect an organisation. First, the risk management process itself makes it possible to avoid some risks and to properly manage others. Changes in the way the organisation is managed may also mitigate potential risks. If the organisation is managed in a transparent and accountable way, many risks associated with public image, funding and stakeholder satisfaction can be avoided. It may also be possible, if not necessary, to change the strategic direction of the organisation. For example, if government policy is turning towards elite sport rather than grass-roots sport, a club that delivers grass-roots sport may wish to reconsider its objectives. At the very least, it should consider how to manage the risk associated with the change in policy. Finally, if the sport is inherently risky, or if there are significant risks facing the organisation, it may be possible to take out insurance to cover the risk. For example, most officials are insured against liability for injuries that occur to athletes under their control. In addition, most sport organisations that stage events insure themselves against injury to spectators. This will be discussed in more detail below.

HEALTH AND SAFETY

(Section contributed by Andy Gray and Sarah James)

Health and safety is often maligned but actually it has very real and genuine objectives, namely preventing people from being harmed or becoming ill. In the UK, health and safety laws[1] achieve this by requiring relevant precautions be put into place and the adherence to best practice. Such is its importance, ignorance is not a defence. It is therefore obviously very important that voluntary sport organisations are fully aware of their obligations and, where necessary, that they seek specialist guidance. That said, complying with health and safety laws is not just about avoiding penalties; it can also prove beneficial day to day in that it can create a positive working environment and increase staff/volunteer retention.

The starting point to meeting health and safety obligations is to assess the nature of the organisation in question. If the voluntary sport organisation employs staff (even if it is just one employee), it is deemed to be a small business. 'Employs' means having individuals (full-time or part-time) under a contract of employment. It does not matter if the contract is written or verbal. Equally the payment of expenses may in some cases constitute a contract. If it has volunteers only, it still has responsibilities but these are as extensive and are centred around the general principle of 'duty of care' (see below).

Duty of care

This is a general legal requirement placed on individuals and organisations to avoid carelessly causing personal injury or damage to property. Importantly, it is owed to all persons. If a person suffers injury, loss or damage ('the claimant') because a person or persons ('the defendant(s)') was at fault he/she can claim compensation through the civil courts. To show fault (or 'negligence', to use the legal term) the claimant must prove that:

- he/she was owed a duty of care by the individual or organisation
- that duty of care was broken
- he/she suffered injury, loss or damage as a result.

The standard of care the law expects individuals to display is that of reasonable care. However, the greater the risk of injury, the higher the standard that must be exercised. Examples of where a duty of care arises in the voluntary sport sector include:

- when occupying premises
- when running fetes/fairs
- when loaning equipment to others.

When exercising a duty of care, different standards must of course be applied towards children and adults.

Businesses

In addition to the general obligations mentioned above, there is an abundance of legislation with which employers must comply, all designed to improve the working environment. Generally speaking, employers must provide:

- a safe and healthy place of work in which they have eliminated/controlled any risks to health (and including providing toilets, washing facilities, drinking water, appropriate lighting and temperature, etc.)
- safe systems of work in place and followed. Any dangerous items/materials must be safely stored
- adequate supervision

234

leigh robinson and dick palmer

- training and information necessary for health and safety, including providing opportunities to raise concerns and influence decisions
- a written policy (see below).

There are also obligations owed by the employee to look after themselves and others, and to cooperate with the employer in matters of health and safety.

Organisations with employees can be found criminally liable if they breach their duty of care obligations to employees and others. If found guilty, the organisation can be liable to pay a fine. Through the principle of vicarious liability, employers are not only liable for their own acts but also for those acts of their employees and agents. Further, whilst it may be possible to insure against civil claims it is not possible to insure against criminal sanctions.

A written health and safety policy is a requirement of law where there are five or more employees. It is also a requirement that this be communicated to all employees and anyone else under the organisation's control (including volunteers and contractors); that it is available for inspection; and that it is reviewed. However, even when an organisation only has volunteers, having the policy is a good idea – it will also help fulfil its duty of care to its volunteers, by putting into place clear procedures and responsibilities.

RISK MANAGEMENT AND PROTECTION

Sport includes risks that vary from minor legal disputes to death. It is therefore good management to accept these risks and take measures to control them and to protect the organisation. A number of risk management and protection tools are presented below.

Insurances

There are a number of ways in which sport needs insurance. First, there is the broad area of cover against physical injury to the insured, which extends to trainers, referees, coaches, officials and spectators. Second, is the cover against injury to someone else. The insured may be a player held liable for injury to another player or for injury to a spectator. The insured may be vicariously liable for the player's acts. Increasingly the insured may have some responsibility for the safety of players, other participants or spectators through the provision of sport facilities, control of the venue or control of the game, either generally or on a particular occasion.

The following types of insurance should be considered where appropriate.

Professional indemnity insurance

Professional indemnity insurance covers individuals for legal liability when there has been an error, omission or neglect by an employee or individual in the carrying out of their professional duties. This is useful insurance for any VSO. Because the error or neglect can lead to the professional being sued for damages, professional indemnity cover insures them against claims for negligence. Policies can include damages for libel and slander. Negligence or accidental error are the key areas to cover and in sport this equates to negligence or error occurring during the instruction by the coaches, managers, physiotherapists or doctors.

Public liability insurance

Owners and occupiers of premises have a responsibility to keep premises in a safe condition so that other persons entering the premises are not injured. Sporting organisations also must use reasonable care and skill to ensure that people coming into or near the ground are not injured in any way as a result of the negligence of the proprietor or sporting participant. Public liability insurance is an important form of insurance since it protects volunteers, employees and members of the organisation. This insurance provides indemnity to the organisation against its legal liability to pay damages arising from accidental injury (including death) and accidental damage to property. This covers claims arising from negligence of the organisation or one of its employees, or from the condition of the premises.

Directors and officers liability insurance

This form of insurance is designed for board members and officers of clubs and organisations who can be sued by their own organisation for acts of negligence. In these cases it is alleged that they have breached the duty of care owed to their organisation. Such insurance is of particular importance to organisations that have large financial turnovers or taxation liabilities.

Property insurance

The insurance plans set out above are designed to protect an organisation and its members against liability claims. However, insurance should also be taken out that protects the organisation's assets. They include:

- Fire: A fire insurance policy is advisable when the organisation owns buildings or flammable equipment.
- Burglary: This covers against the stealing of sporting equipment and saleable goods.
- Money: Since large sums of money are not generally covered under a burglary (contents) policy, separate cover is often required.
- Consequential loss: This covers loss of income suffered by a commercially operating organisation as a result of fire damage to its premises. It also compensates for the increased cost of operating following a fire.

- Pluvius (rain): This generally relates to the cancellation of events as a result of adverse weather conditions.
- Fidelity: This relates to the risk of members stealing the organisation's funds.
- Motor vehicle: Any motor vehicle owned and operated by the organisation will require insurance to protect both its own value, and the value of vehicles owned by other drivers, in the case of an accident.
- Cash in transit: All gate receipts from events and functions organised by the organisation may need to be insured. There are many examples of situations where funds are collected at an event on the weekend and cannot be banked until the following Monday. In such cases a cash-in-transit insurance policy can provide protection from theft or other causes of loss until the money reaches the bank.

Conflicts of interest

To improve accountability and transparency, voluntary sport organisations need to make sure they are not operating with a conflict of interest. Such conflicts occur in several situations. Of primary concern are those that arise out of financial interests between members of the board and anyone providing contracted services. For example, if a board member owns a clothing company, it would be a conflict of interest for that member to decide how much to budget for team uniforms.

Conflicts of interest may exist where a board member or other stakeholder (known as an 'interested party') directly or indirectly profits as a result of a decision, policy or transaction made by the organisation. Examples include situations in which the VSO:

- contracts, buys or leases goods, services or properties from an interested party, such as leasing office space from a board member
- employs an interested party other than a person who is already employed, such as employing a board member to carry out consultancy work
- provides substantial gratuities or favours to an interested party, such as offering to pay for the education of the children of sponsors
- gratuitously provides use of the facilities, properties or services of the organisation to an interested party, such as allowing the club, of which the chair of the NF is a member, to train at the high-performance centre free of charge
- adopts policies that financially benefit an interested party, such as including a staff member's husband on the approved list of suppliers.

In many countries it is illegal to have a conflict of financial interest within the organisation because such conflicts are a primary source of corruption and a threat to a nation's economy. In the event that there are no laws regarding conflicts of interest in the country in which a VSO operates, it is still prudent for

237

the organisation to voluntarily adopt an internal policy on conflicts of interest. This should require members of the board and appropriate staff to agree to and sign an 'interests register' that outlines clearly other interests that they have that may conflict with their role in the organisation. This will limit the possibility of an interested party directly or indirectly benefiting or profiting as a result of a decision, policy or transaction made by the organisation.

Indemnification and waivers

An indemnification clause releases a party from the legal responsibility for the reckless or illegal behaviour of another party, such as members or contractors, with whom the organisation has a legal relationship. This type of clause is a good idea to minimise the risk to the organisation in the event of a lawsuit. Every contract signed should indemnify the organisation from any illegal behaviour on the part of a contracted service provider. Also, it is helpful to only permit membership to people who agree in writing to an indemnification clause.

Waivers of liability are often used to reduce the possibility of a lawsuit in the event of injury or death as a result of participating in an activity of the organisation. Typically, a waiver asks the member to acknowledge the risk of injury and death and release the organisation from any legal responsibility should such injury or death occur. Signing waivers of this nature are often a condition for an athlete's participation in an event. In addition, clubs recognised by an NF might require all participants in a sporting activity to sign waivers of liability. Unfortunately, if this does not happen the organisation may be put at risk.

SUMMARY

There is no doubt that sport is risky and therefore VSOs have to be proactive in the management of risk. Key to this process is that the board needs to understand and accept that risk management is part of the governance process. Once this is established the risk management process needs to be communicated to the rest of the organisation. Having said this, risk management is such an important process, that if the board is slow to accept their role in this, it may need to be driven by a senior member of the organisation. The management of risk requires a structured approach of identifying, quantifying, prioritising and taking accountability for risk. This will then allow appropriate protection mechanisms to be put in place to protect the organisation where necessary.

NOTE

1 There are lots of laws in this area, the majority of which have been created as regulations. An important starting point is the Health and Safety at Work etc Act 1974.

238

leigh robinson and dick palmer

CHAPTER 13

INFORMATION TECHNOLOGY AND VOLUNTARY SPORT ORGANISATIONS

Brian Minikin

The challenges facing voluntary sport organisations in today's 'fast-food' world are many and are discussed in detail in the following chapter. However, not least of these is managing the information and communication demands of sport teams, clubs and associations as they respond to the demands placed on them by the external and internal environment of the organisation. The concept of the 'e-Federation' (Delicado, 2002) has come about in recognition of the heavy administrative workload undertaken by national federations and the advent of an array of modern electronic tools that help to deal with this workload (see Table 13.1). In this chapter, a review of information and communication technologies (ICT) as they apply or might apply to managing voluntary sport organisations is presented.

Sport organisations of all types are required to store and make use of information in one form or another and to communicate with members and the public at large. The means by which they choose to do this depends upon a number of

Table 13.1 The evolution of technology and its impact on communication in VSOs

No technology	Little technology	Advent of technology	E-technology
Word of mouth Manually intensive processes Communication limited to the sphere of influence of one person	Written Notices Notice Boards Use of public media, radio, TV and newspaper notices Random communication not well directed or targeted	Audio communication Phone, fax, taped messages, commentary Extended sphere of influence and the beginnings of messaging networks and responsive communication	Digital communication The computer Email, Web sites Text messaging Automated database driven processes Well targeted and two way interactive communication

239

factors, such as the volume and diversity of information that is generated and the intensity with which information is disseminated, which is usually governed by the frequency and size of events and activities that the organisation is involved with. In the modern world, however, the rapidly changing ICT landscape adds further to the decisions that managers of sport organisations need to make in terms of the ICT they choose to best meet their needs while remaining within their organisational capacity.

There are several forms of information technology that can be used by VSOs:

- telephones – fixed, mobile, via Internet
- computers – mainframes, servers, PCs
- personal digital assistants (PDAs) (often merged with mobile phones)
- cameras – digital, phone, webcam
- video – tape, numeric, Internet streaming video
- Internet – satellite, cable, wireless, dial-up (via telephone lines)
- television – cable, satellite, Internet
- storage – disks, CDs, DVDs, USB keys
- networks – optical fibre cable, wireless, Bluetooth.

Sport organisations are likely to have a diverse range of information needs from a diverse range of sources. The integrated use of several forms of information technology, known as ICT solutions, allows these different purposes to be met in an efficient and cost-effective manner. The decision is how best to integrate ICT into the organisation.

Successful management of information should 'identify and capture information that is crucial to success, translate it into something of value for the organisation and ensure easy access to it' (Camy and Robinson, 2007: 39). ICT solutions help with this and offer many advantages to sport organisations that are looking to efficiently store, retrieve and use information as well as improve the efficiency of communication to stakeholders. However, not all voluntary sport organisations are ready to take on complex solutions, nor do they necessarily even need them. If the solution is too complex and the organisation does not have the capacity to use it, the investment that is made will be wasted.

There are, however, a number of key factors that an organisation must consider before investing a great deal in these technologies. Factors such as organisational culture, attitude and expertise all have an impact on the effectiveness of ICT implementation and use. There are many examples of ICT implementation failing, not because of poor design or functionality, but because people within the organisation did not adopt it. In addition, disseminating knowledge of new ICT requires training, and specific skills must be provided. There are also external factors to consider, such as accessibility to the Internet and the broadband availability in a country. It would be pointless to develop a system that no one can access or that is too slow to operate effectively. However, despite these factors, e-management and accessibility to ICT should be a priority for VSOs.

Thus, the primary challenge for managers is to determine what their needs are and whether or not the organisation has the development in place to make use of the technologies available. Managers then need to determine if the cost and expertise required to use ICT justifies the benefits that are derived by the organisation. For example, there may be little to be gained by having a website as a primary source of information if the members of the organisation or its primary target audience do not have access to the Internet. The following discussion will set out what ICT solutions are available for sport organisations and identify how they have been used in sport organisations.

CONTEXTUAL INFLUENCES ON ICT

There are a number of factors that will impact on a VSO's need for, and capacity to use, ICT solutions. First, voluntary sport organisations have a number of forms and functions (see Chapter 1) and these will have a direct impact on the ICT that is necessary for the organisation. It is not difficult to see that the ICT needs of a local running club will be different from those of the International Amateur Athletics Federation.

Second, the demographic and geographic structure of the membership of the voluntary sport organisation will place pressure on communication and information gathering and dissemination infrastructures. Use of ICT will need to be culturally acceptable and geographically accessible before being an effective tool for VSOs.

Third, VSOs, in particular NOCs and NFs, evolve through different stages of organisational development and depending upon the scope of their activities can vary immensely in their organisational objectives, structure, services and information and communication needs. It appears logical that more complex VSOs or VSOs that are in the process of becoming more complex will require more complex ICT solutions.

For example, 'In their early days, sport organisations assumed their social responsibility through improvised sport activities and volunteer work with which they were able to provide enjoyment, free time leisure and community contact to the youth' (Hernandez, 2002: 49). Such organisations generate small amounts of information that require little more than temporary record keeping, notices and word of mouth communication. The structure of these organisations will differ significantly from well developed organisations, more commonly part of an established sport industry, or even enterprises on the scale of a premier league football club or the fully professional basketball, baseball or football clubs that characterise the American professional sport systems. Such organisations

241

require highly developed information gathering, storage and retrieval systems that can handle the volume and complexity of the information produced. These organisations contrast significantly with so-called 'amateur' sport organisations, such as clubs or national federations in developing countries, which are governed and managed by volunteers, often with little in the way of reliable income to sustain them (Browne, 2008; Minikin, 2009).

Communication and information management should be a core function of a modern VSO, regardless of the context in which it operates. However, the degree to which a sport organisation generates and disseminates information will depend upon its level of development, its diversity, both demographically and geographically, the type of activity that it is involved with and the communication tools that it has available to it to use. The sport organisation can then choose an information gathering, collection and dissemination system that best meets its needs based on what is available and affordable from the context of its external environment. This is demonstrated by Figure 13.1, which shows that as the context becomes more complex in terms of organisational size and development and the geography and demography that the organisation is located in, so does its requirements for the use of information, moving from simply producing

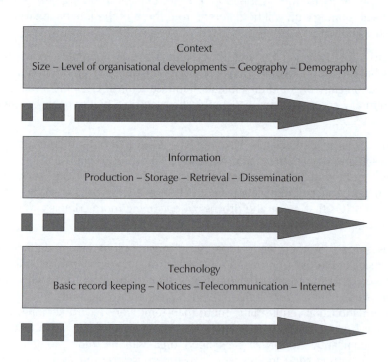

Figure 13.1 ICT continuum for voluntary sport organisations

brian minikin

information to being able to disseminate it. This has obvious implications for the ICT the organisation needs and it will move from basic record keeping to the use of full Internet technologies.

INFORMATION AND VOLUNTARY SPORT ORGANISATIONS

In order to grasp the complexity of the issues surrounding ICT and sport management, it is best to consider the components one at a time and then attempt to bring them together to determine a framework in which information is gathered, stored and then retrieved and communicated as and when required. As set out previously, the type and quantity of information generated by a voluntary sport organisation will depend on the level of development and complexity of the organisation and the type of activities that it is concerned with. However, most VSOs need the information that is set out in Table 13.2.

These lists are by no means exhaustive. Add to this the need to establish brand positioning and marketing and it is not difficult to imagine the information challenges that face managers of sport organisations. However, although the information and communication demands on managers have increased significantly in recent times, so has the technology to assist them with this. For example, Rosendich (2001) describes how the technological revolution has influenced the management of sport organisations, and in particular the role of relational databases that form the core of many sport information gathering and storage solutions. A relational database is an information structure that stores data in tables that can be linked to each other for cross-referencing, such as age and club name. Relational databases make it possible to store and readily retrieve information collected by sport organisations.

Delicado (2002: 6) describes the development of web-based portals that provide access to databases by members and that sport organisations would aspire to establish 'a corporate, vertical portal'. A portal is a virtual gateway to a network of websites with a common interest; a corporate portal is one that focuses on a particular sport, such as basketball. These are thought to lead to the following benefits:

- a more consistent view of the organisation
- improved decision making process as information is more readily available
- better information organisation and search capabilities
- direct access to internal knowledge
- direct links to reports, analysis and queries
- personalised access to information.

Historically reliant on paper filing systems and archives, sport organisations have benefited from the invention of the basic desktop computer to electronically

243

Table 13.2 Information needs of VSOs

Category	Type of information
Membership details	Contact details Biographic information Clothing sizes Passport information Club/team details Skills and preferences Availability
Governance and management	Minutes of meetings Rules and regulations Operations and procedures Planning documents Reports
Records of competitions or activities	Entries for events Team rosters Results Tables Statistics Courses held Reports Qualifications/levels of achievement Honours and awards
Financial matters	Budgets Financial statements Expenditure records Asset records Audit reports Sales and purchase records Income analysis Event entry E-commerce
Facilities and equipment	Training venues Competition venues Equipment inventory Availability of venues Parking capacities Seating capacities Quality and types of services provided

store and retrieve information. The laptop computer has enabled organisations to bring their ICT system to the field of play and even reduced the need for established office space. With the laptop, the physical storage of information is not fixed to a specific location and can be moved to different locations for the collection or retrieval of information. In addition, Flash Drive and external hard drive technology has made it possible to transfer or store large quantities of data away from the primary computer and move this data from one computer to another with ease.

Local Area Networks (LANs) enable data to be shared easily by more than one computer and even allow file sharing and multiple points of input and retrieval within a confined area. The Internet has further diversified this so that the computer has become a device to transfer information to storage on a server using the facilities provided by the Wide Area Network (WAN), which, in its current manifestation, makes full use of the World Wide Web. Consequently, the computer does not now even need to store information as increasing use of virtual file storage systems is developed. The computer becomes simply an access point for storage, retrieval and transfer of information. Furthermore, in recent times, the computer's central position in the ICT framework is being challenged by devices such as mobile phones, PDAs and the new breed of super phones such as the BlackBerry and iPhone.

Delicado (2002) examined the potential benefits for voluntary sport organisations that adopt ICT strategies and recognised the potential advantage of the Internet for VSOs with respect to data collection and storage as well as information management and dissemination. The packages used often start out as generic database software applications, but in recent years a range of sport-specific packages have been developed to meet the customised needs of VSOs.

In addition, ICT also has the potential for educational, societal, commercial and operational application. For example, it allows distance working and nomad management, which is of particular value for VSOs. Volunteers who are working in various locations around a country can access information about organisational objectives and programmes. Coaches can monitor their travelling athletes, who complete online training diaries accessible to coaches from all over the world. In addition, e-learning has enhanced the anti-doping education of local experts in a cost- and time-effective way, allowing these individuals to be trained using material available online or on CD-ROM.

Online platforms driven by relational databases have revolutionised sport information management making information available as and when required from anywhere in the world. This information can include any of the categories listed in Table 13.2 and with the power of a database, the sorting and retrieval process of information is impressive. In particular, the automation of tasks such as the generation of mass emails significantly reduces the time it takes to get information from a source, such as a competition venue, to the public at large via a website or specifically to a list of members, without the operator having to spend time sending or processing information any further. The establishment of corporate portals for sport organisations to collect, store and disseminate information for sport organisations, as described by Delicado (2002) is now a reality and an affordable one at that.

245

Two examples of corporate portals come from cricket and football. The cricket web portal (www.cricinfo.com) provides an example of a database-driven web platform with live scores of matches available online, complete with live commentary and up to the minute statistics of players that are involved in first class cricket worldwide. This is a commercially driven portal that requires a costly investment in human and physical resources. It nevertheless highlights the potential for the future world of sport. The Union of European Football Associations (UEFA) operate an extensive website to provide up-to-date scores and statistics of matches played throughout Europe, access for fans to chat rooms and capability for fans to purchase tickets for games. It is typical of centralised, web-based administration and communication tools (www.uefa.com).

Sites like these require a large staff commitment to input information in order to keep the content up to date. The live match functionality and web streaming of commentary also requires a high level of technical expertise and equipment to drive them. They rely on revenue gained from broadcasting to pay for the support provided by large teams of web managers. For some highly developed VSOs this type of platform is essential but it does require the establishment of a significant infrastructure and can be expensive with respect to the commitment to human resources required to maintain them.

For the less developed and less wealthy sport organisations, there are solutions that can be driven by the organisations themselves or, better still, by its membership base. Examples of these solutions include Leaguenet, who supports grass-roots rugby league in Australia (www.leaguenet.com.au) and Footyweb, who supports grass-roots Australian Football (www.footyweb.com.au). These are examples of web portals for sport that are driven by the membership and rely on regular contributions from member clubs and teams to keep the overall content live. Each contribution is then aggregated through their web portal to be available for all other members to both view and use. Essentially this removes the 'middle man' from the ICT equation and saves significant costs. However, such solutions do require a greater commitment to training and change management strategies throughout the organisation's member base in order to gain acceptance of the technology and generate commitment to contributing.

At an international level, the Oceania National Olympic Committees (ONOC) supports an online database that communicates with an offline platform to enable information to be processed at times when the Internet is not available. This is particularly important for countries where Internet access is limited either because of infrastructure reasons, or because of the instability of the Web. This process, illustrated in Figure 13.2, means that it is now possible for Oceania sport organisations to log in their membership data to an offline database and use it for a variety of functions including the assignment of players to competitions and teams as required without having to re-enter their details again.

246

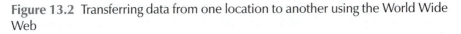

Figure 13.2 Transferring data from one location to another using the World Wide Web

This same data can then be synchronised to an online data server where it can be directed to a specific event database and then retrieved via a similar offline database where the player's details become available for use in an event. Using the Internet means that member information can be generated, stored, retrieved, processed and transferred anywhere in the world, instantly. This has led to the cost of athlete registration for competitions being reduced by more than 50 per cent as a consequence of doing away with the need to enter and re-enter data for individual members.

When integrated into an event management package, the data collection process set out in Figure 13.2 means that the data collected can be used over and over again by a voluntary sport organisation to manage its routine events and competitions (see case study 13.1 below). On a larger scale, using this process could make athlete data available to a succession of host organising committees for the major multi-sport events, such as the Olympic Games or Commonwealth Games. The case study below shows how such technologies have been used at a local level.

Case study 13.1: Melbourne East Netball Association (MENA)

In Melbourne's eastern suburbs is a netball association with a membership of 1500+. As a central venue sport all members converge on the same place each Saturday and a couple of nights midweek to play on the ten courts. Each Saturday at nine separate time slots these courts have matches on them, totalling more than 90 matches per week. Prior to the availability of technology the secretary spent three days processing the match scores and calculating the ladders, which were posted weekly on venue noticeboards. In addition, a fixture book was produced at the beginning of each season at a large cost and those who did not receive it often made weekly calls to find out the time they were playing. In addition to the table/ladder calculations, the most time-consuming tasks were keeping records of the number of matches played by individuals and the redrawing of fixtures when teams withdrew or required an adjustment.

In 2002, MENA introduced the SportingPulse software 'Sportzware', which was designed to automate some of these time-consuming manual tasks. At a cost of

AUS$1 per player, per year, MENA received the software, training and full 24/7 support. The software functions were to manage competitions and the unique variables netball posed and to manage member details, such as the number of games played. Immediately the three days were reduced to 20 minutes over a cup of tea or a glass of wine on a Saturday afternoon, after which time the matches were processed and the tables/ladders calculated and posted online on their website for all to view.

In addition there was a cost saving as there was no need to print the fixture books or field and make calls for those enquiring about their match times. Members' expectations are now raised and if ladders/tables are not posted by 6.00 p.m. the same day, the secretary receives emails from members enquiring why! The MENA website (www.mena.sportingpulse.net) is now the central place for all communication between the association and its members; in addition, clubs (www.nhnc.sportingpulse.net) have their own websites and both are being used to generate income as a stand-alone commercial entity as most months more than 35,000 pages are viewed online (Edwina Ricci, Melbourne East Netball Association).

COMMUNICATION AND VOLUNTARY SPORT ORGANISATIONS

It is one thing to collect and disseminate information and quite another to effect a viable communication system within and between voluntary sport organisations. Communication of information is required within the organisation, between the members, or various departments that might have formed and from the organisation itself to the greater community and its stakeholders, primarily to either promote its activities or to ensure that everyone has the same level of understanding of what is happening within the organisation.

Some organisations have learned to make very good use of technology to enhance the flow of information that is generated while meetings or sport events are in progress, by using wireless networks and distributing voluminous reports electronically. Board and staff meetings can be serviced by making agendas, minutes and discussions available electronically, and communication internally and externally can occur via email. Because the Internet has become a worldwide interface, it offers the potential to upload membership records and information archives to the Web and thus make them available to stakeholders, anytime and anywhere.

Likewise, the use of multimedia aids such as overhead projectors, data projectors, electronic scoring systems and wide screen instant replay facilities and integrated sound systems have greatly enhanced the quality and quantity of information flow during sport events, at meetings and in the educational setting. Communication arguably takes up the largest part of the administrative process of a sport organisation. Information is gathered and must be disseminated so that the people that need the information can get it quickly and without fuss. The ability to then respond and interact becomes increasingly important.

For VSOs, the time taken to communicate might be critical to the success of the organisation's management. The longer the time taken to communicate, the more resources are required and the less efficient the organisation becomes. ICT solutions improve communication by greatly improving efficiency and reducing cost both in terms of human resources and time. The current genre of instant messaging tools such as Skype, MSN and Yahoo Messenger and the various chat room facilities enable communication to occur worldwide and in real time. As email has virtually made the facsimile redundant, so instant messaging may one day make email redundant. As PDAs and Super Phones replace laptop computers, so texting, or Short Messaging Services (SMS), are gaining greater popularity as a cheap method of getting messages out to the public or to a discrete member group, particularly younger members who have often been resistant to more traditional methods of communication.

It is now possible to utilise what were once very expensive conference call facilities or provide online chat and education through applications such as Webinar (www.webinar.com) to conduct meeting and education programmes in a secure and reliable online environment. This type of platform is available from a number of providers and effectively adds to the online education tools that are available already, reducing the need to travel for meetings and seminars and increasing the efficiency and productivity of sport organisations.

When it comes to events, the dissemination of results and stories generated by the event is evolving rapidly. Larger sport organisations have traditionally relied heavily on established media outlets to disseminate and even gather information about events (Manha, 2009). Outlets such as newspapers, radio and television have been, in the past, the only organisations with the capacity to effectively distribute the content generated by a sport event. However, the vast majority of voluntary sport organisations have limited or no access to mainstream media outlets and have therefore had to develop their own methods of disseminating information about their activities.

The advent of the World Wide Web makes it possible for VSOs to take responsibility for disseminating information and they may even publish stories and events before the mainstream media can do so (Manha, 2009). The principles of Web 2.0, as described by O'Reilly (2005), have made it possible for sport organisations to use the Web as a medium for transferring and projecting information in real time, no longer relying on mainstream media to communicate their activities. (A Web 2.0 site allows its users to interact with other users or to change website material, in contrast to non-interactive websites where users are limited to the passive viewing of information that is provided to them.)

249

What started out as a way of publishing material on sport has now become a means of providing information for publication that is visible by all instead of only by the targeted media distributor. The research carried out by Manha (2009) on the challenges facing minor sport organisations in communicating their messages and information through mainstream media concluded that making use of social networking platforms and self-editing websites enable such organisations to generate information and communicate it to the world faster and often more accurately than traditional mainstream media outlets. Traditional media outlets that used to break sport news first now find themselves seeking out their information from sport organisation websites, social networking sites or from the direct feeds from events or matches.

From a stakeholder communication perspective, Butler (2009) conducted an extensive survey of athletes to determine what means of media connection might best improve the level of communication between National Federations and their member athletes. It was found that athletes needed more than emails or notices from their national bodies. The modern use of web technology, including social networking, online chat rooms and other similar media, make it possible for sport administrators to more regularly survey the feelings of the athletes and actively involve the membership in the decision-making process of these organisations.

It is not uncommon to find athletes subscribing to the common social networking sites such as Facebook, Twitter and Bebo. Through such sites, athletes are able to communicate more effectively with their fan base as well as express their own feelings 'unofficially' while preparing for or even during major events or competitions. Melbourne-based sport ICT company, SportingPulse, took this concept a step further with the establishment of 'My Sport', which provides individual members of sport clubs with their own personal 'My Sport' page, a very easy to use and powerful web tool for keeping personal information and profiles that can be shared with other members (www.sportingpulse.com).

By integrating the membership with tools such as 'My Sport', it is possible now for sport organisations to communicate with their members as never before. Multimedia publications, training and coach education and general notices can be published and disseminated in real time through computers, PDAs or by SMS text to the most basic of mobile phones. While these tools may not be of much value to those in rural settings in the developing world, the potential for them to be applied to information strategies involving amateur sport organisations in developed countries is enormous. The key, however, is to ensure that communication is both affordable and accessible.

For the developed world, the Internet has also opened up possibilities for disseminating information on an unprecedented scale. For less developed parts of the world, the Internet is becoming a much cheaper communication medium than phones and faxes, especially if this is combined with wireless technology and satellite access. The Internet and the World Wide Web have the potential to

brian minikin

form sport-specific global communities as international sport organisations lead the way in providing communication networks to their members.

ICT SOLUTIONS FOR THE MANAGEMENT OF VOLUNTARY SPORT ORGANISATIONS

Using electronic solutions for the information management of voluntary sport organisations has many advantages in that they improve efficiencies by reducing the repetitive work processes generated by the older 'paper trail' technologies. Although computers are fundamental to ICT solutions, mobile phones also now dominate the communication landscape in all corners of the world. As technology evolves, the possibilities for communication by VSOs increase exponentially. The need for face-to-face meetings will decline and as communication technology improves, more and more of the day-to-day business of sport organisations will be conducted online. What appears to have started out as a convenient way to store data and save space has led to the use of electronic technologies for all aspects of data collection, storage and dissemination. For the 21st century, this revolves around the use of wireless technology, Flash Memory and the use of the Internet to access relational databases that store and process information.

The initial trend was for ICT companies to provide services such as databases and websites, serviced by the company itself. This was a necessarily expensive exercise, beyond the reach of the average sport organisation. However, the advent of Web 2.0 and its interactive nature encourages a sense of ownership within the communication framework of organisations by embracing input from its consumers as opposed to utilising the Web as a single output-driven media (Boulos and Wheeler, 2007).

Web-based platforms like the IOC's extranet, which is a member-only service that connects the members of the Olympic family in a secure and closed online community, are becoming increasingly popular amongst international sport organisations as a way to store and disseminate information. For the volunteer sport organisation, less expensive solutions are required. Case study 13.2 provides information on a web portal established for sport organisations in the Pacific Region called OceaniaSport.

Case study 13.2: OceaniaSport

Web portals such as OceaniaSport (see Figure 13.3) have made it possible for information gathering, storage and communication to occur for sport organisations grouped geographically, rather than demographically. Recognising that sport organisations in the developing countries of the Oceania Region had one of the lowest Internet penetrations in the world, it was necessary to find

251

a solution that would meet their needs in a combination of offline and online interfaces. More critical was that it could be done economically, as the priority for the majority of these sport organisations was not the implementation of a web-based communications platform.

This portal links all NOCs and their member sport federations in the Oceania Region and provides databases that can upload details and results of competitions to sport federation websites. In addition, it can upload all details of registered members of the respective sport federations to an online database. The members themselves can operate all aspects of the system at the grass roots of their sport. The system includes four main functions:

■ A website for each NOC that is self-editing and accessed through the Oceania portal for sport (www.oceaniasport.com). These websites can integrate with an online database for members.
■ A website for all NFs affiliated to their NOC. These are also self-editing websites that are simple and easy to use and meet the general communication needs of any sport association. It is through these websites that the day-to-day operations of the associations are carried out, in particular the dissemination and logging of competition information and results.
■ Competition management software (CMP) that enables sport associations to generate draws and fixtures as well as print results and statistics. It also

Figure 13.3 OceaniaSport

brian minikin

allows the administration of tribunals. This software permits the organisation to keep a record of members and officials, handle finances and display all this information in hard copy or on the Web.

■ A member database. In addition to the database available in the CMP, which can work offline, all NOCs and their members have access to an online member database that can be used both locally and regionally. It was through this database that accreditation and entries were handled at the 2003 South Pacific Games. The strength of this database is that it can be used repeatedly for the administration of local or regional and single or multi-sport events, handling accreditation, event entries and finances.

The following observations can be made about the context surrounding OceaniaSport.

Before OceaniaSport

All information was gathered, stored and disseminated manually, consequently many files and records have been lost. For example, there is no complete record of results for the South Pacific Games as the paper records were lost during a move of the Games Secretariat some years ago. NOCs and their national federations suffered from poor handover processes as a result of lost records and files. Hence, one executive committee had little opportunity to work and progress onwards from the outcomes of the previous administration. Lack of communication and information sharing between and within countries was also a major obstacle for the development in sport throughout the Pacific Region.

With the low Internet connectivity and penetration experienced in most areas of the South Pacific, it was imperative that there be an offline component to any chosen system so that users without a fast and reliable Internet connection could still use the system. The difficulties of entering and accrediting athletes for regional competitions centred largely on the gathering of information, usually by paper, and either faxing or couriering this information through to the organising committee. Once received, this information was entered into another system for the preparation of accreditation cards and for the entering of athletes into a variety of sport event management systems. Most of this work was either done manually or at best using simple spreadsheets. The selected web portal needed to alleviate this work.

Establishment of a member database

The recognition of the need to establish a regional database of athletes, coaches and administrators was identified for the Pacific Region as early as 1991. Very few national federations kept records of their membership and so the information-gathering exercise was not only significant when it came to a major event, but was often a repeat of a process that had already taken place on numerous occasions previously. NOCs had also failed to keep track of the people who had completed training courses funded by Olympic Solidarity and previous written records of these people had been lost. Thus there was a need for a database to formalise member and training records.

The tangible outcomes of OceaniaSport

As a consequence of investment in the web portal, each Pacific Games now has a website that stores all of the results, images and stories from the Games and will remain a permanent record within OceaniaSport. The biggest challenge when trying to obtain a regional database has been ensuring that the users at the grass-roots level are getting value out of the system. If this is not achieved the system would not be a success. This is what makes the SportingPulse solution unique. Communication and results are the responsibility of the people who run the competitions and without creating additional work they are able to satisfy the media, their competitors/members and the general public as a single task.

It was in this context that the Oceania NOCs, working closely with SportingPulse, created the concept of OceaniaSport. The system has a minimum of centralised support and control, which means that ICT solutions make the best use of the Web 2.0 phenomenon, at an affordable price. It also deals with the so-called 'digital divide', described by Rosendich (2001), by providing an offline database that communicates with the online database and respective sport association websites, at times when the Internet is available.

Using the best features of Web 2.0, the OceaniaSport solution puts the content of websites and the databases into the hands of the users themselves, saving many thousands of dollars, reflected in the efficient administration of sport organisations and reduced costs levied by the system provider. Furthermore it significantly reduces the demand for volunteer time spent in administering the information that surrounds an event and, during the times when sport organisations have trouble retaining their volunteers, this is a very important development.

LIMITATIONS IN THE USE OF ICT

Making use of the new communication technologies has not been as rapid as logic would suggest it might be. Butler (2009), highlighting the work of Lundmark and Westelius (2008), noted that many sport organisations were not making the best use of communication technologies and were often slow to adopt new advances in these areas. This has certainly been observed within the OceaniaSport portal, where the uptake of regular usage of association websites has been less than 30 per cent.

Within the Pacific Islands context, this might well have as much to do with a low penetration of the Internet as anything else; however, the fact that this trend has been noted in societies with more developed IT capabilities suggests that more needs to be done to encourage sport organisations to embrace ICT solutions. This is particularly important within the context of branding and establishing a market position. By maintaining a website, sport organisations that have low member interest or access can still benefit from having their activities visible by parent organisations and potential marketing agents. This idea has led to companies such as Sportgenic Torque to launch a web portal in March 2009 (www.sportgenic.com) that specifically offers opportunities to sport organisations to position themselves for potential marketing agents to adopt.

It would appear that volunteer sport organisations tend to look at new technologies as either too expensive to invest in or involving too much time and effort in the retraining of their existing human resources. The OceaniaSport experience has highlighted the need to not only make a solution affordable but to provide an extensive amount of support and encouragement to ensure that recipient organisations make the most of new ICT solutions. Sport organisations, especially those driven by volunteers, may in fact be slower to take up ICT solutions if the users perceive that it is too difficult to change their working methods. However, for those sport organisations that have made a commitment to embracing modern ICT solutions, the rewards in time saved and organisational efficiency have been immeasurable. See case study 13.3 for an example of this.

Case study 13.3: Mt Martha Lifesaving Club

Mt Martha Lifesaving Club (MMLSC) has grown dramatically in the past eight years. In that time, the governing body of lifesaving (Life Saving Victoria) has undergone major changes including a merger between the two bodies that governed aquatic rescue in this state. As a result, the annual administration required increased dramatically and the stresses this and the dramatic growth created saw the need to streamline these processes.

Life Saving Victoria (LSV) began by supplying all its volunteer lifesaving organisations with a laptop computer and a data projector in 2007. Following this, MMLSC set up a wireless Internet hub enabling administrators to complete online tasks without having to pay Internet costs personally. With a sound infrastructure in place, the software needed to manage the club's activities (competition entries, qualification applications, merchandise purchases and payments, and patrol attendance) was investigated. An online business tool was essential due to the access required by multiple people and one was chosen and implemented. This system has now been working well for the past two seasons, saving hundreds of hours of administration.

The communication to the 1000 member organisation was increasingly important. The cost of information requiring immediate dissemination, such as changes to training schedules due to weather, qualification upgrade offers from LSV and dates of social activities, was becoming prohibitively high using regular mail. The content management website and SMS/email plugin that the club now uses enables instant and inexpensive access to an information hungry membership. Clubs such as MMLSC could not function to their full capacity without the use of ICT tools available today and the volunteer executive committee has ensured that it continues to embrace cutting edge technologies to further assist its membership.

SUMMARY

New ICT developments make the level of information gathering, storage, retrieval and dissemination take on dimensions that were unimaginable only a few years ago. These are centred on hardware developments such as laptop computers, PDAs and hybrid mobile phones as well as the Internet and wireless technology. Solutions that are available to volunteer sport organisations are becoming increasingly affordable and no doubt this trend will continue as new or improved technologies become available.

Coaches are now able to view and analyse athletes' performances via the World Wide Web from anywhere in the world and give instant feedback on performance. Personal blogging, instant messaging and email make it possible to communicate on a scale like never before.

Clearly the prudent acquisition of appropriate technology will enable the people working in sport organisations to make better use of their time by automating many of the processes and functions that are currently duplicated through having to be done manually.

Increasingly, sport umbrella bodies such as NOCs and national sport federations are attempting to develop ICT solutions that encompass their membership within national boundaries. This is also helping to make ICT solutions more available to volunteer sport organisations as well as involve them in the wider national interest in their sport. The IOC and bodies such as the Commonwealth Games Federation now provide web-based information services to their members either through an extranet or via an interactive web site. Web portals like OceaniaSport are leading the way for ICT solutions for sport that cross both national boundaries and sport boundaries. ICT solutions will improve the collection, storage, retrieval and dissemination of information for voluntary sport organisations and this can only be beneficial, even to the most humble of sport organisations.

brian minikin

CHAPTER 14

THE FUTURE OF MANAGEMENT IN VOLUNTARY SPORT ORGANISATIONS

Leigh Robinson, Brian Minikin and Dick Palmer

The voluntary sport sector is fundamental to sport and sporting opportunities, playing a critical role in sport provision through a vast network of organisations that run from small, locally supported clubs, to the most commercial of all – the IOC. Clubs, considered the backbone of the voluntary sport sector, work hard to deliver opportunities at the local level, while their respective NFs are charged with overseeing this and promoting excellence in participation. Mega events such as world cups and the Olympic Games are 'owned' by organisations from the voluntary sporting sector, while the value of volunteer activity has been estimated at £14 billion in the UK alone. The importance of the voluntary sector underlines the need for good practice in the management of VSOs. By ensuring that VSOs are governed properly and then supported by best management practice will allow them to be most effective in their delivery of sport.

The principles set out in the book so far are not always appropriate for all organisations. This could be due to their size, the resources available to them or their overall stage of development. For example, a significant number of VSOs do not have paid staff and therefore the separation between governance and management may not have occurred as it is set out in Chapter 3. However, it is important that all managers of VSOs are able to assess their organisation and determine which of the principles can be adapted and applied to the particular circumstances surrounding their organisation. Although a sport organisation may not have paid staff, there still needs to be a governing board that accepts responsibility for the VSO and determines the activities to be delivered, even if these are delivered by other volunteers or external service providers.

There are management functions that should remain unchanged no matter what the size or stage of development of the VSO. For example, the principles to be followed in the planning process, the management of human resources, the management of performance and the staging or hosting of events should be the same for all VSOs; it is the scale of the function that will differ. All VSOs must be able to audit their environments and manage change as and when required. The viability of a VSO will depend on its ability to respond to change, as there is often little choice about whether to change or not. All VSOs operate within a legal context that they need to understand and all must manage risk by preparing alternative strategies that deal with undesirable circumstances. Finally, opportunities will be lost if VSOs do not take advantage of the ICT that is available to them, no matter what their size or development. The use of modern ICT will improve the efficiency and effectiveness of the organisation by reducing the time commitments required of volunteers while significantly improving the quality and quantity of their output. In these instances, the skill of the voluntary sport manager is to make sure that the management principles set out in this book are scaled to meet the needs of the organisation.

CHALLENGES FOR THE FUTURE

Managers of VSOs will need to spend much of their time identifying and responding to change occurring in their operating environments. Indeed, this is one of the reasons why many sport organisations are now managed in a manner that reflects the practices of the commercial sector – a sector that has traditionally been considered to be more innovative and professional than the voluntary sector.

Managers can not afford to become complacent, as changes to the external environment surrounding VSOs continues to introduce issues that require a response. For example, the 2009 Crawford Report on the future of sport in Australia requires substantial changes on behalf of that country's VSOs. Seven such issues that voluntary sport managers will need to deal with in the next few years are outlined below; responding to these will require innovative and strategic thinking, careful management of staff and resources and a commitment to stakeholders and quality.

The popularity of sport

Sport disciplines and even events within codes are being increasingly subjected to public scrutiny as new sports appear on the scene or alternative activities that are more attractive to the younger person results in a reduction of participation in regular or formal sporting activities. The current debate surrounding the viability of test cricket or even the 50-over format is a cause of great concern for traditional cricket administrators in the face of public preference for the Twenty20 version of the game. Young people's tastes in sports change and will continue to change and therefore the task of promoting and popularising a VSO's sport becomes a very important priority for many governing bodies. The IOC has responded to the growing concern that its product is losing popularity by introducing the Youth Olympic Games, with modified events such as three-a-side basketball, while the 2010 Winter Olympic Games saw the new events such as skeleton, snowboard

258

and freestyle skiing attract a lot of viewing interest. Even within the Summer Games programme there is pressure to remove some of the older traditional sport events in favour of the more popular modern versions, which has led to the inclusion of rugby 7s in the 2016 Games.

There are a number of factors involved:

■ The televising of the sport: Sports that make exciting television promote, in young people, the desire to participate. Those sports that do not present well on television (even those that have been historically popular) make far less impact. This is a challenge for many sports, with some changing aspects of their sport in order to appeal to television audiences.

■ Olympic status: Those sports that have Olympic programme status will, in most countries, be more likely to receive state funding and support than sports not on the Olympic programme. This is out of the control of many managers, but does explain why sports aggressively lobby to be included in the Olympic programme.

■ Access to facilities and equipment: The availability of these can hamper the development of sports. Lacrosse almost died out as a sport after the two world wars due to the lack of hickory for making the sticks. Even the events within a sport such as athletics can be impacted by lack of equipment, e.g. pole-vaulting in various countries in the developing world is hardly practised because the expense and availability of the poles and the landing mats makes the event difficult to organise.

■ The duration of the event: There is a growing interest in sport competitions that can be packaged up and delivered for the 'fast-food' sport market. Twenty20 cricket and rugby 7s are examples of modified versions of traditional sports that are threatening to become more popular and significant than the traditional version of the sport. People appear to be less interested in participating or watching events that take a long time to complete.

■ The cost: The cost of either watching an event or taking part in sport will be a significant factor in the future that sport managers will have to deal with. Traditionally sport was a cheap or even free form of activity. However, as business principles evolve and there is an increase in pressure to package sport in a more entertaining way, so the cost of participating in, and spectating of, sport events also increases. This puts sport in a position where the consumer market, the spectators and participants may be attracted to the idea of spending their money elsewhere.

■ The competition: Increasingly, there are more and more alternatives for people seeking a sport experience. Non-competitive, recreational activities in particular appear to becoming more popular, along with participation in events that are organised outside the mainstream of traditional VSOs, such as 'wild swimming'. VSOs are therefore threatened by the introduction of new activities that appear more attractive than what they offer and also by

the future of management in voluntary sport organisations

organisations that are not membership based and therefore do not require a commitment or effort from participants.

It is not unreasonable to assume that some sports will recede in popularity and other new sports will emerge and take centre stage. Managers of sport organisations will need to monitor the interest in their product, the levels of participation and be innovative in their attempts to attract new participants and spectators.

Increasing professionalism

VSOs are required to do more and do it professionally. Sport promotes itself as contributing to health and the general well-being of society. It professes to have values, such as joy of efforts, fair play, respect for others and the pursuit of excellence, which are perceived as desirable in many contexts. Thus it creates high expectations within society and these expectations are placing increasing pressures on sport organisations to deliver high quality services to the public at large (see below). In exchange for receiving public funds, and indeed public interest, many VSOs will have to become more accountable and manage their performance in a transparent and open way.

The need for professionalism is driven by other aspects of the external environment. In the current climate, VSOs face an increasingly uncertain funding future, which is dependent on external political influences. At the time of writing there was a worldwide recession leading to reductions in government expenditure and it is naive to believe that sport will not be affected. At the very least, there is likely to be an impact on the quality and quantity of sport facilities that are accessible to VSOs as most of these are government funded. There will be increasing impact from legislation that affects safety, in particular child safeguarding, and the emphasis on the role of sport in health will lead to even greater focus on the claims sport makes in this area.

In addition, there are internal expectations that are driving professionalism. Members are expecting much greater 'value for money' in terms of their membership, volunteers are expecting greater professional help from their clubs and NFs and senior staff expect greater levels of professionalism from governing boards. The consequence of this should be greater professionalism from both the voluntary and non-voluntary parts of the organisation. This will require a greater commitment to education and the provision of support services to volunteers, which in turn will impact upon the financial and physical resources required by the organisation to operate effectively. However, an effective manager will understand that the answer lies in the clever application of management principles, rather than spending money and growing the organisation at all cost.

The implications of this are that VSOs need to engage professional people, ensure that their volunteers act in a professional manner and, in some cases, function

260

as a competent and performance-based business. The use of the management principles set out in this book will go a long way to help make VSOs more professional.

Accountability

VSOs are membership-based organisations and as such there has been a general acceptance of the need to be primarily accountable to their membership. The underlying premise of the structure of many VSO governance systems is that the main stakeholder of the organisation is its membership. However, it is possible to argue that this is inappropriate in the case of many VSOs given the resource that comes from outside of the membership base. For example, in many countries the vast majority of funding that is available to an NF comes from government or a government agency. In this instance, why should the needs of the members outweigh the needs of the funding agency? In addition, many NOCs are entirely dependent on funding from Olympic Solidarity and therefore to expect the member NFs to drive the direction of the NOC is perhaps inappropriate.

In reality, these external agencies do have a major impact on policy and strategy. For example, UK NGBs have to develop strategies that allow the objectives of the funding sport councils to be met. Membership objectives can become secondary to those of the funding agencies, especially if the VSO has limited capacity to generate income from its own activities. The challenge for managers of VSOs in this situation will be to balance the demands of accountability to both groups. It is possible to foresee a point where managers will need to explicitly set out to its membership the need for greater accountability to the funding agencies or establish a policy that determines what sources of funding best meet the objectives of its membership. Managers will need to be able to anticipate government policies and ensure that the organisation's goals are in line with these in order to position the organisation to effectively access this valuable source of funding without compromising the aspirations of the membership. Furthermore, the future sport manager should be able to seek out potential sponsors that wish to promulgate their own objectives through the compatible objectives that have been derived by the membership of the organisation. This might require a greater awareness of the social capital than has been required in the past.

Volunteers and volunteering

The lifeblood of sport is its volunteer base; even the professional sport system relies on volunteers at the grass-roots level or from the grass-roots level for its major events. For decades VSOs have been organised and run by armies of volunteers with very little direct support from a national office. However, television,

261

technology, family pressure and urban lifestyles have created other priorities for those who previously would have willingly volunteered to play their part in the administration, coaching and support for sport at all levels. Furthermore, changes in legislation across a number of fronts have required voluntary sport to introduce a more bureaucratic approach to administration, which can act as a disincentive to volunteering, particularly amongst sporting youth.

There is concern that the supply of volunteers is reducing to such an extent that the voluntary sport sector is threatened. However, the future of volunteerism is still intact, but will look very different in the future. In the future, a club volunteer will not consider the club to be a 'lifestyle' choice; they will still volunteer but it will be at a different level of commitment. Targeted, heavily supported and well rewarded volunteers will become the norm. Volunteers will be more likely to volunteer for a specific time period, or project, in a role that plays to their specific skills and abilities and they will expect to be rewarded in some way for this.

This means that managers of VSOs will have to approach their volunteer workforce in exactly the same way they approach their paid workforce. Volunteer positions will need to be filled by targeted recruitment and selection, job specifications will be required and mechanisms for development and support of the selected volunteer will need to be in place. In addition, mechanisms of reward will also have to be identified as it is increasingly clear that volunteers are becoming less willing to fund activities from their own pocket. Rewards do not have to be monetary but, without these, VSOs will struggle to recruit appropriate volunteers. In return, VSOs can expect much more in the way of professional behaviour and performance from their volunteer workforce.

Doping and drug culture

Greater rewards have led to more sportsmen and women seeking to cheat the system with performance-enhancing drugs. Sport has made strenuous efforts to rid itself of the scourge of drugs and doping and has been largely successful in this primarily through investment in detection. This is contrary to the trend of modern society where drug abuse has become more and more prevalent, where social drugs, such as cannabis and ecstasy, have become part of everyday youth culture.

Anti-doping is an expensive process in that education, detection and litigation are all high cost activities. In addition, the constant need to develop and refine detection methods in order to keep up with those who develop and use performance-enhancing drugs is challenging. Yet sport, if it is to retain its high moral ground, has to continue to invest in detection and to take a strong, unwavering stance against drugs. This will require managers of VSOs at all levels to promote the 'drug-free' message and to have in place mechanisms that support this. The keeping of databases of athletes, which includes the tracking of athletes'

leigh robinson, brian minikin and dick palmer

movements now required by the WADA, will further add to the administrative burdens placed on VSOs – although this can be greatly assisted by the use of ICT.

Increasing customer expectations of services

Very few managers of voluntary organisations actually know what their stakeholders expect of them and, as many are in a monopoly position (if people want to play their sport, they have to belong to a club and then the federation), they have often give little thought to stakeholder satisfaction. However, expectations of VSOs are steadily increasing. This is being driven by improvements in service quality within all aspects of society, an increasing culture of seeking and providing feedback to organisations and a strong belief in the concept of value for money. In the commercial and public sport sectors, expectations of services are now at a point where it is becoming extremely difficult for managers to meet them. This is because expectations are either so unrealistic that it is not possible to deliver services of such a high standard, or it is financially very costly to do so.

Managers of VSOs need to work with members and other stakeholders to prevent this unrealistic rise in expectations from occurring in the voluntary sector. The key to this is the management of expectations, which is based on information exchange between the organisation and its stakeholders. Stakeholders can set out their expectations of the VSO and the VSO can explain to stakeholders how their expectations impact on the service and provide information on why all expectations cannot be met. Although this may not solve the problem, it will reduce dissatisfaction as stakeholders become aware of why their expectations are not always being met.

An example of this might be in organising club competitions. For years a club may have successfully organised an annual event held at the local park. Over the years, the popularity of the event increased and the standard of play subsequently improved. As participating teams continued to require more in the way of support services, such as water bottles, uniforms, prizes and ultimately the standard of venue, the cost of hosting the event becomes increasingly prohibitive with the result that participation levels drop as participants seek out other venues or organisations that can provide them with what they want. The ultimate dilemmas facing the voluntary organisation's manager is understanding what level of service to provide, what this costs and what the member base is willing to pay for it.

Partnerships

As resources become harder to attract, stakeholder objectives become more complex and member expectations of what will be provided become greater, the need to work in partnership with other organisations will become increasingly

263

important for VSOs. Partnerships will allow services to be offered that the VSO may not have the capacity to do on its own, or they may be able to address a weakness that has been identified within the organisation. There is likely to be a need for partnerships to be developed with 'non-traditional' partners, such as health organisations, as well as more traditional partners, such as schools. The key will be to identify what organisations may help to add value to what the VSO offers.

For example, as a consequence of British Rowing identifying a weakness in the marketing of their organisation, they entered into a partnership with AstraZeneca, one of the world's leading pharmaceutical companies. AstraZeneca have provided skills and expertise in marketing and branding to the VSO and have encouraged staff to become involved with the organisation. As a consequence of this partnership, British Rowing have rebranded the organisation and launched a targeted product aimed at increasing participation in the sport. The partnership with AstraZeneca, although appearing to be an unusual one, builds on the shared values for health that both organisations have and addresses a weakness identified by the VSO.

CONCLUSIONS

The management of VSOs cannot operate in a vacuum and managers need to take into account and respond to developments in the external environment. This in turn requires managers to be aware of what is happening around them and to respond to these developments positively and logically, using best practice sport management practices. The potential contribution of sport to improved health, the pride of the nation, opportunities for lifelong learning and better social cohesion requires managers to demonstrate efficiency and effectiveness in the allocation of resources, management of staff and quality of service delivery. Failure to do this will lead to sport participation being marginalised in societies that are ever increasingly concerned with sport spectating and home-based activities. Alternatively, if voluntary sport managers do deliver services of good value, then continuity of funding and opportunities for enhanced resources should be forthcoming.

264

REFERENCES

Aaker, D. A. (1991) *Managing Brand Equity: Capitalizing on the Value of a Brand Name.* New York: The Free Press.

Adcroft, A. and Teckman, J. (2009) 'Theories, concepts and the Rugby World Cup: using management to understand sport.' *Management Decision,* 46(4), 600–625.

Amateur Swimming Association (2008) The Amateur Swimming Association Annual Report and Accounts 2007–2008, Loughborough: ASA.

American Marketing Association (2007) http://www.marketingpower.com/aboutama/pages/definitionofmarketing.aspx.

Andersen, B., Henriksen, B. and Aarseth, W. (2006) 'Holistic performance management: an integrated framework'. *International Journal of Productivity and Performance Management.* 55(1), 61–78.

Australian Bureau of Statistics (2008) *Sports and Physical Recreation Volunteers: Perspectives on Sport.* Adelaide: The National Centre for Culture and Recreation Statistics.

Barbeito, C. L. (2004) *Human Resource Policies and Procedures for Nonprofit Organizations.* New Jersey: John Wiley and Sons.

Berrett, T. (1993) 'The sponsorship of amateur sport – government, national sport organizations, and corporate perspectives'. *Society and Leisure,* 16(2), 323–346.

Bodet, G. and Meurgey, B. (2005) 'Comprendre la satisfaction dans le contexte des services sportifs associatifs (SSA): une analyse à partir du modèle tétraclasse'. *Revue Européenne de Management du Sport,* 14, 19–34.

Booms, B. H. and Bitner, M. J. (1981) 'Marketing strategies and organization structures for service firms', in Donnelly, J. H. and George, W. R. (eds), *Marketing of Services.* Chicago, IL: American Marketing Association, Chicago.

BOOST (2005) *Building on Olympic Strength to Transition to a State-of-the-art Organisation.* Internal document. Lausanne: IOC.

Boulos, M. N. K. and Wheeler, S. (2007) 'The emerging Web 2.0 social software: an enabling suite of sociable technologies in health and health care education'. *Health Information and Libraries Journal,* 24(1), 2–23.

Bratton, J. and Gold, J. (1999) *Human Resource Management,* 2nd edition. Basingstoke: Palgrave Publishers Ltd.

Browne, T. (2008) 'Measuring the performance of Olympic sports organisations – a Caribbean perspective'. *MEMOS project.* Lausanne: Switzerland.

Butler, C. (2009) 'Determining the best e-tools for the IAAF and its member federations to communicate with elite track and field athletes'. *MEMOS Project,* Lausanne: Switzerland. www.memosXII.com (available as at 1 January 2010).

Camy, J and Robinson, L. A. (eds) (2007) *Managing Olympic Sport Organisations.* Champaign: Human Kinetics.

Canadian Heritage (2002) *The Canadian Sports Policy.* Research Report, Canada: Canadian Heritage.

Chappelet, J.-L. and Bayle, E. (2005) *Strategic and Performance Management of Olympic Sport Organisations.* Champaign: Human Kinetics.

Crawford, D. (2009) *The Future of Sport in Australia.* Canberra: The Australian Government.

Cutlip, S.M., Center, A. H. and Broom, G. M. (1997) *Effective Public Relations,* 8th edition. Englewood Cliffs, NJ: Prentice Hall.

DCMS (Department for Culture, Media and Sport) (2000) *A Sporting Future for All.* London: Department for Culture, Media and Sport.

Delicado, N. (2002) E-federations. *Memos Project.* Lausanne, Switzerland.

Deloitte & Touche (2003) *Investing in Change.* London: Deloitte & Touche.

Desbordes, M. and Tribou, G. (2007) 'Sponsorship, endorsements and naming rights', in Beech, J. and Chadwick, S. (eds) *The Marketing of Sport.* Harlow: Prentice Hall, FT.

Doherty, A. (2003) *A Study of the Volunteers of the 2001 Alliance London Jeux du Canada Games.* London, Ontario: University of Western Ontario.

Doherty, A. and Murray, M. (2007) 'The strategic sponsorship process in a non-profit sport organisation'. *Sport Marketing Quarterly,* 16(1), 49–59.

Enjolras, B. (2002) 'The commercialization of voluntary sport organizations in Norway'. *Nonprofit and Voluntary Sector Quarterly,* 31(3), 352–376.

Ferrand, A. and McCarthy, S. (2009) *Marketing the Sports Organisation. Building Networks and Relationships.* London: Routledge.

Ferrand, A., Torrigiani, L. and Camps i Povill, A. (2007) *Routledge Handbook of Sports Sponsorship: Successful Strategies.* London: Routledge.

Ferreira, M. and Armstrong, K. L. (2002) 'An investigation of the relationships between parent's causal attributions of youth soccer dropout, time in soccer organisation, affects towards soccer and soccer organisation, and post-soccer dropout behaviour'. *Sport Management Review,* 5(2), 149–178.

Finlay, P. (2000) *Strategic Management: An Introduction to Business and Corporate Strategy.* Harlow: Prentice Hall.

FITA (2007) *Archery World Plan 2007–2012.* Internal document. Lausanne: FITA.

FIVB (2002) *The Volleyball World Vision 2008: Report to the FIVB World Congress in Buenos Aires.* Internal document. Lausanne: Fédération internationale de volley-ball.

Flyvbjerg, B. (2004) 'Phronetic planning research: theoretical and methodological reflections'. *Planning Theory and Practice,* 5(3), 283.

Flyvbjerg, B., Bruzelius, N. and Rothengatter, W. (2003) *Mega Projects and Risk: An Anatomy of Ambition.* Cambridge: Cambridge University Press.

Getz, D. (2007) *Event Studies: Theory, Research and Policy for Planned Events.* Oxford: Butterworth-Heinemann.

Gilgeous, V. (1997) *Operations and the Management of Change.* Harlow: Prentice Hall.

Gratton, C. and Taylor, P. (2000) *The Economics of Sport and Recreation.* London: E & FN Spon.

Gray, A. (2009) 'The structure of voluntary sport', personal communication 12.11.09.

Heino, R. (2000) 'New sports: What is so punk about snowboarding?' *Journal of Sport and Social Issues,* 24(2), 176–191.

Hernandez, R. A. (2002) *Managing Sport Organisations.* Champaign: Human Kinetics.

IOC (2002) *Operational and Financial Audit. Consolidation of Operations. Pursuit of Excellence.* Lausanne: Internal document for the IOC Session in Dec. in Mexico City.

IOC (2007) *Olympic Charter. In force as from 7 July 2007.* Lausanne: IOC. Available from IOC website www.olympic.org.

IOC (2008) *Basic Universal Principles of Good Governance of the Olympic and Sports Movement. Preliminary Document.* Lausanne: IOC. Available from IOC website www.olympic.org.

IOC (2009) *Corporate Development with a Focus on Corporate Plan.* Lausanne: Presentation for the AISTS Master in Sport Administration programme.

James, J., Trail, G. T., Wann, D. L., Zhang, J. J. and Funk, D. C. (2006) 'Bringing parsimony to the study of sport consumer motivations: Development of the Big 5'. *Symposium at the North American Society for Sport Management Conference.*

Johnson, G., Scholes, K. and Whittington, R. (2008) *Exploring Corporate Strategy: Text and Cases.* Harlow: Prentice Hall.

Kaplan, R. and Norton, D. (1996) *The Balanced Scorecard.* Boston, MA: Harvard Business Press.

Kikulis, L. (2000) 'Continuity and change in governance and decision making in national sport organizations: institutional explanations'. *Journal of Sport Management,* 14, 293–320.

Kirkpatrick, D.L. (1994) *Evaluating Training Programs: The Four Levels.* San Francisco, CA: Berrett-Koehler.

Kotler, P., Dubois, B. and Manceau, D. (2004) *Marketing Management,* 11th edition. Paris: Pearson Education.

Kotter, J. P. and Schlesinger, L. A. (1979) 'Choosing strategies for change'. *Harvard Business Review,* 57, 106–124.

KPMG (Klynveld Peat Marwick Goerdeler) (2001) *Achieving Measurable Performance Improvement in a Changing World. The Service for New Insights.* London: KPMG International.

Kübler, B. and Chappelet, J.-L. (2007) 'The governance of the International Olympic Committee', in Parent, M. and Slack, T. (eds) *International Perspectives on the Management of Sport.* Burlington, VI: Elsevier.

Kyle, G., Absher, J., Norman, W., Hammitt, W. and Jodice, L. (2007). 'A modified involvement scale'. *Leisure Studies,* 26(4), 399–427.

Langeard, E., Bateson, J. E. G., Lovelock, C. H. and Eiglier, P. (1981) *Marketing of Services: New Insights from Consumers and Managers.* Cambridge, MA: Marketing Sciences Institute.

Leisure Industries Research Centre (2003) *Sports Volunteering in England 2002*. London: Sport England.

Lewin, K. (1951) *Field Theory in Social Science*. New York: Harper and Row.

Loret, A. (1995) *Génération Glisse*, Série Mutations edn, Autrement.

Lundmark, E. and Westelius, A. (2008) 'Internet-based changes in organisational communication', in Dwivedi Y.K. et al (eds). *Handbook of Research on Global Diffusion of Broadband Data Transmission*. London: Information Science.

Manha, J. Q. (2009) 'Minor sports in emerging media – strategy to enhance sports exposure in Portugal'. *MEMOS Project, Lausanne Switzerland*. www.memosXII.com (available as at 1 January 2010).

Marchand, D. (2008) *The International Olympic Committee: Transforming the Organisation Behind the Olympic Games*. Case study 3-1885. Lausanne: IMD.

Mass, S. (2007). 'Bringing the values to life', *Olympic Review*, April-June: 29–45.

McCurley, S. (1993) 'How to fire a volunteer and live to tell about it'. *Grapevine*, February 8–11.

McGraw, P. (2001) 'Attracting, selecting and recruiting people', in CCH, *Australian Master Human Resources Guide*. Sydney: CCH Australia Ltd.

Meinhard, A. (2006) 'Managing the human dimension in nonprofit organizations', in Murray, V. (ed.) *Management of Nonprofit and Charitable Organizations*. Toronto: LexisNexis/Butterworth.

Minikin, B. (2009) 'A question of readiness'. *MEMOS project,* Lausanne Switzerland. www.memosXII.com (available as at 1 January 2010).

Moler, C. (2000) 'Wanted: not-for-profit to take money'. *Parks and Recreation,* 35, 164–172.

Mullins, L. J. (2004) *Management and Organisational Behaviour*, 7th edition. London: Financial Times/Prentice Hall.

Nichols, G., Taylor, P., James, M., Garrett, R., Holmes, K., King, L., Gratton, C. and Kokolakakis, T. (2004) 'Voluntary activity in UK sport'. *Voluntary Action* 6(2), 31–54.

Nolan (Lord) (1995) *Nolan Report – The Seven Principles of Public Life*. First Report, London: HMSO.

Olympic Solidarity (2005) *2001–2004 Quadrennial Report*. Lausanne: IOC. Available from IOC website www.olympic.org.

O'Reilly, T. (2005) *What is Web 2.0? – Design Patterns and Business Models for the Next Generation*. www.oreilly.com/web2/archive/what-is-web-20.html (available as at 1 January 2010).

Pettigrew, A. (1987) 'Context and action in the transformation of the firm'. *Journal of Management Studies,* 26(4), 649–670.

Piekarz, M. (2009) 'Risk management and the sport manager', in Bell, K. (ed) *Sport Management*. Exeter: Learning Matters.

Pynes, J. (2004) *Human Resources Management for Public and Nonprofit Organizations*, 2nd edition. San Francisco, CA: Jossey-Bass, Inc.

Robinson, L. and Crowhurst, M. (2001) *Quality Programmes in Public Leisure Services*. Melton Mowbray: ISRM.

Roche, M. (2000) *Mega-events and Modernity: Olympics and Expos in the Growth of Global Culture*. London: Routledge.

Rosendich, T. J. (2001) 'Information technology for sports management'. *The Sports Journal,* 4(2). www.thesportjournal.org/article/information-technology-sports-management (available as at November 2009).

Sanderson, I. (1998) *Achieving Best Value Through Performance Review*. Warwick/DETR Best Value series, Paper No. 5, Coventry: Warwick University.

Seippel, O. (2006) 'The meanings of sport: Fun, health, beauty or community?' *Sport in Society,* 9(1), 51–70.

Sloman, J. and Sutcliffe, M. (2001) *Economics for Business*, 2nd edition. London: Prentice Hall.

Sport England (2002) *Sports Volunteering in England in 2002*. London: Sport England.

Sporting Pulse (2010) Oceania Sport, personal correspondence, Feb, 2009.

Stone, R. (1998) *Human Resource Management*, 3rd edition. Brisbane: John Wiley and Sons.

Taylor, P., Robinson, L. A., Bovaird, A., Gratton, C. and Kung, S. (2000) *Performance Measurement for Local Authority Sports Halls and Swimming Pools*. London: Sport England.

Taylor, P., Barrett, R. and Nichols, G. (2009) *Survey of Sports Clubs 2009*. London: CCPR.

Taylor, T., Doherty, A. and McGraw, P. (2008) *Managing People in Sport Organizations: A Strategic Human Resource Management Perspective*. Oxford: Elsevier.

USOC (2004) *Game Plan*. Colorado Springs, CO: United States Olympic Committee internal document.

USTA (United States Tennis Association) (2006) *Diversity Plan: Multicultural Focus 2006–2008*. www.usta.com/USTA/Global/Active/News/Diversity/Diversity/370458_Diversity.aspx (available as at 13 March 2009).

WADA (2007) *Strategic Pan 2007–2012*. Version 4 May 2007. Montreal: WADA. Available from WADA website www.wada-ama.org.

Wilson, D. and Butler, R. (1986) 'Voluntary organisations in action: strategy in the voluntary sector'. *Journal of Management Studies,* 23(5).

Yeh, C., Taylor, T. and, Hoye, R. (2009).Board roles in organisations with a dual board system: empirical evidence from Taiwanese nonprofit sport organisations'. *Sport Management Review,* 12(2), 91–100.

Zeithaml, V. A., Bitner, M. J. and Gremler, D. D. (2009) *Services Marketing. Integrating Customer Focus Across the Firm*, 5th edition. Singapore: McGraw-Hill International Edition.

INDEX

272

274

index

Brain, Mind, and the Narrative Imagination